Communications in Computer and Information Science 1562

Editorial Board Members

Joaquim Filipe
Polytechnic Institute of Setúbal, Setúbal, Portugal

Ashish Ghosh
Indian Statistical Institute, Kolkata, India

Raquel Oliveira Prates
Federal University of Minas Gerais (UFMG), Belo Horizonte, Brazil

Lizhu Zhou
Tsinghua University, Beijing, China

More information about this series at https://link.springer.com/bookseries/7899

Alexander V. Tuzikov ·
Alexei M. Belotserkovsky ·
Marina M. Lukashevich (Eds.)

Pattern Recognition and Information Processing

15th International Conference, PRIP 2021
Minsk, Belarus, September 21–24, 2021
Revised Selected Papers

 Springer

Editors
Alexander V. Tuzikov 🆔
United Institute of Informatics Problems
of The National Academy of Sciences
of Belarus
Minsk, Belarus

Alexei M. Belotserkovsky 🆔
United Institute of Informatics Problems
of The National Academy of Sciences
of Belarus
Minsk, Belarus

Marina M. Lukashevich 🆔
Belarusian State University of Informatics
and Radioelectronics
Minsk, Belarus

ISSN 1865-0929 ISSN 1865-0937 (electronic)
Communications in Computer and Information Science
ISBN 978-3-030-98882-1 ISBN 978-3-030-98883-8 (eBook)
https://doi.org/10.1007/978-3-030-98883-8

© Springer Nature Switzerland AG 2022
This work is subject to copyright. All rights are reserved by the Publisher, whether the whole or part of the material is concerned, specifically the rights of translation, reprinting, reuse of illustrations, recitation, broadcasting, reproduction on microfilms or in any other physical way, and transmission or information storage and retrieval, electronic adaptation, computer software, or by similar or dissimilar methodology now known or hereafter developed.
The use of general descriptive names, registered names, trademarks, service marks, etc. in this publication does not imply, even in the absence of a specific statement, that such names are exempt from the relevant protective laws and regulations and therefore free for general use.
The publisher, the authors and the editors are safe to assume that the advice and information in this book are believed to be true and accurate at the date of publication. Neither the publisher nor the authors or the editors give a warranty, expressed or implied, with respect to the material contained herein or for any errors or omissions that may have been made. The publisher remains neutral with regard to jurisdictional claims in published maps and institutional affiliations.

This Springer imprint is published by the registered company Springer Nature Switzerland AG
The registered company address is: Gewerbestrasse 11, 6330 Cham, Switzerland

Preface

This book contains selected extended papers from the 15th International Conference on Pattern Recognition and Information Processing (PRIP 2021), which was held during September 21–24, 2021, and hosted (online) by the United Institute of Informatics Problems of the National Academy of Sciences of Belarus.

The PRIP conference has a long history. It began in 1991 as the First All-Union USSR Conference on Pattern Recognition and Image Analysis in Minsk. PRIP was organized alternately by the Institute of Engineering Cybernetics of the Belarusian Academy of Sciences, the Belarusian State University, and the Belarusian State University of Informatics and Radioelectronics. Currently, it is organized under the Belarusian Association for Image Analysis and Recognition (BAIAR), which was officially accepted by the International Association of Pattern Recognition (IAPR) in March 1993 as a national representative of Belarus at IAPR. To date, 15 editions of PRIP conference have been held.

The onset and continuation of the COVID-19 pandemic in 2020 and 2021 changed the international landscape, and thus PRIP 2021 took place purely online although it was still endorsed by the International Association for Pattern Recognition (IAPR). For the first time, the conference was endorsed by the Asia-Pacific Artificial Intelligence Association (AAIA) and GÉANT, an association of collaborating European National Research and Education Networks (NRENs).

This year, the conference had a single track for which we received 90 submissions. Of these, only 53 papers (representing 142 co-authors) were accepted after peer review for presentation at the conference. In total, 75 speakers (including keynotes and invited speakers) from 18 countries took the floor.

PRIP usually includes theoretical and applied aspects of computer vision, recognition of signals and images, the use of distributed resources, and high-performance systems. This year it was significantly expanded with the inclusion of issues related to artificial intelligence. The conference had the motto "Artificial Intelligence: Facing the Challenges".

Proceedings of PRIP conferences are regularly published by conference organizers. The current book includes the best papers from the conference, which were selected by PRIP Program Committee. The final papers were reviewed again after being revised and extended following presentation at the conference.

The book is aimed at researchers working in pattern recognition and image analysis; knowledge processing; and knowledge-based decision support system.

December 2021

Alexander V. Tuzikov
Alexei M. Belotserkovsky
Marina M. Lukashevich

Organization

The 15th International Conference on Pattern Recognition and Information Processing (PRIP 2021) was hosted by the United Institute of Informatics Problems of the National Academy of Sciences of Belarus in cooperation with the Belarusian State University, the Belarusian State University of Informatics and Radioelectronics, and the Belarusian Association for Image Analysis and Recognition.

General Chair

Alexander Tuzikov   United Institute of Informatics Problems of the National Academy of Sciences of Belarus, Belarus

General Co-chair

Sergey Ablameyko   Belarusian State University, Belarus

Program Committee Co-chair/Chief Event Officer

Alexei Belotserkovsky   United Institute of Informatics Problems of the National Academy of Sciences of Belarus, Belarus

Program Committee Co-chair

Marina Lukashevich   Belarusian State University of Informatics and Radioelectronics, Belarus

International Program Committee

Astsatryan, Hrachya   Institute for Informatics and Automation Problems of the National Academy of Sciences of the Republic of Armenia, Armenia

Belokonov, Igor   Samara University, Russia

Bogonikolos, Nikos   Aratos Group, Greece

Chemeris, Alexander   Institute for Modelling in Energy Engineering, Ukraine

Deserno, Thomas M.   Technische Universität Braunschweig, Germany

Doudkin, Alexander	United Institute of Informatics Problems of the National Academy of Sciences of Belarus, Belarus
Dziech, Andrzej	Jan Kochanowski University of Kielce, Poland
Frucci, Maria	Institute for High Performance Computing and Networking, Italian National Research Council (ICAR-CNR), Italy
Gallo, Luigi	Institute of High Performance Computing and Networking, Italian National Research Council (ICAR-CNR), Italy
Golenkov, Vladimir	Belarusian State University of Informatics and Radioelectronics, Belarus
Golovko, Vladimir	Brest State Technical University, Belarus
Gurevich, Igor	Institute of Informatics Problems of the Russian Academy of Sciences and Hetnet Consulting Corp., Russia
Hiromoto, Robert	University of Idaho, USA
Kharin, Yuriy	Belarusian State University, Belarus
Kovalev, Vassili	United Institute of Informatics Problems of the National Academy of Sciences of Belarus, Belarus
Krasnoproshin, Viktor	Belarusian State University, Belarus
Madani, Kurosh	University of Paris-Est Creteil, France
Marcelli, Angelo	University of Salerno, Italy
Mariage, Jean-Jacques	Université Paris, France
Nedzved, Alexander	Belarusian State University, Belarus
Nystrom, Ingela	Uppsala University, Sweden
Piuri, Vincenzo	University of Milan, Italy
Roth, Hubert	University of Siegen, Germany
Sachenko, Anatoly	Ternopil National Economic University, Ukraine
Sanniti di Baja, Gabriella	Italian National Research Council, Italy
Shmerko, Vlad	University of Calgary, Canada
Starovoitov, Valery	United Institute of Informatics Problems of the National Academy of Sciences of Belarus, Belarus
Subbotin, Sergey	Zaporizhzhya National Technical University, Ukraine
Tatur, Mikhail	Belarusian State University of Informatics and Radioelectronics, Belarus
Uchida, Seiichi	Kyushu University, Japan
Yanushkevich, Svetlana	University of Calgary, Canada
Ye, Shiping	Zhejiang Shuren University, China
Yingke, Xu	Zhejiang Shuren University, China

Zaitseva, Elena	University of Zilina, Slovakia
Zalesky, Boris	United Institute of Informatics Problems of the National Academy of Sciences of Belarus, Belarus
Zalewski, Janusz	Florida Gulf Coast University, USA
Zhao, Qiangfu	University of Aizu, Japan

Additional Reviewers

Alexander Tuzikov	United Institute of Informatics Problems of the National Academy of Sciences of Belarus, Belarus
Sergey Ablameyko	Belarusian State University, Belarus
Marina Lukashevich	Belarusian State University of Informatics and Radioelectronics, Belarus
Alexei Belotserkovsky	United Institute of Informatics Problems of the National Academy of Sciences of Belarus, Belarus
Eugen Efimov	United Institute of Informatics Problems of the National Academy of Sciences of Belarus, Belarus
Natalia Lapitskaya	Belarusian State University of Informatics and Radioelectronics, Belarus
Victor Bucha	Business Intelligence Quants, Belarus
Pavel Lukashevich	United Institute of Informatics Problems of the National Academy of Sciences of Belarus, Belarus

Partners

- The National Academy of Sciences of Belarus
- Business Intelligence Quants
- National Research and Education Network BASNET
- GÉANT Association
- The International Association for Pattern Recognition
- The Asia-Pacific Artificial Intelligence Association

Contents

Classification of Histology Images Based on a Compact 3D Representation

Nadia Brancati[1], Crispino Cicala[2], Maria Frucci[1],
and Daniel Riccio[3(✉)]

[1] Institute for High Performance Computing and Networking, National Research
Council of Italy, Naples, Italy
{nadia.brancati,maria.frucci}@cnr.it
[2] Computer Scientist, Milan, Italy
[3] University "Federico II", Naples, Italy
daniel.riccio@unina.it

Abstract. Although the Convolutional Neural Networks (CNNs) have been widely adopted for the classification of histopathology images, one of the main drawbacks of CNNs is their inability to cope with gigapixel images. To deal with the high resolution of Whole Slide Image (WSI), many methods focus on patch processing which can result in improper representation if the patches are analyzed independently, losing the context information that is fundamental in digital pathology. In this study, the WSI is mapped into a compressed representation preserving the topological and morphological information relating to spatial correlations of neighboring patch features of the WSI. Such a representation is used to train a CNN to solve a classification task of breast histological images. The effectiveness of the suggested framework is demonstrated through experiments on Camelyon16 dataset. The results show the performance of our approach when three different ways to incorporate the spatial correlation in the tensor are used singly or in combination, highlighting that it is comparable with the state of the art.

1 Introduction

The development of medical image CAD algorithms for diagnostic and prognostic evaluation of digitized biopsy images pose preliminary challenges. For instance, gigapixel WSI cannot be fed directly into deep learning models due to their very high resolution. Over the years, the approaches for the computational classification of WSIs were primarily based on partitioning the entire WSI image into patches small enough to be processed independently by a deep network. However, in most of these methods, the class of the entire WSI is usually inferred by combining the decisions obtained for the individual patches [1–3] without exploiting the information provided by relationships between patterns presented by individual patches. This makes the prediction of the CNN an isolated result because the overall structure of the tumour as well as some further sub-structures present in the slide cannot be taken into account during the process of analysis. Indeed, the prediction could require the analysis of the structure, resolution, and spatial correlation of most parts of the whole tumour or gland.

© Springer Nature Switzerland AG 2022
A. V. Tuzikov et al. (Eds.): PRIP 2021, CCIS 1562, pp. 1–11, 2022.
https://doi.org/10.1007/978-3-030-98883-8_1

Some recent approaches [4–6] transform the WSI in a compressed version, by using a grid-based representation, where each patch is replaced by a feature vector. The aim of this representation is to preserve spatial correlations between patches, while compressing the original image. The grid representation can be easily fed as input to a CNN, but the contextual analysis of each point of the grid still remains too local, since a 3 × 3 neighbourhood is usually considered. In order to preserve both detail and contextual information by widely extending the contextual analysis of each patch, a new solution for applying CNNs to histopathological images that works on the entire image is proposed in this work. A set of reference patches coming from a given set of reference WSI is mapped into a high dimensional deep features space, and is subsequently clustered to obtain a bag of deep features words, which is built once and for all. To classify a new whole slide image, all non-overlapping patches are extracted and projected into the same high dimensional deep features space to search for co-occurrences of the deep features words and to build a 3D tensor that represents the entire image in a more compact way. To establish the effectiveness of our approach, we trained and tested our model on the Camelyon16 dataset for the binary classification task of breast cancer. Finally, we compared classification results of our approach with state of the art deep learning networks based on Bidirectional Generative Adversarial Network (BiGAN), a Variational AutoEncoder (VAE), a discriminative model based on contrast training, and Attention networks (AN). We achieved the highest performance accuracy of 75%. Thus, the proposed method can represent giga-pixel images in an alternative way, while preserving the ability to discriminate images by classes even at a higher level of abstraction.

The rest of the paper is organised as follows: Section 2 is devoted to the description of the proposed approach; Section 3 reports the experimental setup, comparative strategies and results. Finally, Section 4 draws some conclusions.

2   Method

This approach consists of two stages that are training and classification. In a training phase, a set of WSI images is considered a reference set. Each WSI is partitioned into non-overlapping patches that are mapped into a deep features space independently through a suitably fine-tuned CNN. The K-means algorithm is then applied to group similar patches into a small number of clusters, whose centroids are considered as deep feature words. In the classification phase, a WSI undergoes the same process of patching and projection. However, the extracted deep features are used to identify the similarity with the deep feature words and their number of occurrences in the image. Both of these information concur to build a 3D tensor generated by Tensor-based Feature Extractor module. The tensor is then given as input to the Tensor-based Classifier which assigns it to one of the two classes benign/malignant.

2.1   Cluster Data Preparation

The bags of deep features words are the basis of the WSI compression process. They are extracted once and for all from a set of annotated WSIs that is considered as a training set. The WSIs were manually annotated by the pathologists, who marked Regions of Interest (ROIs) as tumor, while all the rest of the non-annotated image is considered to be normal tissue. A set of Reference Patches (RP) was extracted from these WSIs, which then include normal and tumor patches of size $S \times S \times 3$. In particular, tumor patches are extracted from the marked ROIs, while the normal patches are obtained by partitioning the non-marked parts of WSIs. Thresholding is applied before partitioning to avoid patch extraction in correspondence of the background. Post-processing is applied to balance the number of tumor and normal patches. The set of RPs is divided into two parts: training and test sets. Both sets include a perfect balance of patches of normal and tumor tissue. The training data set contains about 90% of the data of the RP set and is adopted to fine-tune a pre-trained ResNet-18 [7] for a binary classification task, i.e. in order to distinguish between malignant and benign tissue. The trained network is then used to extract a feature vector of length H for each considered patch, that is mapping the patch into a H-dimensional deep features space. The set of deep features vectors extracted from training patches of RP undergo a clustering process that is performed by K-means to form a set of K bags of deep features words. The feature vectors of the testing patches are used to estimate the number K, for which the resulting clusters are mainly composed of elements of the same type.

Finally, for each cluster i, the corresponding centroid V is stored in the i-th row of a matrix MV of size $K \times H$. The matrix MV will be used to assign patches extracted from an input WSI to the corresponding cluster. In other words, MV allows assigning a patch to the corresponding bag of deep features words.

2.2   Tensor-Based Feature Extractor and Classifier

Centroids of the clusters stored in MV are used to build a compact representation of each WSI, in such a way that preserves both features and spatial relationships between patches extracted from the WSI.

Given an input WSI, namely W, with size $N \times M \times 3$, it is partitioned in non-overlapping patches of size $S \times S \times 3$. Each patch is fed to the fine-tuned ResNet-18 and the outcoming deep feature vector is considered to assign it to the cluster showing the minimum Euclidean distance. A cluster matrix CM of size $N/S \times M/S$ is constructed, where each (i,j) stores the cluster label k of the patch $p_{i,j}$ in W. See Fig. 1.

Starting from this representation, a 3D tensor, with size $K \times K \times D$, is generated to store information on the relationships between each couple of different patches lying at distance less or equal to D in the WSI input. Let us denote this tensor with T. The distance D is the value of the proximity radius determining the contextual area considered for each patch, i.e. D is the maximum distance between two different patches of a WSI for which the relationship between the corresponding features can be taken into account. In the following, two different patches of a WSI at distance less or equal to D will be indicated as adjacent patches.

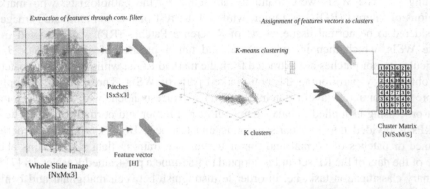

Fig. 1. The Matrix cluster building process. A WSI is divided into a set of patches that are independently mapped to a feature vector by using a pre-trained ResNet-18. Each feature vector is assigned with the label of the cluster whose centroid is at minimum distance. The set of labels is rearranged in a matrix according to the original spatial arrangement of the patches.

The tensor T is dealt as the union of two equivalent prisms P_{dis} and P_{cor} each of them of height D and with bases formed by orthogonal triangles with legs of length K. The prism P_{dis} contains the information related to the distribution of clusters among the adjacent patches of W, while P_{cor} includes information on the correlations between the feature vectors of the adjacent patches of W. Precisely, for each couple of different patches with a given distance $d \leq D$ and with feature vectors belonging to two defined clusters k and k', P_{dis} specifies the occurrence in W of the selected pattern $\{k, k', d\}$ (or also $\{k', k, d\}$), while P_{cor} includes the sum of correlation indexes between the feature vectors associated to the patches of the selected pattern in W. The correlation is given by the value of the Pearson coefficient [8]. See Fig. 2.

A normalization process is applied on each slice of T to obtain values between -1 and 1. This operation is performed adopting the mapping function [9] that is a quasi sigmoid normalization. Finally, the normalized tensor T is fed to a VGG-11 network [10].

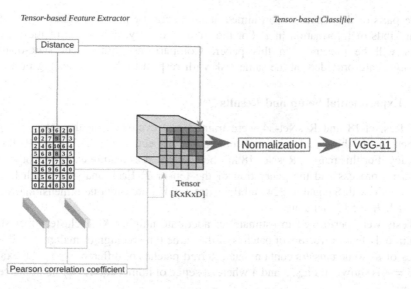

Fig. 2. Our tensor-based network. For each couple of different patches with a given distance $d \leq D$ and with feature vectors belonging to two defined clusters, two different sets of features are extracted on the basis of the information of the cluster matrix and feature vectors of the patches. These sets are stored in two different symmetric volumes (red and orange part) of the tensor T. The red part specifies the occurrence in W of the selected pattern, while the orange partincludes the sum of correlation indexes between the feature vectors associated to the patches of the selected pattern in W. Then, the tensor T is normalized and is fed a deep network for the classification tasks. (Color figure online)

3 Experiments and Results

The performance of the proposed method has been evaluated on the publicly available histopathology image Camelyon16 dataset [11].

The Camelyon16 dataset contains 400 H&E WSIs of sentinel lymph nodes of breast cancer obtained splitted into 270 WSIs (160 of normal tissue and 110 containing metastasis) for the training phase and 130 WSIs (80 of normal tissue and 50 containing metastasis) for the test phase. This original splitting was preserved in our experiments. All WSIs of the training set containing metastases are accompanied by manual annotations that have been used for both the training of the ResNet-18 and the selection of patches used for the clustering processes. In particular, 120156 patches have been extracted from the WSI training set to fine-tune the ResNet18 and 15000 patches coming from the WSI test set were used for clustering. The involved patches were appropriately selected from many different images, equally distributing them according to their type, normal or tumor tissue.

Different experiments have been performed to select: a) the deep networks both for feature vector extraction and for classification; b) the patches set for the clustering process; c) the normalization function and finally, d) the values of K and D. Moreover, different strategies have been considered for training of our network, considering either single parts or the whole tensor, aimed at assessing the potential contribution of different kinds of information in T. For the sake of brevity, only some of these experiments will be presented in this paper. Comparisons with recent state-of-the-art techniques are provided on the same task with respect to the same testing protocols.

3.1   Experimental Setup and Results

Both ResNet-18 and ResNet-34 were trained and evaluated on the set of reference patches for the binary classification obtaining, respectively, 97.75% and 97.08% of accuracy. For this reason, ResNet-18 has been adopted as feature extractor for both the clustering process and the generation of the tensor T. Each analyzed patch has size $S \times S \times 3$, with S equal to 224 and the extracted features are one-dimensional vectors of length $H = 512$ elements.

Tests were performed to estimate an adequate number K of clusters that should contain only feature vectors of patches of the same type (benign or malignant). For low values of K, some clusters contain data referred patches of different types. An example for $K = 8$ is shown in Figs. 3 and 4 where absence of homogeneity occurs in the central clusters.

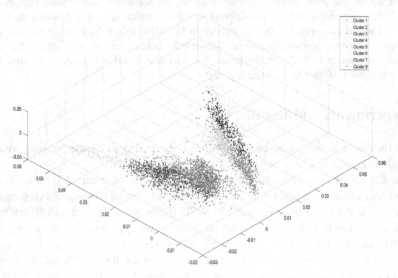

Fig. 3. Representation of the distribution of feature vectors in space and associated clusters with $K = 8$.

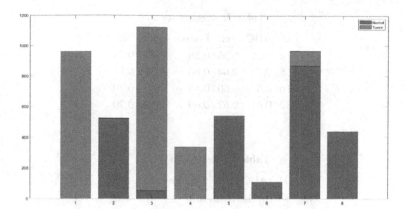

Fig. 4. Final composition of the clusters for $K = 8$. The cluster identifier is shown on the abscissas, the number of elements contained in them on the ordinates.

With higher values of K, the homogeneity of the clusters is more guaranteed. Thus, the value of K was set to 256. Figure 5 shows the representation of the 256 clusters.

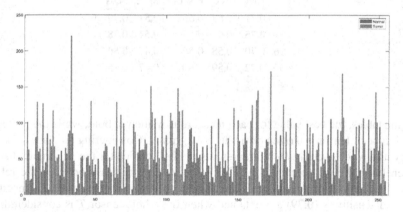

Fig. 5. Final composition of the clusters for $K = 256$. The cluster identifier is shown on the abscissas, the number of elements contained in them on the ordinates.

We propose three different scenarios for the classification, depending on whether only one part of T (P_{dis} or P_{cor}) or the whole tensor T is involved in the analysis.

For each strategy, the results have been evaluated with tensors at different depths, in particular for $D = 4, 8, 16$ and 32.

The performance of different approaches has been compared in terms of standard metrics, namely Accuracy, F-score, Specificity and Sensitivity. The Area under the ROC Curve (AUC) has been also considered. The numerical results of these experiments are reported in Table 1, 2 and 3 for T, P_{dis} and P_{cor}, respectively.

Table 1. Results for T

	D	AUC	Acc	F-score	Spec	Sens
T	4	0,61	0,56	0,56	0,45	0,73
	8	*0,72*	**0,64**	0,66	**0,51**	*0,79*
	16	0,61	0,60	0,66	0,48	0,70
	32	0,61	0,62	*0,69*	0,50	0,70

Table 2. Results for P_{dis}

	D	AUC	Acc	F-score	Spec	Sens
P_{dis}	4	0,51	*0,62*	**0,77**	–	0,62
	8	*0,55*	*0,62*	**0,77**	–	0,62
	16	0,50	0,62	0,73	0,50	*0,66*
	32	0,49	0,44	0,51	0,32	0,56

Table 3. Results for P_{cor}

	D	AUC	Acc	F-score	Spec	Sens
P_{cor}	4	0,71	*0,63*	*0,65*	**0,51**	0,79
	8	**0,75**	*0,63*	*0,65*	**0,51**	0,78
	16	0,70	0,58	0,56	0,47	**0,80**
	32	0,72	0,59	0,60	0,47	0,75

In the tables, the best value for each measure is written in bold, while the best result for each type of tensor is written on a blue background. Considering the values for each strategy as a whole, setting $D = 8$ represents the best choice for the maximum distance between two different patches of a WSI for whose relationship between the relative features can be taken into account. The highest values of accuracy (0,68), specificity (0,51) and sensitivity (0,79) are obtained when the whole tensor T is considered. The highest value of F1 score (0,77) is provided by P_{dis} (0,66 for T and 0,65 for P_{cor}). The best performance in terms of AUC (0,75) is obtained considering P_{cor} (0,72 for T and 0,55 for P_{dis}). The remaining measures for P_{cor} show values similar to those obtained for T. Thus, the best strategy can be considered the one based on P_{cor} and for D = 8. For this configuration, Fig. 6 shows the confusion matrix and the ROC curve.

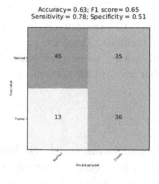
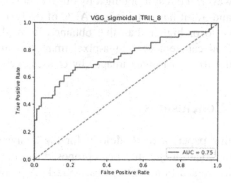

Fig. 6. Confusion matrix and ROC curve of the network, taking into account only P_{cor} with $D = 8$.

Other experiments were performed considering the cosine similarity and the chi-square distance for the correlation measure. The results in terms of AUC are lower than those obtained by adopting the Pearson coefficient: 0.69 and 0.62 for cosine similarity and chi-square distance, respectively.

Also, different classifiers were considered adopting as in the case of the VGG-11, Adam optimizer with learning rate = 0.0001 and CrossEntropyLoss: the Attention model presented in [5], the Support Vector Machine (SVM) and the AlexNet architecture. Comparing the results shown in Table 4 for $D = 8$ and P_{cor}, the Attention Model architecture provides a better performance in terms of F-score, but with a lower sensitivity than VGG-11. The remaining classifiers show a low performance in AUC and accuracy.

Table 4. Comparison between different classifiers

	AUC	Acc	F-score	Spec	Sens
A.M	0,58	0,62	**0,71**	0,50	0,68
SVM	0,63	0,60	0,65	**0,59**	0,60
AlexNet	0,59	0,52	0,46	0,43	0,76
VGG-11	**0,75**	**0,63**	0,65	0,51	**0,78**

The classification result in terms of AUC is comparable with those of the studies in [4] and [5]. The capacity of these methods to reduce the whole-slide images into a compact format was tested in [4] by using three different networks: the Bidirectional Generative Adversarial Network (BiGAN), a Variational AutoEncoder (VAE) and a discriminative model based on contrast training, while the method [5] is based on two Attention networks (AN). The AUC of the BiGAN, VAE and contrastive networks are respectively 0.70, 0.67 and 0.65, while AN provides an AUC equal to 0.71. The results are in line with many of those obtained from the method presented in this study, in which the level of abstraction of whole-slide image representation has increased.

However, the result obtained by our model is quite relevant, since for depth levels 4, 8, 16 and 32, it has obtained an AUC of 0.71, 0.75, 0.70 and 0.72 respectively, which is equal to or higher than that obtained from [4] and [5] methods. Thus, the proposed method can represent giga-pixel images in an alternative way, while preserving the ability to discriminate images by classes even at a higher level of abstraction.

4 Conclusions

In this paper, a methodology for the analysis of gigapixel Hematoxylin and Eosin histological images has been proposed and the experiments have been performed for a breast cancer binary classification task. A preprocessing is adopted to generate a set of clusters of the feature vectors extracted from annotated ROIs. Starting from this set, information related to the proximity of the patches, in which a WSI input is partitioned, can be extracted. Such information is stored in different 3D tensors allowing compact representations of WSIs that can be processed by deep learning techniques. Our method is independent of WSI size and can process large dimensional images without losing the resolution details and preserve relationships along with feature-based correlation among the extracted patches from the WSI. Experimental results have shown that the tensor including information obtained by considering a proximity radius of 8 patches and the correlation measures between the different patches provides the best performance. The results of the proposed approach exceed those obtained by recent studies proposed in the literature, opening up to the future possibility of extending this approach to further reduce the amount of data to be processed, while still obtaining good results in classification tasks.

Acknowledgments. This work was supported by the project "Campania Oncotherapy - Fighting tumor resistance: an integrated multidisciplinary platform for an innovative technological approach to oncotherapies - Regione Campania".

References

1. Cruz-Roa, A., et al.: High-throughput adaptive sampling for whole-slide histopathology image analysis (HASHI) via convolutional neural networks: application to invasive breast cancer detection. PLOS ONE **13**(5), e0196828 (2018). https://doi.org/10.1371/journal.pone.0196828
2. Das, K., Conjeti, S., Chatterjee, J., Sheet, D.: Detection of breast cancer from whole slide histopathological images using deep multiple instance cnn. IEEE Access **8**, 213502–213511 (2020). https://doi.org/10.1109/ACCESS.2020.3040106
3. Vang, Y.S., Chen, Z., Xie, X.: Deep learning framework for multi-class breast cancer histology image classification. In: Campilho, A., Karray, F., Romeny, B.H.J. (eds.) ICIAR 2018. LNCS, vol. 10882, pp. 914–922. Springer, Cham (2018). https://doi.org/10.1007/978-3-319-93000-8_104
4. Tellez, D., Litjens, G., van der Laak, J., Ciompi, F.: Neural image compression for gigapixel histopathology image analysis. IEEE Trans. Pattern Anal. Mach. Intell. **43**(2) (2019)

5. Tomita, N., Abdollahi, B., Wei, J., Ren, B., Suriawinata, A., Hassanpour, S.: "Attention-based deep neural networks for detection of cancerous and precancerous esophagus tissue on histopathological slides. JAMA Network Open **2**(11), e1 914 645–e1 914 645 (2019)
6. Brancati, N., De Pietro, G., Riccio, D., Frucci, M.: Gigapixel Histopathological Image Analysis using Attention-based Neural Networks. arXiv:2101.09992 (2021)
7. He, K., Zhang, X., Ren, S., Sun, J.: Deep residual learning for image recognition. In: Proceedings of the IEEE Conference on Computer Vision and Pattern Recognition, pp. 770–778 (2016)
8. Stigler, S.: Francis Galton's account of the invention of correlation. Stat. Sci. **4**(2), 73–79 (1989)
9. Marsico, M., Riccio, D.: A new data normalization function for multibiometric contexts: a case study. In: Campilho, A., Kamel, M. (eds.) ICIAR 2008. LNCS, vol. 5112, pp. 1033–1040. Springer, Heidelberg (2008). https://doi.org/10.1007/978-3-540-69812-8_103
10. Simonyan, K., Zisserman, A.: Very Deep Convolutional Networks for Large-Scale Image Recognition. arXiv:1409.1556 (2014)
11. Bejnordi, B.E., et al.: Diagnostic assessment of deep learning algorithms for detection of lymph node metastases in women with breast cancer. Jama **318**(22), 2199–2210 (2017)

Smart Tiling for Program Optimization and Parallelization

Alexander Chemeris$^{(\boxtimes)}$ [iD], Sergii Sushko [iD],
and Svetlana Reznikova [iD]

Pukhov Institute for Modelling in Energy Engineering, NAS of Ukraine,
Kyiv, Ukraine
a.chemeris@ipme.kiev.ua

Abstract. The process of automatic program optimization and parallelization is considered in this chapter. The problem is very important especially considering speed of computations, used resources, power consumption that depends on system elements activity and others. This is very important for mobile, embedded and standalone systems, especially those based on multicore microprocessors. Huge potential for parallelization is concentrated in cyclic sections of algorithms, since that main part of computations is performed here. In this chapter the authors consider the way of automatic parallelization of loops that use an iterative process to find out an optimal solution. As a core of this process Particle Swarm Optimization (PSO) Method is used. It gives a solution that is close to optimal one and moreover it reduces time of optimal parallel program development. The authors show how to parallelize iterative space of program loops by using PSO Method in cycling process. This method was named Smart Tiling Method. Some experiments show the positive effect on execution time of parallelized program by Smart Tiling Method.

Keywords: Parallelization · Loop parallelization · Tiling · Particle swarm optimization · Smart Tiling

1 Introduction

Fast growth of multiprocessor computer systems (CS) requires an improvement in development of parallel software. In particular, this is parallelizing compilers, since a creation of parallel software with providing no computational errors and dead-end branches is a nontrivial task.

Parallelization of serial program operations is a distribution of set of operations which work with data memory on processor units with some topology. To reduce idle state of CS processors, it is necessary to perform a load balancing of processor elements, which leads to decreasing execution time of parallel program. Another task of increasing of computational performance is a minimization of data transfers between nodes of CS. A resolving of this task will allow to efficiently parallelize a software.

The highest performance in CS can be achieved if structure of algorithm of solving task corresponds to CS's architecture. Therefore, a distribution of computations should be done in such way to provide minimum amount of data transfers between CS

© Springer Nature Switzerland AG 2022
A. V. Tuzikov et al. (Eds.): PRIP 2021, CCIS 1562, pp. 12–32, 2022.
https://doi.org/10.1007/978-3-030-98883-8_2

microprocessors and a transfer of data between processor and memory with the same computational load of CS microprocessors. All of the above also applies to loop sections of algorithms in which largest part of computational work of software is located.

Providing of such principles of distribution of computations in loops requires performing a variety of tasks. Such tasks include: definitions of dependencies in a program – both data dependencies and control dependencies, based on a set of dependencies, which must be either exact or excessive. It is necessary to determine potential parallelism, which operations can be performed in parallel; detection of atomic computations, i.e. those grains of algorithm that cannot be interrupted by synchronization or data exchange and which must be executed on one microprocessor; distribution of operations between virtual processors and determination of their execution order (space-time mapping); combining atomic operations into blocks and assigning them to real processors of operating system (blocking and mapping); coordination of data assignments and operations on operating system microprocessors to reduce data transfers; setting of optimal order of operations' execution based on synchronization of computations and data locality.

In addition to the mentioned tasks, also there are different tasks which required effective solutions on level of architecture of CS, such as: minimizing of number and size of temporary data arrays, organization of efficient data transfer, assembly of efficient executable code, automation of parallelization, etc. Thus, this section of the monograph is devoted to one of most effective ways to create a parallel software with parallelization of loop parts of algorithms.

During developing tools for compiling computer programs, an important part is devoted to code optimization processes. This applies to both serial and parallel programs. However, special attention is focused on automatic parallelization of algorithms.

Automatic parallelization generally consists of three stages of algorithm processing based on some logical representation of algorithms or on structural level in form of some diagram, for example, by using UML, or at the system level, by using code of high-level language. On the first stage, an algorithm is analyzed, on the second stage, rules for transformation of the algorithm are developed, and on the third stage, code generation for a parallel computing system is performed.

This section discusses a possibility of using optimization methods to improve an efficiency of partitioning of iteration space of loop operators. On the beginning of the section, dependencies in programs and loops are considered, as well as various models of iteration space. Further, an attention is devoted to methods of partitioning and transformation of iteration space. Then an iterative process of partitioning of space of loop operators and an intellectual method of partitioning (Smart Tiling Method) are proposed, as well as the experiments showing advantages of the method.

2 Dependencies Between Operators in Programs

Before performing transformations in programs related to optimization or parallelization, it is necessary to determine dependencies between operations and data in algorithm. Dependencies appear when it is necessary to access the same memory cell in different moments of time. So, if the operator S_1 refers to a memory cell x and then S_2 refers to x, then it means that S_2 depends on S_1 in x.

Definition. There is a dependence between two operators S_1 and S_2 if they both access to the same memory cell, and at least one of these calls is a memory write [1].

It is known that programs have four types of dependencies associated with access to the same memory cells.

Consider two operators S_i and S_j ($S_i \prec S_j$) and, in accordance with [2], define types of dependencies in a program. Sign '$\prec$' is used here, which determines a lexicographic order of the operators S_i and S_j. It means that operator S_i precedes the operator S_j in program. Both commands perform read-write operations in computer's memory.

Definition. A lexicographic order (ordered sequence) of n-dimensional Cartesian multiplication $A^n = A \otimes A \otimes \ldots \otimes A$ is defined as follows: let $a = (a_1, a_2, \ldots, a_n)$ and $b = (b_1, b_2, \ldots, b_n)$, then $a \prec b$, if $a_1 < b_1$ or $a_1 = b_1$, $a_2 = b_2$, ..., $a_k = b_k$, and $a_{k+1} < b_{k+1}$, where $1 \leq k \leq n - 1$.

Dependence by data (data-flow dependence) between operators S_i and S_j ($S_i \prec S_j$) appears when operator of program S_j reads data calculated in S_i.

S_i: $X = F_1(\text{In}(S_i))$;
S_j: $Y = F_2(\text{In}(S_j))$; $X \in \text{In}(S_j)$ & $j \geq i + 1$;

where $\text{In}(S)$ is a set of input variables of operator S. A data dependence is determined by so-called "write before read" order [4].

Dependence by output (output dependence) of two operators S_i и S_j ($S_i \prec S_j$) appears when the same variable is written in both operators, i.e.

S_i: $X = F_1(\text{In}(S_i))$;
S_j: $X = F_2(\text{In}(S_j))$; $j \geq i + 1$.

This dependency prevents of usage when executing any current statement of invalid X values.

Antidependence between operators in program S_i и S_j ($S_i \prec S_j$) occurs if reading of variable made before when it was written in computer memory, i.e.

S_i: $X = F1(\text{In}(Si))$; $Y \in \text{In}(Si)$.
S_j: $Y = F2(\text{In}(Sj))$; $j \geq i + 1$.

Antidependence prevents S_i from changing to S_j, which can lead to incorrect values.

There is another type of dependence, namely dependence of control. It is determined by program operators that change an order of execution of operators depending on a certain condition. So, for example, in C code snippet:

S_i: if(x = = 0).
S_j: y = ToDo(arg);

Thus, the above types of dependencies between operators of programs were defined. These dependencies are typical for any part of program. However, some specific types of dependencies are defined for loop sections. The classification of dependencies is shown in Fig. 1.

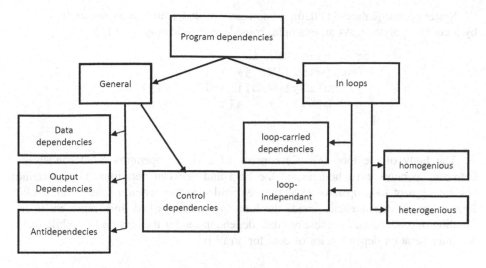

Fig. 1. Classification of dependencies in a program

One of the main ways to represent dependencies in a program is to display dependencies in the form of graphs. For this, flow graphs, graphs based on Petri nets, lattice graphs and others are used. When a loop is represented as an expanded graph, dependencies between loop iterations are determined.

Definition. An expanded dependence graph of an algorithm is a directed graph obtained as follows: each operation $S(J)$ generates a vertex $V(J)$ of the graph, each dependence $S(I) \rightarrow S^*(J)$ generates an edge $(V(I), V^*(J))$.

In general, consider nested loops, each of loops defines its own index variable. Set of index variables determines an index vector of nested loop $I = (I_1, I_2, ..., I_n)$. For any loop in which loop index I changes from the value L to U with a step S, an iteration number i is equal to value $(I - L + S)/S$, where I is an index value for this iteration [5].

For nested n loops, an iteration vector I for the innermost loop is a vector containing an integer number of iterations for each loop, in nesting order of loops. In other words, an iteration number of a multidimensional nested loop is determined in accordance with the form $I^k = \{i_{11}^k, i_2^k, ..., i_n^k\}$, where i_k, $1 \leq k \leq n$, is an iteration number loop for nesting level k.

Definition. An iteration space of loop is a set of all integer vectors $I = (I_1, I_2, .., I_n)$ which satisfies the system of inequalities [6]:

$$Li \leq xi \leq Ui, \ where \ i = 1...n \tag{1}$$

System of inequalities (1) defines boundaries of loops and limits an iteration space by a convex polytope. As an example, consider the following loop [7]:

```
for( i=1; i<N; i++)
    for(j=1; j<N; j++) {
        a[i,j] = b[i,j-1] + c[j+1];
        b[i+1,j] = a[i,j] + d;
    }
```

The body of the loop (Fig. 2) consists of a set of operators S. Dependencies between operators exist both inside the loop and between iterations. Let's imagine several steps of loop operator execution, expanded in the iteration space. Here, solid lines represent dependencies inside the loop body, and dashed lines represent inter-iteration dependencies. So, there are data dependencies for the array a[]. While there are inter-iteration dependencies of data for array b[].

j \ i	1	2	3	4
1	a[1,1]=b[1,0]+c[2]; b[2,1] = a[1,1] + d	a[1,2]=b[1,1]+c[3]; b[2,2] = a[1,2] + d	a[1,3]=b[1,2]+c[4]; b[2,3] = a[1,3] + d	a[1,4]=b[1,3]+c[5]; b[2,4] = a[1,4] + d
2	a[2,1]=b[2,0]+c[2]; b[3,1] = a[2,1] + d	a[2,2]=b[2,1]+c[3]; b[3,2] = a[2,2] + d	a[2,3]=b[2,2]+c[4]; b[3,3] = a[2,3] + d	a[1,4]=b[2,3]+c[5]; b[3,4] = a[2,4] + d
3	a[3,1]=b[3,0]+c[2]; b[4,1] = a[3,1] + d	a[3,2]=b[3,1]+c[3]; b[4,2] = a[3,2] + d	a[3,3]=b[3,2]+c[4]; b[4,3] = a[3,3] + d	a[3,4]=b[3,3]+c[5]; b[4,4] = a[3,4] + d

Fig. 2. Dependencies inside loop iterations and between iterations

For loops, a conception of dependence distance [1] was introduced, which actually determines after how many iterations this variable will be used. This value can be a constant value or variable value and is determined by a linear or non-linear expression.

In n nested loops a set of distance vectors is approximated by an integer l from the interval $[1, n]$, which is defined as the largest integer, so that the first $l-1$ components of a distance vectors are zeros. A dependence at l_n level means that a dependence manifests itself at level of l-th nest of loops, i.e., at a given iteration $l-1$ outer loops. In this case, a dependence is said to be an inter-iteration dependency and such dependencies are called loop-carried at l level. If $l = \infty$, then a dependence occurs inside a loop body between two different operators (independent). A value of l is called level of dependence.

3 Graph Models of Iteration Space

An expanded dependency graph is defined above. To adapt this graph when representing loop program fragments, a loop should be expanded according to values of index variables, which determines an order of execution of statements which builds up a loop body.

Other graph models are also used to represent dependencies in loop program statements. A brief description is provided below.

Reduced Loop Graph
Due to existence of different types of dependencies, in many cases it is impossible to execute a program code in parallel without preliminary analysis and further reduction of dependence. In order to facilitate a generation of parallel program code, after obtaining a set of loop dependencies, a so-called reduced dependence graph (RDG) is created [9]. This is a directed graph $G = (V, E)$, a structure of which is determined by dependencies in loop body. Vertices of a graph correspond to set of operators in loop's body. Further, all strongly connected components are defined that are a maximal subgraph $S = (V', E')$, in which for each vertex $u \in V \& u \notin V'$ there is no other vertex $v \in V'$ between which there is a connection $(u, v) \in E$. So, there is a directed graph's edge between two vertices of subgraph S. A reduced dependence graph, an edge of which are denoted by dependence levels, is called a reduced level dependence graph.

Graphs of such type are a basis for constructing of parallelization based on polyhedral model which represents an iteration space of loop operators. A space is represented in this model by a convex polyhedron, which is formed by an intersection of planes constructed on basis of system inequalities of index variables of loop operators.

Lattice Loop Graphs
A concept of a lattice graph is considered in details in [1, 5, 9] and others. A definition of a lattice graph is based on a concept of support spaces. This concept allows to consider not only closely nested loops, but also loops of an arbitrary structure. Depending on which nested loops operator belongs to, it is accordingly located in a certain reference space.

If in nodes of iteration space, which corresponds to points with coordinates equal to value of index variables of nested loop, we place the graph vertices corresponding to loop body for different values of index variables, and connect these vertices with edges that correspond to inter-iteration dependencies, then a result will be a lattice dependency graph of nested loop.

Iteration Space and Presburger Arithmetic
In [10, 11] Omega test for obtaining dependencies in an analytical form is described. There are used concepts of sets, tuples and relations, which analytically represent a graph of dependencies of program loop operators. Data transformations are performed based on operations of set and relations theory and by using of Presburger arithmetic [12].

For example, here is a program fragment containing a two-dimensional nested loop:

```
for i=1 to 6 do
    for j=1 to 10 do
        a(i+j, 3*i+j+3) = a(i+j+1, i+2*j+4)
    endfor
endfor
```

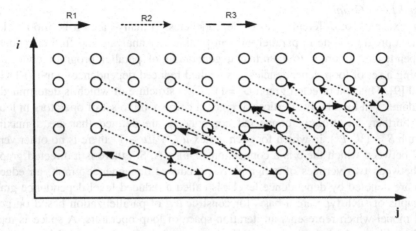

Fig. 3. Example of iteration space

A traditional view of dependence graph with a division of dependencies by type is shown in Fig. 3. Usage of Omega test gives a representation of the iterative space of loop in the form of an analytical system of relations:

```
anti   R1={[i,2i]->[i,2i+1]: 1 <= i <= 4}
anti   R2={[i,j]->[i',i+i'+1]: j = 2i' && 1 <= i < i'<=5}
flow   R3={[i,j]->[j-i-1,2i]: 2i+2<= j <=i+7, 10 && 1<=i}
```

The iteration space is defined by bounds of the loop indices. Since there are two nesting loops, we consider a two-dimensional case in which the loop variables change in the range $1 \leq i \leq 6; 1 \leq j \leq 10$. An integer range enclosed by these values represents an iteration space. For two-dimensional case, this is a rectangle shown in Fig. 3. Here, each point of an integer space is associated with a loop iteration with the corresponding values of the iteration variable. Analyzing the dependencies, it can be determined that the operator has three inter-iteration dependencies.

So, relation $R1 = \{[i, 2i] \rightarrow [i, 2i + 1] : 1 \leq i \leq 4\}$ determines dependence between the vertices with indices $[i, 2i]$ and indices $[i, 2i + 1]$ for the interval $i = (1, 4)$. In Fig. 3 this dependence is marked with a solid line. The dependence according to data $R3 = \{[i,j] \rightarrow [ji - 1, 2i] : 2i + 2 \leq j \leq i + 7, 10 \&\& 1 \leq i\}$ has   a   more   complex expression and defines the dependence between the vertices $[I,j]$ and $[ji-1, 2i]$ within subscript domain $2i + 2 \leq j \leq i + 7, 10\ \&\&\ 1 \leq i$.

In general, there can be several types of R_k dependencies in loop body. In this case, an expression

$$R(L) = \bigcup_{k=1}^{K} R_k \qquad (2)$$

where K is a dimension of system of dependencies in iteration space, which has dimension L.

Thus, an iteration space model of loop consists of a set of tuples with integer coordinates and a system of relations that defines a graph of dependencies between nodes of iteration space.

4 Parallelization Task

In task of automatic parallelization, a conclusion can be obtained that most of computational work is concentrated in loop fragments of algorithms. An efficiency of one or another approach to automatic parallelization of programs is determined by finding a number and type of dependencies in algorithms. The basis of automatic parallelization methods is a dependence graph, presented in form of a particular model. How accurately and completely a dependence graph will be built determines an efficiency of resulting program. After a construction of dependence graph of algorithm, problems of distribution of computations on microprocessors of computing system are solved.

In this case, objects for solving of these problems are three types of spaces. Each space can be considered as points of a one-dimensional or multi-dimensional structure.

1. An iteration space is a set of dynamically computed loop iterations, that is, a set of value combinations based on loop indices. An iteration space is a set of iterations whose identifiers are specified by values stored in index variables. A nested loops of depth n (i.e., n nested loops) has n index variables and, accordingly, is modeled in n-dimensional space. An iteration space is limited by lower and upper bounds of loop indices.
2. Data space is a set of array elements which are accessed. It's about arrays of data (vectors, matrices, etc.) represented by index variables. In general, on logical level of abstraction, a data array has dimension N. Physically, in memory of microprocessor, it is a linear one-dimensional array of cells.
3. Processor space is a set of processors in a computing system. Typically, processors are numbered. It's assumed that processor space is a p-dimensional array, depending on architecture of particular computing system. For computing systems with shared memory, which include multithreaded architectures, a processor space is a one-dimensional data array.

In fact, it is necessary to determine an effective combination of these three spaces for specific architectures of computing systems. For this, a general approach to analysis and parallelization of programs in a high-level language is provided below. A feature of this approach is an iterative nature of parallelization procedure, due to transformation procedure and requirements to refine the parallelization result through usage of objective function of optimization methods.

5 Methods of Transformation of Iteration Space

Computational loops of computer programs can be transformed in various ways. Accordingly, iteration spaces, which are a way of describing computational loops, can also be transformed.

Consider main methods of transformation of computational loops [13]:

- fission – transformation of a computational loop into several other computational loops with the same range of indices, but different parts of initial loop;
- fusion – combining of adjacent computational loops into one loop with the same range of indices;
- loop-invariant code motion – moving those parts of code outside of loop body which are inside a loop, but which do not depend on calculations inside a loop;
- parallelization – simultaneous execution of same operations of a computational loop on different computing devices;
- pipelining – modification of loop body for the most efficient pipeline of commands or computational blocks;
- scheduling – dividing of loop body into multiple parts that can work simultaneously on several processors;
- skewing – moving iterations of a multidimensional computational loop in order to move dependencies of iterations into outermost computational loop;
- splitting – simplification of the computational loop or elimination of dependencies by splitting the loop body into several computational loops that have the same commands, but with a smaller iteration range;
- tiling – reorganization of computational loop to reduce usage of amount of loop data in order to improve data locality;
- vectorization – grouping of several loop iterations to use vector operations;
- unrolling – unrolling the loop body into an equivalent number of non-loop operations.

As it follows from the list above, the methods for modifying of computational loops are quite diverse and not always universal [14]. It is also possible to use several methods for transformation of computational loops at the same time. In any case, it is possible to estimate a practical speed up of execution of a computer program only by results of launching and measuring of execution time. Thus, a choice of methods for transformation of computational loops for each specific program code is a unique task and requires an individual selection.

In practical transformation of loops of computing programs in order to optimize a software, a developer can manually change a sequence of command execution, ranges of iteration, or transform computational loops in a different way.

Another approach looks much more promising when a source code of computational loop is transformed into an iteration space, which, in turn, can be used by various methods of transformation of iteration space [8]. Performing a transformation of iteration space in accordance with some chosen methods, full mathematical correspondence to the methods is achieved. In addition, several transformations of the iteration space can be performed in serial. After all conversions have been done, an iteration space can be converted back to modified source code of a program.

Despite of mentioned advantages of software optimization through transformation of iteration space, rather than working with program code itself, this approach has some disadvantages. Work with iteration space requires understanding some software packages and understanding of used mathematical background. It should also be kept in mind that automatically generated source code of program has poor readability and is difficult for a developer to understand.

Let's consider some of the methods of transformation of iteration space more detailed.

Parallelization is a well-known method of transformation of iteration space. Usage of this method is most effective in order to optimize computer programs in terms of execution speed [1]. Indeed, on beginning of 2022 year, it is difficult to find a type of computing device that has only one core in its composition. PCs, embedded systems, telecommunications equipment, phones, tablets, televisions – all of them have multiple computing cores. Perhaps one of only types of computing devices where a position of single-core microprocessors is still quite strong is microcontrollers. At the same time, multi-core and more efficient devices appear for this type of devices also.

Considering multicore computing systems as a global trend in the development of microelectronics, a problem occurs to maximize usage of all computing cores. It is a distribution of computational load on all available computational nodes that is the main task of parallelization. The big difficulty for using parallelization is that not all algorithms can be easily parallelized, as well as the fact that algorithms were originally developed for single-core processing. Thus, despite of obvious efficiency from usage of parallelization, usage of this method is not so simple and straightforward.

It should be noted that depending on algorithm itself, not all calculations can be fundamentally parallelized and there will always be some part of code that cannot be parallelized. An understanding of this fact was realized time ago and resulted in Amdahl's law:

$$S_p = 1 \Big/ \left(1 + \left(1 - \alpha/p\right)\right) \tag{3}$$

where S_p is an acceleration of execution time of a serial-parallel program; p is a number of processors; α is a fraction of calculations that can only be calculated serially. Accordingly, part of calculations 1-α may be parallelized.

As it follows from formula (3), even an increase a number of processors to infinity it cannot reduce a program execution time lower than an execution time of its serial part. Common usage of most parallel algorithms and parallelization of algorithm to microprocessors is the most effective method to reduce program execution time.

Another method of transformation of iteration space is tiling method [15]. Unlike parallelization, a practical advantage of using this method is not so obvious at first glance. The essence of tiling method is that an iteration space is additionally divided into smaller blocks named tiles. From point of view of computational loops, it means that several other, maximally nested loops are added to existing computational loops. A number of additional nested loops may differ, but usually two nested loops are used. In this case, tiling occurs on two-dimensional tiles.

For example, a two-dimensional computational loop can be represented by an iteration space, as shown in Fig. 4 on left side. Right side shows the same computational loop by using of tiling method with 4 × 3 tiles.

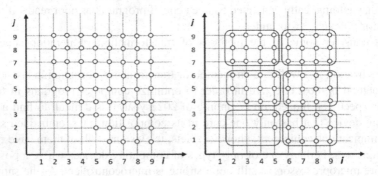

Fig. 4. Example of tiling with 4 × 3 tiles

The example above shows a different flow of operations in smaller blocks than initially. The main advantage of tiling method is an improved data locality, which in turn leads to fewer cache misses. In practical tasks, dimensions of computations can reach hundreds of thousands and millions. Therefore, processing in small blocks is even more appropriate from point of view of improving data locality [16].

It should be noted that tile method is an optimization on the level of transformation of iteration space. The transformed iteration space can be converted back to obtain a modified source code. Thus, methods which perform tiling do not have to be implemented directly in a compiler. Tiling method can be used by utilities separately from compilers, which, based on results of their work, generate a transformed source code. At the moment, there are several software packages that implement tiling method by converting source code to source code.

Two mentioned transformations of iteration space (parallelization and tiling method) approach to problem of speeding up of execution of programs in completely different ways. It should be noted that it is possible to use these two methods together. Since tiling method involves obtaining a larger number of processing threads, if there are no data dependencies between tiles, one can expect an additional gain when using parallelization.

6   Cyclic Partitioning of Iteration Space

An availability of a large number of existing software optimization methods produces a problem of optimal choice of optimization methods for each specific computational loop. Moreover, some methods are parametric, and efficiency of optimization methods will depend from an accuracy of choice of its parameters.

Suppose that there is a certain finite set of optimization methods M and a certain finite set of optimization parameters P, and an optimization criterion (objective function) of the i-th loop is F. F can be any optimization criterion set in advance – program execution time, program code size or data, or any other parameter that needs to be improved.

Then general formula for choosing of optimal methods and optimization parameters can be represented by the formula:

$$F_i = argmin(f(M_i, P_i)) \tag{4}$$

where f – is some unknown relation.

An *argmin* function denotes such a value of the input parameters $f(x)$, at which minimum value of function is reached:

$$argmin_x(f(x)) \in \{x | \forall y : f(x) \leq f(y)\} \tag{5}$$

Obviously, when M and P are empty sets, then optimization methods are not used and value of objective function is equal to its initial (not optimized) value.

Searching of optimal methods and parameters of optimized function (4) in general case is a task of selecting optimization methods and then refining their parameters. In a practical sense, searching among a limited number of methods is most applicable. In cases where optimization parameters significantly affect to objective optimization function, it may be sufficient to choose one or several optimization methods, but at the same time perform a very accurate selection of parameters of these methods.

Returning to tiling method, it can be noted that sizes of tiles are its parameters and can hold any integer values. In this connection, a question occurs how much tile sizes affects to possible optimization criteria. The authors performed a series of experiments to identify an influence of tile size on execution time of test programs.

To check time and energy efficiencies of automatic program, which performs tiling method based on polyhedral model, Pluto 11.4 package was chosen [17]. The test hardware is a desktop PC with an Intel Core i5-4670K quad-core processor and a 64-bit Ubuntu 14.04 LTS operating system. The benchmark applications used to estimate execution time and power consumption were taken from the PolyBench/C 4.1 benchmark suite [18].

The first step was to measure execution time and energy consumption. The experimental results are given in [19]. The authors have shown that for most of the test programs, tiling method shows an acceleration of program execution in 5–20%, depending on the test. Separately, a significant further increase in performance should be noted with mixed usage of tiling method and parallelization. Some test programs did not get any speedup from the method.

At the second stage of experiments in [20], the authors performed a discovery of tile sizes. The results obtained revealed two most important facts: tiling method is very sensitive to tiling sizes, while an execution time of programs varies greatly, and experiments have shown that the graphs of the execution time dependencies vary greatly for each test algorithm and do not have any specific pattern. Examples of execution time dependencies on tile sizes are shown in Fig. 5 and 6.

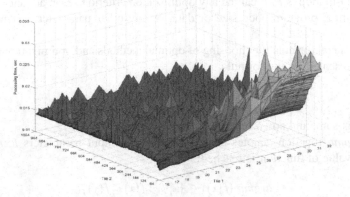

Fig. 5. Example 1 of dependency of execution time on tile sizes for the test program

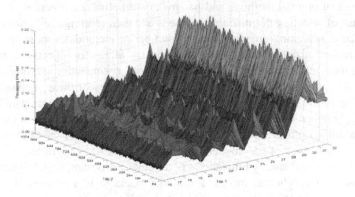

Fig. 6. Example 2 of dependency of execution time on tile sizes for the test program

Taking into account a significant scatter of objective function's values and significantly different nature of dependencies, two conclusions can be done:

- selection of tile sizes has a profound effect on execution time of test programs;
- it is impossible to determine a priori which exactly tiling sizes will be optimal for each specific case.

Thus, a problem occurs to select an optimal tile size. The complexity of dependence between tiles sizes and execution time indicates that selection of optimal tiling blocks should be performed iteratively, by sequentially selecting best values. In general case, it is necessary to enumerate all possible admissible values of tile sizes. Among obtained results, one can obviously choose the best one. In a practical sense, a direct search is inappropriate. Checking of execution time for each pair of tiles takes some time to compile and execute a program in order to measure an execution time. Thousands of such operations will take enormous time [21]. Therefore, a certain algorithm should be used, which, based on existing measurement results, will offer new options for choosing tile sizes.

7 Smart Tiling

Considering all variety of existing algorithms for finding minimum of a function of several variables, the authors have adopted Discrete Particle Swarm Optimization Method as a basis, as a method that searches by using a variety of search agents, and thus, although it does not guarantee searching for a global minimum, it significantly increases a probability to find out a global minimum in comparison to algorithms with one searching agent.

Various methods are used to find an extremum in complicated multidimensional functions. Evolutionary methods represent a separate class of search methods [22]. A special case of evolutionary methods is Particle Swarm Optimization Method.

Particle Swarm Optimization Method provides many extremum searching agents, which are informationally related to each other and, during a certain number of iterations, perform a serial search for an extremum. The authors call this method by analogy with a swarm of bees, behavior of the inhabitants of which is associated with searching for honey from all bees in hive.

A feature of the method is that each particle on next iteration of searching takes into account both its own found minimum and global minimum of all particles and adjusts its current search point also taking into account a global minimum. Also, change in coordinate on current iteration takes into account previous change in coordinate of previous iteration.

The set of particles is denoted by $P = \{P_i, i \in \overline{1..N}\}$, where N is a number of particles in a swarm or population. At times $t = 0,1, 2,\ldots$ coordinates of particle P_i are determined by the vector $X_{i,t} = (x_{i,t,1}, x_{i,t,2}, \ldots, x_{i,t,n})$, and its velocity by the vector $V_{i,t} = (v_{i,t,1}, v_{i,t,2}, \ldots, v_{i,t,n})$. r_1 and r_2 are random numbers in range from 0 to 1. An initial coordinates and velocities of particle P_i have form $X_{i,0} = X_i^0$ and $V_{i,0} = V_i^0$, respectively.

$$v_{i,t+1} = wv_{i,t} + c_1 r_1 \left(m_{i,t} - x_{i,t} \right) + c_2 r_2 (g_t - x_{i,t}) \tag{6}$$

Particles change their coordinates and velocities on each iteration. Number of particles and iterations can be as large as possible.

As applied to searching for optimal set of tile sizes, particles are pairs consisting of two sizes of tiles. Accordingly, a target function is a program execution time.

Since nodes of iteration lattice of loops are strictly integer numbers, a Discrete Particle Swarm Optimization Method was used. Main difference of which is a rounding of both coordinates and particle velocities, which achieves a transition from continuous to discrete integer processing. The determination of work efficiency was performed on basis of classical distribution of particle swarm optimization method, when initial coordinates are scattered over entire range of permissible values.

Based on tiling method together with Discrete Particle Swarm Optimization Method, the authors proposed an intelligent tiling method named Smart Tiling Method. The method performs an iterative search for the best parameters of tiling method. The block diagram of the proposed algorithm is shown in Fig. 7.

Let's consider the proposed algorithm more detailed. On initial stage, main parameters of method are chosen – choice of computational loops for which an optimization will be performed; choice of size ranges of tiles, choice of number of particles, iterations and search criterion (objective function). The search criterion is necessary for early completion of search for optimal values of tile sizes. Given an iterative nature of Smart Tiling Method, a direct search for optimal values can take a very long time. Therefore, usage of search completion criterion is quite justified. The search completion criterion can be an achievement of a certain time of program execution. On other hand, a maximum possible acceleration of program is not initially known. In this case, a criterion for completion of search may be an absence of acceleration of execution time in several last iterations of search.

In addition, it should be noted a choice of initial positions of particles and a vector of their initial motion. In original particle swarm optimization algorithm, it was assumed that particles are located randomly in a valid search area. Subsequently, researchers proposed different initial coordinates of particles. After analyzing test cases of search and carrying out various experiments, it turned out that classical Particle Swarm Optimization Method in some cases finds global minimum very poorly if it is located on the edge of search area. In this case, neither an increasing of number of particles, nor an increase of number of search iterations lead to finding a global minimum of program execution time. In connection with mentioned above, additional experiments were performed, which showed sufficient efficiency of initial placement of particles on edges of search area with an initial velocity directed to middle of search area. With such initial placement of particles, a searching for a global minimum, which is on edge of search area, is much more likely.

8   The Experiments

To confirm an efficiency of the proposed Smart Tiling Method, several series of experiments were performed.

Initially, the experiments were performed for test programs in order to determine an efficiency of tiling methods separately and then together with parallelization. Evaluation of efficiency was performed in terms of program execution time and computational energy efficiency [23]. Energy efficiency refers to total amount of electrical energy required to calculate a specific task. In case of using parallelization, a consumption of electrical energy per second can significantly increase due to usage of all microprocessor cores. At the same time, a computation time itself is dramatically reduced. Energy efficiency allows to quantify a reduction in computing power consumption. In general, the experiments show that if tiling method speeds up computations, then its

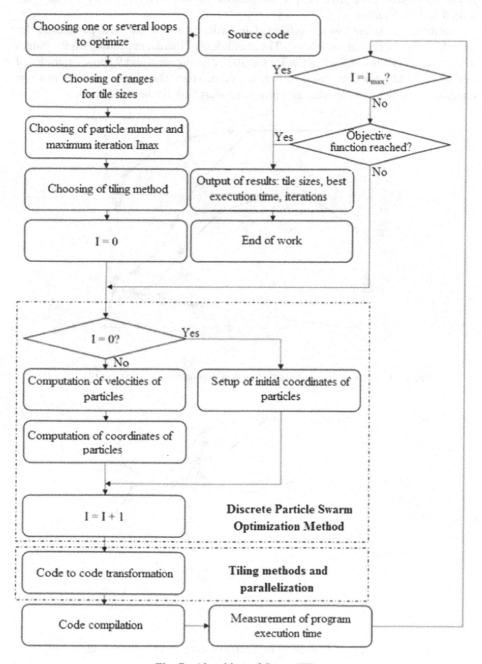

Fig. 7. Algorithm of Smart Tiling

use in conjunction with parallelization leads to an improvement in energy efficiency of computations. Also, a comparison was made of energy efficiency of computations on different computing platforms [24].

The next stage of the experiments was to measure an execution time of test programs for different tile sizes [25]. Examples of the obtained results are already presented in Fig. 5 and 6.

Further experiments were performed in order to select the best parameters for particle swarm optimization method. The coefficient of inertia, depending on the values of these coefficients of speed can differ significantly. Figure 8 and 9 show examples of finding best tile sizes by using different coefficients. The figures depict how the coordinates of the particles change during the searching for best tile sizes.

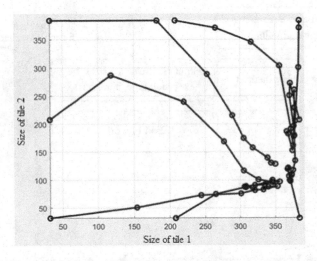

Fig. 8. Example 1 of searching of function's minimum for different tile sizes

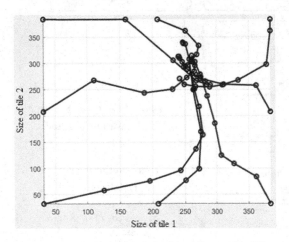

Fig. 9. Example 2 of searching of function's minimum for different tile sizes

As a result of numerous experiments, coefficients w = 0.5, c1 = 0.75, c2 = 0.75 were chosen, which provide a fairly extensive search for particles, and not only around the first found minimum.

On the final stage of the experiments, an efficiency of the proposed Smart Tiling Method was evaluated. For comparison, the results of the initial program execution time and with tiling method were used. In order to estimate a relative speedup of execution time, a result of the execution time without usage of optimization was set as 100%. An acceleration of the optimized results was calculated as a fraction of the initial execution time according to the formula (7):

$$P = \frac{T_{opt}}{T_{start}} \times 100\%, \tag{7}$$

where P is a relative execution time, T_{opt} is an execution time of optimized program, T_{start} is an execution time of initial (non-optimized) program.

The comparison results of these methods are shown in Fig. 10 and 11.

As it follows from the presented diagrams, usage of Smart Tiling Method further improves the existing tiling methods.

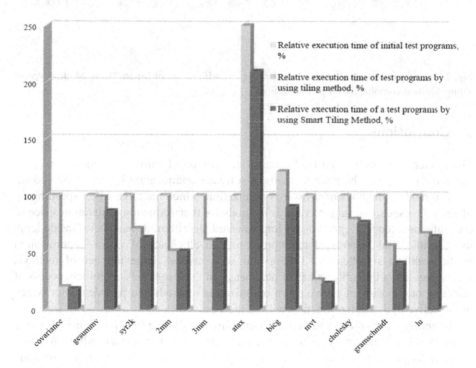

Fig. 10. Comparative acceleration of test programs with usage of Smart Tiling Method versus classical Tiling Method

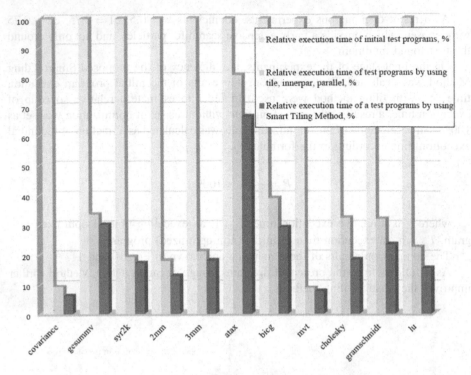

Fig. 11. Comparative acceleration of test programs with usage of Smart Tiling Method versus Tiling Method combined with parallelization

9 Conclusions

The modern approaches and mathematical description of software optimization problem are considered. The main methods of software optimization by speed are shown.

The modern methods of software optimization, which are targeted on speeding up of software execution, suggest various methods for transformation of iteration space of computational loops. Depending on implemented algorithm, dependencies inside loop, used architectural features of microprocessor, an efficiency of various optimization methods differs significantly. Taking into account both large number of methods themselves and admissible values of parameters of these methods, a problem occurs of selecting or choosing of such a set of optimization methods and parameters for which an objective optimization function will be the best.

In general case, in order to find the minimum of objective function, it is required to perform a complete enumeration of methods and their parameters, which is unacceptable for practical use due to huge time required for measuring a program execution time for each possible set of methods and parameters. The authors propose to restrict such methods to parallelization and tiling method as main optimization methods and to search for the best parameters of tiling sizes, which will allow finding the best execution time for these optimization methods. This approach does not allow finding the best execution time for all existing methods, however, iterative selection of the parameters of tiling method allows to get better execution times than with a random selection of these parameters.

The authors propose Smart Tiling Method as an improvement of classical Tiling Method by iterative usage of Discrete Particle Swarm Optimization Method. By finding the best tiling sizes of the method, it was possible to further speed up an execution of test programs with usage of new method.

Smart Tiling Method can be applied for computational loops of computer programs written in programming languages C or C++, for computational loops of arbitrary dimension, with using of various compilers and on any hardware platform. In general, additional speedup of test programs execution when using Smart Tiling Method without parallelization was 1–18% and 4–33% by using tiling methods together with parallelization.

References

1. Voevodin, V.V., Voevodin, Vl.V.: Parallel Computing, 608 p. BHV-Petersburg, St. Petersgurg, ISBN 5–94157–160–7 (2002). (in rus.)
2. Kennedy, K., Randy, A.: Optimizing Compilers for Modern Architectures - A dependence based approach. Morgan Kaufmann Publishers, San Francisco, San Diego, New York (2001)
3. Steinberg, B.Ya.: Mathematical Methods of Parallelization of Recurrent Program Loops on Supercomputers with Parallel Memory, 192 p. Rostov University Press, Rostov-on-Don (2004). (in rus.)
4. Huang, T.-C., Yang, C.-M.: Data dependence analysis for array references. J. Syst. Softw. **52**, 55–65 (2000)
5. Banerjee, U., et al.: Time and parallel processor bounds for fortran-like loops. IEEE Trans. Comput. **9**, 660–670 (1979)
6. Darte, A., Robert, Y., Vivien, F.: Loop parallelization algorithms. In: Pande, S., Agrawal, D. P. (eds.) Compiler Optimizations for Scalable Parallel Systems. LNCS, vol. 1808, pp. 141–171. Springer, Heidelberg (2001). https://doi.org/10.1007/3-540-45403-9_5
7. Creusillet, B., Irigoin, F.: Interprocedural Analyses of Fortran Programs. Ecole des Mines de Paris, Paris (1997)
8. Feautrier, P., Lengauer, C.: Polyhedron model. In: Padua D. (eds.) Encyclopedia of Parallel Computing. Springer, Boston, MA (2011). https://doi.org/10.1007/978-0-387-09766-4_502
9. Lim, A.W., Lam, M.S.: Maximizing parallelism and minimizing synchronization with affine partitions. Parallel Comput. **24**(3–4), 445–475 (1998)
10. Pugh, W., Rosser, E.: Iteration space slicing and its application to communication. In: Proceedings of the International Conference on Supercomputing, pp. 221–228 (1997)
11. Bielecki, W., Siedlecki, K.: Extracting synchronization-free threads in perfectly nested loops using the Omega project software. In: SEPADS'05 Proceedings of the 4th WSEAS International Conference on Software Engineering, Parallel & Distributed Systems, Salzburg, Austria (2005)
12. Boigelot, B.: On iterating linear transformations over recognizable sets of integers. Theor. Comput. Sci. **309**, 413–468 (2003)
13. Wolf, M.E.: Improving locality and parallelism in nested loops. Ph.D. Dissertation CSL-TR-92-538 (1992)

14. Lazorenko, D.: Method of high-level transformations of source code of description of digital systems to reduce their energy consumption. In: Collection of scientific works of G.E. Pukhov Institute for Modelling in Energy Engineering, vol. 38, pp. 41–53 (2007) (in rus.)
15. Darte, A., Silber, G., Vivien, F.: Combining retiming and scheduling techniques for loop parallelization and loop tiling. Parallel Process. Lett. **7**, 379–392 (1997)
16. Lam, M.S., Rothberg, E.E., Wolf, M.E.: The cache performance and optimizations of blocked algorithms. In: Proceedings of the 4th International Conference on Architectural Support for Programming Languages and Operating Systems, April 1991, pp. 63–74 (1991)
17. Boundhugula, U., Ramanujam, J., Sadayappan, P.: Pluto: A Practical and Fully Automatic Polyhedral Parallelizer and Locality Optimizer. Louisiana State University, Columbus (2007)
18. Pouchet, L.: PolyBench/C the Polyhedral Benchmark suite. http://web.cse.ohio-state.edu/~pouchet/software/polybench/#description. Accessed on 28 Dec 2021
19. Sushko, S., Chemeris, A.: Comparison of the efficiency of the automatic optimization based on the polyhedral model. In: Proceedings of the II International Conference Summer InfoCom 2016, Kyiv, 1–3 June 2016, pp. 74–76 (2016) (in rus.)
20. Sushko, S., Chemeris, O.: Influence of tile sizes on program execution time. In: Modeling and Informational Technology, vol. 82, pp. 110–117. Kyiv (2018) (in Ukrainian)
21. Feautrier P.: Parametric integer programming. RAIRO Recherche Op'erationnelle **22**(3), 243–268 (1988)
22. Kureichik, V., Kazharov, A.: Using of swarm intelligence in resolving of NP problem. In: News of YUFU. Technical Science, vol. 7, issue 120, pp. 30–37 (2011) (in rus.)
23. Chemeris, A., Sushko, S.: Investigation of performance and power consumption during automatic optimization by tiling and parallelization methods for computations on X64 platform. In: Modeling and Informational Technology, vol. 80, pp. 52–60. Kyiv (2017) (in rus.)
24. Sushko S., Chemeris O.: Determination of energy efficiency of computations on different computer systems. In: Modeling and Informational Technology, vol. 85, pp. 34–39. Kyiv, (2018) (in Ukrainian)
25. Chemeris A., Sushko S.: Estimation of decreasing of execution time of test programs with using of automatic optimization based on polyhedral model on Raspberry Pi 3. In: Proceedings of the International Conference Winter InfoCom, 1–2 December 2016, pp. 63–65. Kyiv (2016) (in rus.)

Digest of Blockchain Technologies to Design System for Big Image Data Provenance and Security

Igor Zakharov[1]([✉]), Jonathan Anderson[2], Garrett Parsons[1],
Michael D. Henschel[1], Bryan Ewenson[1],
and Christopher Papanagiotou[1]

[1] C-CORE, Ottawa, ON, Canada
{igor.zakharov, garrett.parsons, michael.henschel,
bryan.ewenson, christopher.papanagiotou}@c-core.ca
[2] Memorial University, St. John's, NL, Canada
jonathan.anderson@mun.ca

Abstract. Data quantities are rapidly increasing in many industry sectors due to the development of new sensors, mobile and cloud technologies, advancements in IoT and AI, and growth of social and entertainment media. Many applications (e.g., in finance, healthcare, government data) have strict information security requirements for simultaneous access, record updating, and validation in an immutable manner, which can be achieved with distributed ledger technology (DLT). In this paper we review and analyze sixty-three currently available blockchain (BC) systems and their components in context of the DLT for big image data storage, provenance tracking, replication, and sharing. We also elaborate the key BC system components and architecture for major information security concerns.

Keywords: Distributed ledger technology (DLT) · Blockchain · Information security · Big image data

1 Introduction

Data volumes are rapidly increasing across different industries and governments due to the development of new sensors, mobile and cloud technologies, advancements in IoT and AI, and growth of social and entertainment media. The amount of data created, captured, copied, and consumed within an organization can reach volumes on the order of 100s of terabytes to multi-petabytes [1] with millions and even billions of records approaching to big data scales (beyond computing power of modern data centers).

Information security measures to protect data from internal and external cyber threats include access control (authentication and authorization), data integrity maintenance, encryption and digital signatures, and monitoring [2, 3]. Beyond these traditional measures, centralized digital ledger recordkeeping enables verifiable transaction logs to be created and maintained by a central authority to simplify auditing mechanisms [4].

© Springer Nature Switzerland AG 2022
A. V. Tuzikov et al. (Eds.): PRIP 2021, CCIS 1562, pp. 33–47, 2022.
https://doi.org/10.1007/978-3-030-98883-8_3

In contrast to the centralized ledger, the distributed ledger is a decentralized database which is synchronized and accessible across different users (nodes) on a network. In multiple applications, such as finance, legal services, medicine, Earth observation etc., the distributed ledger technology (DLT) can be used to meet requirements in secured transactions, simultaneous data access, validation, record updating and storing in an immutable manner [5, 6]. The immutability provides DLT access to a different point in the consistency-availability-protection (CAP) trade-off space [7, 8] than the traditional solutions [9]. In addition to the key mechanisms, such as, database, consensus algorithm, peer-to-peer (P2P) network and transactions logging, the main DLT features also include [1]: immutability (new data can only be appended, but not changed or deleted), and cryptography.

Distributed ledgers enable the formation and maintenance of consensus in terms of the existence, status and evolution of a set of shared facts [2]. The major differences between distributed ledgers and traditional distributed databases (distributed across sites in a network) are the use of an adversarial threat model and a very different view of authority.

Blockchains (BCs) can be considered to be a subset of distributed ledgers that share the same adversarial threat model (assuming that not all nodes are trustworthy) over a P2P network and have additional characteristics, such as [1], linked blocks which chronologically store transactional data. Beside BCs, DLTs also include [1, 2] Directed Acyclic Graphs (DAGs), shared and hybrid ledgers. Systems based on DAG structure demonstrate scalability and efficiency in saving storage space up to 97% [3].

In general, the implementation of a custom, private permissioned blockchain from scratch is a difficult task [4] and therefore a digest of currently available BCs is essential to achieve advanced performance. The goal of our paper is to review and analyze the currently available BC systems in context of the DLT component configuration for big data management. The novelty of the paper also includes a digest of current BC technologies and the elaboration of possibilities for BC implementation for information security of big image data.

2   BC Surveys

Numerous publications provided comprehensive and systematic literature reviews of BC technology analyzing its concept, architecture, components and implementation focusing on:

- evolution and architecture [5, 6],
- performance evaluation [7],
- identity management [8],
- post-quantum cryptography [9],
- use by cryptocurrencies [10],
- industrial IoT applications [11],
- healthcare application [12],
- data management [13],
- engineering and manufacturing applications [14],

- supply chain management applications [15],
- connection with cloud computing [16],
- connection with communication networks [17],
- electronic voting system [18],
- and other numerous applications [19–23].

A survey on BCs for several smart applications (city, healthcare, transportation and grid), which can generate big data [24], discussed approaches, opportunities, challenges and future directions for secure big data acquisition, data storage, data analytics, and data privacy preservation. BC architecture for massive data storage was recently analyzed and implemented [25] to improve scalability and performance. Various aspects of BC-enabled cyber-physical systems, including security, privacy, immutability, fault tolerance, interoperability, data provenance, atomicity, automation, data/service sharing, and trust were reviewed in [26]. BCs can be categorized as permissionless and permissioned (requiring authorization). Based on the usage and ownership the BCs can be divided [22] into public, private and consortium (to record cross-organizational transactions).

3 Blockchain

3.1 Transactions

A transaction is the smallest unit of a work process, consisting of an exchange between two or more participants or systems (ISO 2008). Transactions can take many forms depending on their intended purpose. For instance, if provenance of data is a desired feature of the given blockchain, then its transactions will contain the information necessary to build a chain between versions of the data (references to specific versions, symbolic links, etc.). An example of the lifecycle of user transactions through a Hyperledger Fabric Blockchain Network can include ordering and validation-committing stages [27].

3.2 Block Structure

The block structure includes a block header and block body [22]. The block header specifies the metadata, including various fields: hash (ID) of previous block (to connect its previous block called a parent block), hash of current block, timestamp (creation time of the block), nonce (relates to consensus mechanism for validation), Merkle root (to store the transactions for efficient data verification).

The block's header may also contain other information, for example, block version (software/protocol version), nBits (target threshold of a valid block hash) [28] and confirmation [17]. The block body (also called as block data) stores transactions (work process resulting in a state change) which are assembled using cryptographic functions. All performed transactions (e.g., transfers of money) are hashed and hash values are structured into a Merkle DAG. The linked blocks form a BC.

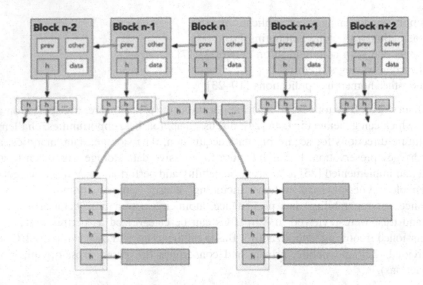

Fig. 1. Blockchain structure.

3.3   BC Architecture

The three main components which enable BC technology are a decentralized P2P network, distributed consensus and cryptographically secure algorithms [23]. Works [2, 27] highlight the importance of ledger and validity rules (when transactions are considered valid and how the ledger is updated). The high-level BC architecture implemented in Hyperledger Fabric is shown in [29].

The paper [30] describes four layers of a BC system: application, distributed computing, platform, and infrastructure. The architectural components can also be described [22] using the following six layers:

1. Application,
2. Contract (script, algorithm, smart contract),
3. Incentive (issuance and allocation mechanisms),
4. Consensus,
5. Network (P2P network, communication and verification mechanisms),
6. Data (block information in Fig. 1).

3.4   Smart Contract

A smart contract is a computer program deployed and executed in BC system to enable control and addition transactions and blocks to the ledger when the predefined conditions are met. Smart contract may also provide API functionality to external applications including Distributed Applications (DApps), which are the programs that, while they are not stored there, interface with the blockchain through the use of smart contracts. DApps expose blockchain-backed functionality to end users.

4 Information Security with BC

4.1 Security Threats

Distributed Ledger Technology increases the difficulty of manipulating the ledger via a single malicious node, but there are several major categories of blockchain vulnerabilities [23]:

- fork (nodes in the network have diverging views of the chain),
- stale or orphaned blocks.
- other (e.g., 51%, DNS, DDoS, selfish mining, consensus delay, double-spending).

Some of these vulnerabilities are specific to cryptocurrency applications and associated with public permissionless BCs. In permissioned BC, multiple validation nodes are trusted to maintain the consensus. To avoid certain nodes accepting inconsistent messages, consensus mechanisms (e.g. PBFT, PoA, DPoS + BFT) are used; decisions are encoded using digital signatures with hashing algorithms (e.g. Elliptic Curve Cryptography and SHA-256 [23]).

4.2 Consensus Mechanisms

BC networks are designed to function with no single trusted network node [22]. Consensus mechanisms enable agreement among decentralized nodes before a block is included into the blockchain. Consensus also can be an agreement among DLT nodes that validates a transaction. Three major types of consensus protocols are (i) compute-intensive-based (e.g. proof of work (PoW)), (ii) capability-based (e.g. Proof of Authority (PoA)) and (iii) voting-based (e.g. Practical Byzantine Fault Tolerance (PBFT)) [30]. A systematic review of 66 known consensus protocols was conducted [31] to facilitate protocol selection focusing on their features and sector preference and environment. More recent publications reviewed consensus protocols analyzing their properties, applications, and performance [32]; taxonomy and classification of 28 new protocols [33]; evolution and comparative analysis of 130 consensus algorithms using a novel architectural classification [34] based on publications in academic journals and industry websites for different application domains. These reviews indicated that several consensus mechanisms, such as BFT-SMaRt and PoA, demonstrate high performance and efficiency for applications requiring large volumes of transactions. The procedure of discerning authorities results in the centralized configuration of PoA, which makes this approach appropriate for private consortiums to accept a proposed block once it is accepted by the majority of authorized entities. Comparison [35] of PoA and PBFT for permissioned blockchains, deployed over the internet with Byzantine (malicious or misleading) nodes, advocates that PoA requires less message exchanges thus enabling higher performance, however without providing adequate consistency guarantees for scenarios where data integrity is essential.

Increasing the number of nodes improves network availability for the users, but for certain consensus mechanisms can lead to longer consensus agreement times. Some affected consensus mechanisms were developed to decrease times by creating different types of nodes, not all of which participate in the consensus process.

The major data security advantages related to using BCs include decentralization, transparency, immutability, auditability and integrity. The significant benefit which can be achieved with BC is the automation of data and transaction flow processes.

5 Digest of BC Technologies

5.1 Implementations of BC and Other DLT Systems

The key aspects described in the above sections (block structure and BC architecture) have to be implemented and customized based on the type of application and considering the data to be stored, secured and managed with the BC. BC application areas are varying between finance, government, IoT, legal and other industries. The block components, algorithms and protocols have to follow the latest standards and meet the defined requirements. In order to identify available BC technologies, the digest of BC and other DLT technologies was performed using internet search engines, GitHub and comprehensive review and analysis of research publications available via IEEE Xplore and the Memorial University library catalogue. Multiple resources (e.g. [30, 36]) previously analyzed different available BC and other DLT frameworks and platforms.

In total 63 BCs/DLTs were analyzed in this paper. There are many BCs for specific use cases, solutions, projects and applications (e.g. in healthcare [37]) which were not included into the digest due to their commercial nature and confidential aspects of implementation. A comprehensive list of BC and DLT systems identified on November 24, 2021 is provided in Table 1. This list includes both frameworks (e.g. Ethereum, Hyperledger, Qtum) and the implementations of BCs for specific applications. These implementations were analyzed in context of their applicability and demonstrated capability to big data applications (in this case the name of BC is highlighted by the bold font). The Italic font of BC name indicates that a technology is less applicable to big data (e.g. not sufficient information, inactive GitHub for three or more years). Table 1 includes the following columns:

- number and name,
- application area (or use case),
- technology (consensus mechanism, database (DB), programming language and other details), and
- a category of documentation availability and internet address.

The documentation is important for efficient implementation and usage of BC/DLT systems. In Table 1 the documentation and other supplementary information was categorized in three levels of availability:

1 - low (or not identified nor available),

2 - moderate (basic setup and user's guides, examples and code snippets, stack overflow),

3 - good (in addition to the moderate level of documentation/information, may include video tutorials, thorough guides, whitepapers and research publications, test network, multiple communities, documented API/Features).

Table 1. BC and other DLT technologies.

#	Name	Application	Technological aspects	Documentation
1.	Aion	Cryptocurrency, transfer and trade custom assets	Unity, a hybrid PoS/PoW; Java, Rust	2; aion.theoan.com
2.	**ADAPT**	Data/image provenance	BigchainDB, Cryptographic-FS, Tendermint; MongoDB, Python	2; adapt-sys.com
3.	**ArcBlock**	Development **platform** (for e.g. supply chain management, data marketplace)	OACP (Open Chain Access Protocol), Uses IPFS, NodeJS, SDK (Python, Java, Elixir)	3; arcblock.io
4.	Ardor	**Platform** securing IoT devices, DB, sensitive data, cryptocurrency (NXT)	PoS; Java	3; www.jelurida.com/ardor
5.	**BigchainDB**	Development **platform**; supply chain management, provenance tracking	Tendermint; MongoDB; Python, JavaScript, NodeJS, Java	3; www.bigchaindb.com
6.	*Binded*	Copyright **platform**, images	JavaScript	1; binded.com
7.	Bitcoin	Popular blockchain implementation; Cryptocurrency (BTC)	PoW; Minsc (SC), C++	2; bitcoin.org
8.	*BlocHIE*	Healthcare information exchange	PoW; Python	1
9.	Signum	Cryptocurrency (SIGNA), fungible custom tokens for use within the network	PoC+; H2 or MariaDB; forked from now-defunct Burstcoin; Signum SmartJ, Java	2; burst-coin.org signum.network
10.	Cardano	Cryptocurrency (ADA)	PoS and Ouroboros; PostgreSQL; Custom languages Marlowe and Plutus, Haskell	3; cardano.org
11.	Chain core	Track and transfer balances in a token format	A variant of BFT; PostgreSQL; Go, SDK (Java, Ruby, Node)	2; chain.com
12.	**Corda**	Financial sector, CorDapps	Raft; Kotlin, Java	3; corda.net
13.	Credits	Issuing tokens and automating of fintech services, cryptocurrency	Proof of Agreement (on + BFT); C++, Java	3; credits.com
14.	**Cosmos** SDK, Tendermint	Application that conform to Inter-Blockchain Communication protocol (IBCP)	Tendermint; Go, Starport	3; cosmos.network
15.	Democracy Earth	Blockchain-based decision-making (voting)	Proof of Identity, JavaScript	2; democracy.earth

(continued)

Table 1. (*continued*)

#	Name	Application	Technological aspects	Documentation
16.	**Elements**	**Framework** to design, build, and operate of sidechain-capable blockchains	Built on Bitcoin's codebase; Strong Federation; C++, drivers (Python, C#, Ruby, Node, Go, Perl, Java)	3; elementsproject.org
17.	Enigma	Cryptocurrency (SCRT)	Tendermint; Rust, Go	3; enigma.co
18.	EOS	**Platform** for building, deploying, and running applications	DPoS, Asynchronous BFT Secret Contracts; C++	3; eos.io
19.	**Ethereum**	**Framework,** Cryptocurrency (ETH)	PoS; Go, resources (Rust, Python, JavaScript, C#, Delphi, smart contract (Solidity, Vyper)	3; www.ethereum.org
20.	Exonum	**Framework,** for government land registry and academic certificates	Similar to PBFT; RocksDB; Rust, Java SDK, light client (JavaScript, Python)	3; exonum.com
21.	Follow My Vote	**Platform** for rapid development and deployment of secure dApps	Based on Graphene; C++	1; followmyvote.com
22.	*Graphene*	Focus on transaction processing speed	DPoS; C++, SDK (Java, Python, JavaSrcipt, iOS)	1; cryptonomex.com
23.	*Hydrochain*	Water consumption analysis and billing process with IoT	JavaScript	1;github. com/UltimateRoman/Hydro-chain
24.	Hydro Blockchain	Secure accounts, identities; wallet, virtual cards	Solidity, JavaScript	hydrogenplatform.com
25.	Hyperledger Besu	Ethereum client for public and private/permissioned network use cases	Multiple consensus options (Ethash (PoW), Clique (PoA), IBFT 2.0 (PoA), QBFT (PoA); Java, NodeJS, Solidity	3; besu.hyperledger.org
26.	Hyperledger Iroha	**Platform** for developing applications	YAC; C++, SDK (Java, Python, JavaSrcipt, iOS)	3; hyperledger.org
27.	**Hyperledger Fabric**	**Framework** for developing permissioned blockchain applications or solutions with a modular architecture	Go SDK (Go, Java, Node.js, Python, JavaScript)	3; hyperledger.org
28.	Hyperledger Indy	SDK, tools, libraries, and reusable components for digital identities	Redundant RBFT, Python	3; hyperledger.org
29.	Hyperledger Burrow	Single-binary blockchain **framework**	PoS, EVM and WASM; Go, Javascript API, Solidity	3; hyperledger.org
30.	Hyperledger Sawtooth	Enterprise blockchain **framework**	PBFT, PoET, and Raft; Python, SDK (Go, Java, JavaScript, Python, Rust, Swift)	3; hyperledger.org

(*continued*)

Table 1. (*continued*)

#	Name	Application	Technological aspects	Documentation
31.	ICON	Cryptocurrency (ICX), connecting heterogeneous blockchains	Powered by Goloop; Tendermint, DPoS, DPoC; RocksDB; Go, SDK (Python, Java, Swift)	3; icon.foundation
32.	**IOTA**	Multi-asset **platform** for use with IoT	DAG; based on PoS, PoW; Go, Rust, client library (C, Go, JavaScript, Java, Python)	3; iota.org
33.	KSI Blockchain	**Platform**, EOGuard for satellite data provenance	SDK (Java, C, Go)	2; guardtime.com
34.	Komodo	Ecosystem, wallet, Komodo token (KMD)	Delayed PoW, zk-SNARKs; C++, C, Python, AtomicDEX	3; komodoplatform.com
35.	Lisk	Application **platform**	Delegated PoS, Lisk-BFT; JavaScript, Lisk-SDK	3; lisk.com
36.	*MedRec*	Electronic health record	Based on Ethereum; Go-Ethereum (Geth), Solidity	1; medrec.media.mit.edu
37.	*MediaChain*	Connecting applications to media	DAG; JavaScript, Go	1; mediachain.io
38.	MultiChain	Commercial service and **platform** to build and deploy applications	Compatibility with the Bitcoin ecosystem; C++, C	2. www.multichain.com
39.	*ModelChain*	Medical applications	PoW, research stage	1
40.	**Neblio**	Service and consulting (e.g. for supply chain, records management, asset tracking)	C++, Python, JavaScript, Go, Java, Ruby, C#, PHP	3; nebl.io
41.	NEM	**Platform** for exchange, cryptocurrency (XEM)	Proof of Importance (PoI), Java, C, Javascript	1; nem.io
42.	NEO	**Platform** for exchange	DBFT, interoperability with Ethereum; C#, Go, Python, Java, or TypeScript	3; Neo.org
43.	NXT	NXT Token, asset exchange	PoS, Java	2; jelurida.com
44.	OmniPHR/EHR	Clinical data management and sharing **platform**	Groovy, JavaScript	cablabs.com
45.	OpenChain	Open source DLT	Based on Bitcoin Blockchain PoW; C#, JavaScript	3; docs.openchain.org
46.	**Qtum**	**Platform**, service, QTUM token	PoS; C++, Python, JavaScript	3; qtum.org
47.	**Quorum**	Protocol, **platform**	Derived from Ethereum; Raft; Go, Javascript, GoQuorum	3; kaleido.io

(*continued*)

Table 1. (*continued*)

#	Name	Application	Technological aspects	Documentation
48.	*Paperchain*	Access streaming revenue, NFT	Proofs of Consumption; Papergres; Go	1; paperchain.io
49.	Parity/Polkadot	Infrastructure, **framework**	Cross-Consensus Messaging Format (XCM), ABFT, PoA Nominated PoS; Rust	3; parity.io
50.	*Po.et*	Was a protocol for publishing industry, token (POE)	Bitcoin blockchain; Typescript, JavaScript	1
51.	Propy	Automation of the real estate sales process, token (PRO)	Ethereum, JavaScript	1; propy.com
52.	Ripple	Financial solutions, API for money transfer	XRP Ledger, C++, JavaScript	2; ripple.com
53.	Rubix	BAAS, smart contracts, NFT	Proof of Harvest; JavaScipt, Shell	1; rubix.network
54.	Smilo	Control digital assets, identities and securities, wallet	Proof of Resource and Time (SPoRT), Go, JavaScript	2; smilo.io; didux.io
55.	Stellar	Money transfer	Stellar; Go, Java, JavaScript, SDK (Python, C#.NET Ruby, Scala, Qt/C++, Flutter)	3; www.stellar.org
56.	Stratis	BAAS, development platform	Based on Bitcoin; PoS, PoA, PoW; C#	3; stratisplatform.com
57.	Tezos	**Platform** for assets and applications for industries, tokens (TEZ)	PoS; Python, Ligo, OCaml, Golang, TypeScript, JavaScript	3; tezos.com
58.	Ubitquity	**Platform**, BAAS for real estate, documentation	Files can be stored on IPFS, StorJ, Vultr; Python	2; ubitquity.io
59.	Ujomusic	Music software services company	IPFS; OrbitDB, Postgres; Ethereum based; Go, JavaScript	1; blog.ujomusic.com
60.	Verisart	Certification service for NFTs, video, digital art, paintings, collectibles	Based on Bitcoin blockchain	1; verisart.com
61.	Wanchain	Wallet, exchange and mobile payments, token (WAN)	PoS; Solidity, Go, JavaScript	3; wanchain.org
62.	Waves	Wallet, cryptoasset exchange	FPoS, Waves-NG protocol; Ride, Python, JavaScript	2; waves.tech
63.	Zilliqa	**Platform** to scale 1000/s transactions, token (ZIL)	Practical BFT and PoW; Scilla, C++, JavaScript, Golang	1; zilliqa.com

5.2   Summary of BC Technologies

BCs and other DLTs in Table 1 can be categorized in three groups:

- frameworks – are well supported and documented technologies, which can be implemented to develop BC applications from scratch or using modules,
- platforms – is the cloud service designed to accelerate the BC development and operation for the users relying on existing blockchain infrastructure.
- implementations - allow the users to adopt or execute applications on the provider's blockchain network.

Frameworks and platforms are highlighted by the bold font in "Application" column of Table 1. In addition to the listed 18 platforms, the largest cloud service providers (e.g. AWS, IBM, Azure, Oracle, GCP) have already developed environments for deploying BC applications. Multiple platforms also provide blockchain as a service (BaaS).

The most popular programming languages used for BC implementations are Java family (JavaScript is used by 29 BCs and Java by 20 BCs), 20 BCs use C family (C++, C, C#), 19 use Python and 18 use Go. Also, the following languages are also used: Ruby, Node, Kotlin, Delphi, Swift, Groovy, Ride, Scala. The number of BCs provide software development toolkit (SDK) in multiple languages for rapid implementation. Smart contracts are often implemented using Java and JavaScript, Solidity (used by 6 BCs), Rust (5 BCs) and other languages including custom designed (Signum SmartJ, Marlowe, Plutus, Starport, Minsc. Vyper, Yul, NodeJS, Ligo, Scilla).

The ledger technology relies on DB (NoSQL or SQL) for storage blocks and transactions. The popular DBs used for BCs are PostgreSQL and MongoDB; other technologies, such as H2, MariaDB, RocksDB, BerkeleyDB, OrbitDB, were also identified.

Other technological aspects identified during review and analysis of BCs include:

- instant check of provenance (Verisart);
- consensus protocol may process transactions without confirmation (Zilliqa);
- blocks can be created at regular time intervals regardless of the presence of transactions (KSI);
- various DAG data structures (not only Merkle tree) where each message is attached to previous ones (e.g. IOTA);
- processing capacity of 14K (Cosmos) and 100K (Graphene) transactions per second can be achieved;
- a partial mesh network, which means that every node is only connected to a small subset of nodes in the network (e.g. Lisk).

6   BC for Big Image Data

6.1   Implementation

BC implementation has to take into account vulnerabilities and the performance of the hash function considering the data size and file system. The BC system can be implemented for increasing level of information security of large and growing data volumes in data centers and cloud environments. In a cloud environment, the usage of BC enables multiple nodes to participate in maintaining transparent and immutable provenance information for tracking data transactions and detect malicious activities [23]. The API and web user interface can be used to monitor BC activity and visualize provenance records.

The development activities to achieve the best performance and security capabilities of BC system were conducted to define, select and design its technological elements, including block structure and information, hash function and consensus mechanism.

6.2   Performance

An important problem in BC is scalability, which coincides with growing data volumes. An increasing number of transactions (and block validations) from an increasing number of users, leads to communication overhead that limits the network scalability [30]. BC systems for massive data storage can potentially enable scalability with acceptable performance [25]. To address issue of redundant massive data storage, a secure data storage and recovery scheme in the BC-based network was proposed [38] by improving the real-time monitoring, and supporting the dynamic storage, and update of distributed data. DLT systems based on DAG structures can also be used to save storage space [3].

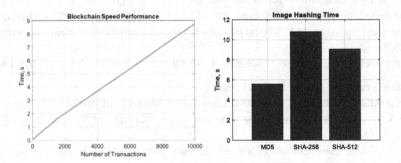

Fig. 2. AMBC speed performance: transaction processing (left) and hashing large (1.8 GB) image (right).

The processing speed (Fig. 2) achieved with a MATLAB-based BC prototype on a single core of Intel Core i7-4770 CPU @ 3.40 GHz is with 32 GB RAM was 1,115 transactions per second using MD5 hashing algorithm for transaction and block information only (without hashing image data). Higher BC processing speeds, if required, can be achieved with parallel implementation of BC cryptographic services module (Fig. 2) or using hashing algorithms with higher performance.

6.3 Image Data Hashing

The BC system applications for sharing and enabling integrity of large data files such as medical [39] and Earth observation [40] images provide examples of the required definition and design activities. The assurance in immutability of image data may also be required for other applications (e.g. multimedia). An immutable cryptographic signature (ciphertext) can be used to assign a unique hash value to an image. Generating hash value (i.e. hashing) of image is one of the bottlenecks for big data because image file size can be more than 1 GB. Computational time for hashing an EO image with popular hashing functions (MD5, SHA-256 and SHA-512) implemented in Java on a single core is shown in Fig. 2. The best performance (5.58 s for a SAR image of 1.8 GB size) was achieved using MD5 function. Faster functions, such as xxh3 and crc32, implemented in PHP programming language, can potentially provide up to 20 times higher hashing speed than MD5 [41], however these algorithms may provide weaker security in exchange for performance improvements. A parallel or GPU-based hashing of large number of images can also be used to achieve higher performance.

7 Conclusions

This paper reviewed and analyzed current concepts, applications and implementations of BC systems. In total, 63 BC technologies including platforms and frameworks were identified. The main elements of a BC system to enable information security of big data were analyzed and defined. The demonstrated BC speed performance and capabilities, as it is demonstrated with the current technologies and experiments, are sufficient for big image data applications.

References

1. Lange, M., Leiter, S.C., Alt, R.: Defining and delimitating distributed ledger technology: results of a structured literature analysis. In: Di Ciccio, C., et al. (eds.) BPM 2019. LNBIP, vol. 361, pp. 43–54. Springer, Cham (2019). https://doi.org/10.1007/978-3-030-30429-4_4
2. Hileman, G., Rauchs, M.: 2017 Global blockchain benchmarking study. SSRN J. (2017). https://doi.org/10.2139/ssrn.3040224
3. Yang, W., Dai, X., Xiao, J., Jin, H.: LDV: a lightweight DAG-based blockchain for vehicular social networks. IEEE Trans. Veh. Technol. **69**, 5749–5759 (2020). https://doi.org/10.1109/TVT.2020.2963906
4. Knirsch, F., Unterweger, A., Engel, D.: Implementing a blockchain from scratch: why, how, and what we learned. EURASIP J. Inf. Secur. **2019**(1), 1–14 (2019). https://doi.org/10.1186/s13635-019-0085-3
5. Bhutta, M.N.M., et al.: A survey on blockchain technology: evolution architecture and security. IEEE Access **9**, 61048–61073 (2021). https://doi.org/10.1109/ACCESS.2021.3072849
6. Yang, W., Aghasian, E., Garg, S., Herbert, D., Disiuta, L., Kang, B.: A survey on blockchain-based internet service architecture: requirements, challenges, trends, and future. IEEE Access **7**, 75845–75872 (2019). https://doi.org/10.1109/ACCESS.2019.2917562

7. Fan, C., Ghaemi, S., Khazaei, H., Musilek, P.: Performance evaluation of blockchain systems: a systematic survey. IEEE Access **8**, 126927–126950 (2020). https://doi.org/10.1109/ACCESS.2020.3006078

8. Rathee, T., Singh, P.: A systematic literature mapping on secure identity management using blockchain technology. J. King Saud Univ. – Comput. Inform. Sci. S1319157821000690 (2021). https://doi.org/10.1016/j.jksuci.2021.03.005

9. Fernandez-Carames, T.M., Fraga-Lamas, P.: Towards post-quantum blockchain: a review on blockchain cryptography resistant to quantum computing attacks. IEEE Access **8**, 21091–21116 (2020). https://doi.org/10.1109/ACCESS.2020.2968985

10. Rehman, M.H.ur., Salah, K., Damiani, E., Svetinovic, D.: Trust in Blockchain Cryptocurrency Ecosystem. IEEE Trans. Eng. Manage. **67**, 1196–1212 (2020). https://doi.org/10.1109/TEM.2019.2948861

11. Alladi, T., Chamola, V., Parizi, R.M., Choo, K.-K.R.: Blockchain applications for industry 4.0 and industrial IoT: a review. IEEE Access **7**, 176935–176951 (2019). https://doi.org/10.1109/ACCESS.2019.2956748

12. Namasudra, S., Deka, G.C. (eds.): Applications of Blockchain in Healthcare. SBD, vol. 83. Springer, Singapore (2021). https://doi.org/10.1007/978-981-15-9547-9

13. Paik, H.-Y., Xu, X., Bandara, H.M.N.D., Lee, S.U., Lo, S.K.: Analysis of data management in blockchain-based systems: from architecture to governance. IEEE Access **7**, 186091–186107 (2019). https://doi.org/10.1109/ACCESS.2019.2961404

14. Kasten, J.E.: Engineering and manufacturing on the blockchain: a systematic review. IEEE Eng. Manag. Rev. **48**, 31–47 (2020). https://doi.org/10.1109/EMR.2020.2964224

15. Chang, S.E., Chen, Y.: when blockchain meets supply chain: a systematic literature review on current development and potential applications. IEEE Access **8**, 62478–62494 (2020). https://doi.org/10.1109/ACCESS.2020.2983601

16. Gai, K., Guo, J., Zhu, L., Yu, S.: Blockchain meets cloud computing: a survey. IEEE Commun. Surv. Tutorials **22**, 2009–2030 (2020). https://doi.org/10.1109/COMST.2020.2989392

17. Rehmani, M.H.: Blockchain Systems and Communication Networks: From Concepts to Implementation. Springer International Publishing, Cham (2021). https://doi.org/10.1007/978-3-030-71788-9

18. Jafar, U., Aziz, M.J.A., Shukur, Z.: Blockchain for electronic voting system—review and open research challenges. Sensors **21**, 5874 (2021). https://doi.org/10.3390/s21175874

19. Cagigas, D., Clifton, J., Diaz-Fuentes, D., Fernandez-Gutierrez, M.: Blockchain for public services: a systematic literature review. IEEE Access **9**, 13904–13921 (2021). https://doi.org/10.1109/ACCESS.2021.3052019

20. Shen, C., Pena-Mora, F.: Blockchain for cities—a systematic literature review. IEEE Access **6**, 76787–76819 (2018). https://doi.org/10.1109/ACCESS.2018.2880744

21. Ali Syed, T., Alzahrani, A., Jan, S., Siddiqui, M.S., Nadeem, A., Alghamdi, T.: A comparative analysis of blockchain architecture and its applications: problems and recommendations. IEEE Access **7**, 176838–176869 (2019). https://doi.org/10.1109/ACCESS.2019.2957660

22. Xie, J., et al.: A survey of blockchain technology applied to smart cities: research issues and challenges. IEEE Commun. Surv. Tutorials **21**, 2794–2830 (2019). https://doi.org/10.1109/COMST.2019.2899617

23. Shetty, S.S., Kamhoua, C.A., Njilla, L.L.: Blockchain for Distributed Systems Security. Wiley (2019)

24. Deepa, N., et al.: A Survey on Blockchain for Big Data: Approaches, Opportunities, and Future Directions. arXiv:2009.00858 [cs]. (2021)

25. Chen, X., Zhang, K., Liang, X., Qiu, W., Zhang, Z., Tu, D.: HyperBSA: a high-performance consortium blockchain storage architecture for massive data. IEEE Access **8**, 178402–178413 (2020). https://doi.org/10.1109/ACCESS.2020.3027610
26. Zhao, W., Jiang, C., Gao, H., Yang, S., Luo, X.: Blockchain-enabled cyber-physical systems: a review. IEEE Internet Things J. **8**, 4023–4034 (2021). https://doi.org/10.1109/JIOT.2020.3014864
27. Nijssen, S., Bollen, P.: The Lifecycle of a user transaction in a hyperledger fabric blockchain network part 2: order and validate. In: Debruyne, C., Panetto, H., Guédria, W., Bollen, P., Ciuciu, I., Meersman, R. (eds.) OTM 2018. LNCS, vol. 11231, pp. 150–158. Springer, Cham (2019). https://doi.org/10.1007/978-3-030-11683-5_16
28. Zheng, Z., Xie, S., Dai, H., Chen, X., Wang, H.: An overview of blockchain technology: architecture, consensus, and future trends. In: 2017 IEEE International Congress on Big Data (BigData Congress), pp. 557–564. IEEE, Honolulu, HI, USA (2017). https://doi.org/10.1109/BigDataCongress.2017.85
29. Hyperledger Fabric – A Platform For Business Solutions. https://www.edureka.co/blog/hyperledger-fabric/. Accessed on 20 Dec 2021
30. Ismail, M.: Article a review of blockchain architecture and consensus protocols: use cases, challenges, and solutions. Symmetry **11**, 1198 (2019). https://doi.org/10.3390/sym11101198
31. Shahaab, A., Lidgey, B., Hewage, C., Khan, I.: Applicability and appropriateness of distributed ledgers consensus protocols in public and private sectors: a systematic review. IEEE Access **7**, 43622–43636 (2019). https://doi.org/10.1109/ACCESS.2019.2904181
32. Kaur, S., Chaturvedi, S., Sharma, A., Kar, J.: A research survey on applications of consensus protocols in blockchain. Secur. Commun. Networks **2021**, 1–22 (2021). https://doi.org/10.1155/2021/6693731
33. Bouraga, S.: A taxonomy of blockchain consensus protocols: a survey and classification framework. Expert Syst. Appl. **168**, 114384 (2021). https://doi.org/10.1016/j.eswa.2020.114384
34. Lashkari, B., Musilek, P.: A comprehensive review of blockchain consensus mechanisms. IEEE Access **9**, 43620–43652 (2021). https://doi.org/10.1109/ACCESS.2021.3065880
35. Angelis, S.D., Aniello, L., Baldoni, R., Lombardi, F., Margheri, A., Sassone, V.: PBFT vs Proof-of-Authority: Applying the CAP Theorem to Permissioned Blockchain. In: ITASEC (2018)
36. TechnoDuet: A Comprehensive List of Blockchain Platforms, technoduet.com. Accessed on 15 July 2021
37. Coravos, A.: Where are the healthcare-related blockchains? https://github.com/acoravos/healthcare-blockchains. Accessed on 11 July 2021
38. Liang, W., Fan, Y., Li, K.-C., Zhang, D., Gaudiot, J.-L.: Secure data storage and recovery in industrial blockchain network environments. IEEE Trans. Ind. Inf. **16**, 6543–6552 (2020). https://doi.org/10.1109/TII.2020.2966069
39. Sultana, M., Hossain, A., Laila, F., Taher, K.A., Islam, M.N.: Towards developing a secure medical image sharing system based on zero trust principles and blockchain technology. BMC Med Inform Decis Mak. **20**, 256 (2020). https://doi.org/10.1186/s12911-020-01275-y
40. Burzykowska, A., Iapaolo, M., Priit, A., Sisask, A.: EO Data Provenance with KSI Blockchain. ESA (2020)
41. PHP.Watch: PHP Hash Algorithm Benchmark. https://php.watch/articles/php-hash-benchmark

Formalisation of Motion Description in Microscopy Images

Olga Nedzved[1]([✉]), Igor Gurevich[2], Vera Yashina[2], Ren Tiaojuan[3],
Ye Fangfang[3], and Sergey Ablameyko[1,4]

[1] Belarusian State University Minsk, Minsk, Belarus
{onedzved,ablameyko}@bsu.by
[2] Federal Research Center "Computer Science and Control" of the Russian
Academy of Sciences Moscow, Moscow, Russia
igourevi@ccas.ru
[3] Zhejiang Shuren University Hangzhou, Hangzhou, China
cliney@zju.edu.cn
[4] United Institute of Informatics Problems of NASB, Minsk, Belarus

Abstract. In this paper, a formalization of the task of monitoring cell population movement in microscopic video-sequences is proposed. The method for solving the task is proposed that is based on integral optical flow and motion maps to identify different types of cell movements. Three types of motion are analyzed: directional motion, aggregation and dispersion. Integral optical flow is used to create motion maps and these maps are used to analyze and describe motions in any region of interest. The results of experiments for cell population analysis in video sequences obtained are presented.

Keywords: Dynamic objects · Cell populations · Microscopic images

1 Introduction

For a structural description of possible algorithms for solving these problems of motion analysis on video, we need a formal instrument that allows us to describe and justify the chosen way of solution. As formalization tools, we chose the algebraic approach, which should provide a unique form of procedures for describing the objects images and transformations of dynamical objects on video. The need to develop a mathematical language that ensures that solutions of problems of image processing, analysis, and understanding may be uniformly described by structural algorithmic schemes is justified by the following factors: (1) there are many algorithms (designed and introduced into practice) for analysis, estimation, and understanding of information represented on video-sequences; (2) the set of algorithms is neither structured nor ordered; (3) as a rule, methods for motion analysis and understanding are designed on the basis of intuitive principles, because the information represented on sequence of images is hardly formalized; (4) the efficiency of these methods is estimated (as is usual in experimental sciences) by the success in solving actual problems—as a rule, the problem of rigorous mathematical justification of an algorithm is not considered.

© Springer Nature Switzerland AG 2022
A. V. Tuzikov et al. (Eds.): PRIP 2021, CCIS 1562, pp. 48–63, 2022.
https://doi.org/10.1007/978-3-030-98883-8_4

Recently, the topic of image algebra has been actively developing. One of the first conceptions of it based on the basis of mathematical morphology [1]. In this theory, the image algebra made it possible to represent algorithms for image processing in the form of algebraic expressions, where variables are images and operations are geometrical and logical transformations of the images.

However, there is the impossibility of constructing a universal algebra for image on the morphological algebra. It depends from the limitation of the basis consisting of the operations set of addition and subtraction in Minkowski's sense [2].

G. Ritter [2] proposes to use a more general algebraic representation of operations of image processing and analysis. Such Image algebra generalizes the known local methods for image analysis, including mathematical morphology.

The most general approach to the algebraic description of information for recognition algorithms is Grenander's general pattern theory [3, 4]. This algebra unites metric theory with probability theory for certain universal operation of combinatorial type. It based on the structure of recognizing elements. The Grenander's theory is based on knowledge about patterns that may be expressed in terms of regular structures.

There are three principles of such theory: atomism, combinatory, and observability. The atomism follows to existing of structures that are composed of certain basic elements. The combinatory is supported by rules that are formulated for definition of structures. The observability is related to the search for identification rules for determining equivalence classes. But this theory corresponds to only processing of a different algebraic construction.

There are no rigorous mathematical models for weakly formalized sciences such as biology or medicine. The general foundation of the algebraic approach to synthesis and analysis of recognition algorithms was described Yu.Zhuravlev in [5, 6]. Zhuravlev's algebra made systematization of separated heuristic algorithms for classification problem. This tool is intended to solve problems with incompletely formalized and partially contradictory data. The basic idea is based on model construction that is based on heuristic arguments. Such solution is very efficient in many applications. Therefore, it is sufficient to construct a family of such heuristic algorithms for solving appropriate problems and, then, to construct the algebraic closure of this family, which contains the required solution [7]. In this paper, we try to use algebra formalization for video of movable cells and develop tools that allow to create algebra for motion in video.

Video analysis can be used to study cell growth, cell migration, proliferation, inflammation, and tissue regeneration. In addition, it can be used to study the growth and invasion of tumors, to study the dynamics of individual cells and cell populations in response to drug exposure. These processes can vary significantly in duration: from a few seconds to several days. At the same time, the requirements for the quality and processing speed of the extracted diagnostic information are increasing, especially when carrying out analysis in real time.

Most of the existed algorithms are based on monitoring of movement of separate cells [8, 9]. There are two problems with the work of these algorithms: the quality of cell detection and redundancy information. Investigated cells are alive and there are many processes inside them. Sometime a border of cell is no contrasting and cell is not detected and missed during tracking as result.

Important part of live cell monitoring is the investigation of dynamical properties of cells, cell conglomerates and cellular interactions including detection of spatiotemporal localization of mitosis events. Every mitosis event is the division of cell into two daughter cells, which includes a change in size, shape and brightness of the area around cells and daughter cells movement. In paper [10], optical flow and motion maps were used formalize and detect group object motion types.

In this paper, we propose a formalization of for the task of analysis of movement of a cell population with a movable internal structure, which is characterized by a change in shape and size. This requires taking into account the movement of individual cells that are included in the population. We also develop a scheme for monitoring of dynamic object motion and show practical results.

2   Formalization of a Dynamic Object

The collective movement of objects in the video between two points in time is called the field of flow. Determining algorithms for measuring the flow field and extracting information about the movement of objects are the key tasks of video analysis.

The solution of problems of complex dynamical systems can be described using tensor calculus. For example, Lagrange equations of the second kind are used to analyze the motion of complex mechanical systems. These equations are:

$$\frac{d}{dt}\left(\frac{\partial T}{\partial \dot{q}^i}\right) - \frac{\partial T}{\partial q^i} = Q_i i = \overline{1, s}$$

where s is number of degrees of freedom of a mechanical system; q^i is generalized coordinate; $T = T(\vec{q}, \dot{\vec{q}})$ is kinetic energy of a mechanical system; Q^i is generalized force.

After performing a threefold differentiation of the kinetic energy, linear combinations of the second derivatives of generalized coordinates and linear combinations of the products of their first derivatives were obtained.

The vector method of specifying the movement of a point determines the change in the position of a point in space using a radius-vector, which is a function of time (see Fig. 1):

$$\vec{r} = \overrightarrow{r(t)}$$

Then the velocity and acceleration of point is:

$$\vec{v} = \frac{d\vec{r}}{dt}; \quad \vec{a} = \frac{d\vec{v}}{dt} = \frac{d^2\vec{r}}{dt^2}$$

The radius vector, velocity and acceleration are vectors, which means they can be considered as tensors of rank $(1,0)$. Cartesian coordinate system and curvilinear coordinates can be used:

$$q^i = q^i(t), i = \overline{1, s}$$

where q^i is set of independent parameters characterizing the position of a point in space uniquely. The number of parameters depends on the number of degrees of freedom s.

The speed of movement of a point is:

$$\vec{v} = \frac{d\vec{r}}{dt} = \frac{\partial \vec{r}}{\partial q^i}\frac{dq^i}{dt} = \frac{\partial(q^i \vec{e_j})}{\partial q^i}\frac{dq^i}{dt} = \frac{dq^i}{dt}\vec{e_i}$$

where $\frac{\partial(q^i \vec{e_j})}{\partial q^i} = \vec{e_i}$ are coefficient at the differentiable component. This expression corresponds to the expansion of the velocity vector in a curvilinear basis; contravariant velocity vector components:

$$q^i = \frac{dq^i}{dt}$$

The acceleration vector is:

$$\vec{a} = \frac{d\vec{v}}{dt} = \frac{\partial \vec{v}}{\partial q^i}\dot{q}^i$$

Derivative of the velocity vector is formed along the generalized coordinate:

$$\frac{\partial \vec{v}}{\partial q^i} = (\frac{\partial \dot{q}^k}{\partial q^i} + \Gamma_{ji}^{k}\dot{q}^j)\vec{e_k},$$

where $\Gamma_{ji}^{k}\dot{q}^j$ are Christoffel symbol of the second kind.

Then the acceleration is:

$$\vec{a} = (\frac{\partial \dot{q}^k}{\partial q^i} + \Gamma_{ji}^{k}\dot{q}^j)\dot{q}^i\vec{e_k} = (\frac{\partial \dot{q}^k}{\partial q^i}\dot{q}^i + \Gamma_{ji}^{k}\dot{q}^j\dot{q}^i)\vec{e_k},$$

Taking into account the expression for the contravariant components of the point acceleration vector $\frac{\partial \dot{q}^k}{\partial q^i}\dot{q}^i = \ddot{q}^i$, it looks as follows:

$$a^k = \ddot{q}^k + \frac{\partial \dot{q}^k}{\partial q^i}\dot{q}^i$$

The most common case of motion with conservation of the constraints imposed on the point is the case of motion of a point along the surface. Its coordinates can only take on values that define the motion surface.

The law of change of coordinates is:

$$\tilde{q}^i = q^i + \delta q^i$$

where q^i is generalized coordinate at which the point remains on the surface of the defining connection, δq^i is generalized coordinate variation.

Displacement of point in this case is:

$$\delta \vec{r} = \frac{\partial \vec{r}}{\partial q^i} \delta q^i = \vec{e}_i \delta q^i$$

Vector $\delta \vec{r}$ corresponds to the movement of a point, directed tangentially to the surface of movement. Thus, the key characteristic of the dynamics of an object is the displacement $\delta \vec{r}$ and variations of the generalized coordinates δq^i.

It allows to define a moving point as a dynamic object. To combine points into a group, it is necessary to select a set of points at which an associative operation is defined, in which there is a neutral element, and each element of the set has an inverse analogue.

In this case, to determine the motion, variations of the generalized coordinates δq^i are used, where $\delta q^i = 0$ corresponds to absence of movement, $\delta q^i < 0$ corresponds to reverse movement. The change in velocity $\vec{v}$ is determined in the same way $\vec{v} = 0$ is neutral element, $\vec{v} < 0$ corresponds to reverse movement. Similar conversions are possible for acceleration $\vec{a}$, specifying that $\vec{a} = 0$ corresponds to uniform rectilinear motion.

3 Formalization of Motion

Thus, the concept of simple motion for a dynamic object can be easily transformed into the concept of an algebraic field.

For a dynamic object, non-empty sets for coordinate displacement, velocity and acceleration can be specified $G(q^i, \vec{v}, \vec{a})$, with the specified offset operation $\{*\}$: $G + G \rightarrow G$, for which the following axioms are satisfied:

- Associative property:
  $\forall (a, b, c) \in G : (a * b) * c = a * (b * c)$ for motion components (displacement, velocity, acceleration);
- Neutral element presence:
  $\exists e \in G \quad \forall a \in G : (a * e = e * a = a)$ for conservation of the type of movement;
- Presence of inverse element:
  $\exists e \in G \quad \forall a \in G : (a * (-a) = (-a) * a = e)$ for inverse motion.

More complex is the description of behavioral movement, which includes aggregation (movement towards a common center) and dispersion (movement from the center) (see Fig. 1).

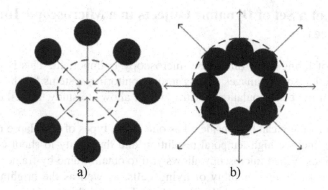

Fig. 1. Elements of the behavioral movement: aggregation (a) and dispersion (b)

There are the following signs of aggregation: several objects are moved to one area of the video from other areas and the speed of this movement is greater than the speed of chaotic movement.

Signs of dispersion include: several objects move in the direction from their common center to other areas of the video and the speed of this movement is greater than the speed of chaotic movement.

For these types of movement, it is also possible to define the algebraic concepts of the group, based on the presence of a hypothetical center of movement. Thus, the presence of an algebraic element is defined as a movement towards the center, a neutral element as the absence of movement and an inverse element as a movement from the center. Associative property is present in this case.

For movement, algebraic groups of events such as simple movement and movement relative to a hypothetical center. This allows us to consider the problem of motion from an algebraic point of view. Displacement vectors for pixel δq^i can be obtained based on the calculation of optical flows. The vectors of the integral optical flow $\tilde{q}^i$ are additionally used. Therefore, the displacement vector obtained on the basis of the integrated optical flow can be expressed as follows:

$$\tilde{q}^i = \sum_j \delta q^i_j,$$

где j is frame change index in the video sequence.

For statistical analysis of motion, only pixels that are actually moving should be considered. This, only trajectories for which the start position differs from the end position are taken into account.

To determine the type and directions of motion in a video sequence motion maps are used. In this case, the motion is described for all points through which the moving pixels pass.

4   Motion of a Set of Dynamic Objects in a Microscopic Image Sequences

In the study of living cells, time-lapse microscopy is important. This is a sequential recording of microscopic images in long-term monitoring systems for the observation and analysis of the cell population in vitro, which allows to study the cell dynamics in detail.

Video-microscopy can be considered as one of the types of time-lapse microscopy. Its advantages include high temporal resolution and the ability to shoot continuously over long periods. Video-microscopy allows you to obtain frame-by-frame recording of changes in the shape and mobility of living cells, as well as the brightness of their images. Cell motion can be described based on dynamic objects [11].

The currently existing technologies for video sequences analysis are focused mainly on the motion of individual objects rather their moving aggregates, which combine the motion of the entire system with the motion of its components [12].

One of the ways to track the motion of cells is the method of tracking dynamic objects, which is a continuous determination of the position of the object [13, 14]. In this paper, we analyze the motion of dynamic objects and scenes, formalize this process and demonstrate the results.

An elementary dynamic object is a small movable localized object with physical parameters such as volume, density or mass. Their motion can be rotational, rectilinear, accelerated, or even barely noticeable. The complexity of detection and tracking is determined by their size, change in shape, and the nature of motion.

Dynamic objects in microscopic videos can be divided into the following classes:

- Individual small objects that are a movable component of the background and can be removed when sorting by size;
- Large background components with small displacement due to stochastic motions in a specimen;
- Fragments of the environment around moving objects that are changed due to their optical characteristics.

Cells in microscopic specimens are mobile objects; three types of cell motility can be distinguished:

- Real cell motion;
- Displacement of intracellular structures;
- Changes in cell shape.

The scene with dynamic objects can be defined as static, with the added time variable. 3D motion is estimated by modeling forward and backward flow of objects as dense three-dimensional vector fields.

A continuous scene can be represented as a 5D vector function, where the input determines a three-dimensional location $x = (x, y, z)$ and the viewing direction 2D (θ, φ). The output corresponds to the color of the pixels and can be defined as $c = (r, g, b)$ and volume density σ. In practice, the direction is expressed as a three-dimensional vector in Cartesian space d. This continuous 5D representation of the scene can be approximated by a network MLP F Θ: (x, d) → (c, σ), where Θ means the weight to match each 5D input coordinate with the corresponding volume density and corresponding color. Dynamic objects can be described in the same way.

The key problem of monitoring a dynamic scene is to separate the background and objects that can be static or change over time. In this case, the direction of motion plays an important role, it can be divided into the following levels:

– Background motion generated by camera motion;
– Background motion formed by a change in the surrounding space;
– Object motion;
– Motion inside objects;
– Motion of groups of objects.

Thus, in the first step, it is necessary to divide the image field into different types of motion. For this purpose, motion maps based on optical flow calculations can be used [10].

Obviously, for a uniform motion of the optical system, the background is formed in the form of a constant flow, which has a unique image. Depending on the motion of the camera, the image has its own unique characteristics (see Fig. 2).

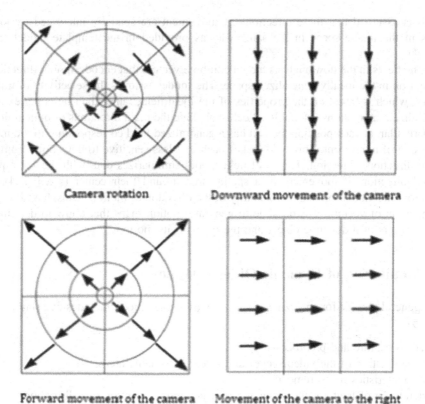

Camera rotation   Downward movement of the camera

Forward movement of the camera   Movement of the camera to the right

Fig. 2. Direction of the optical flow field when the camera moves.

The behavior of system of objects is determined by group motion. In this case, motion maps are used, they determine general trends and can indicate individual events in motion [15]. Motion mapping based on the summation of vectors in a local area of the video. But simple summation can lead to the same values for different motion patterns (see Fig. 3). Thus, the result of the movement must be determined using several different maps.

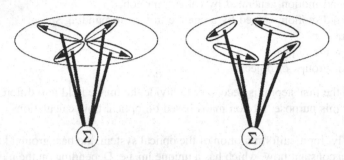

Fig. 3. Two cases when the adder gives the same result for different patterns of motion.

It is assumed that these directions of movement are spatially integrated by local cells in the image space in the same way as provided in the template model (See Fig. 4).

The fields in the flow analysis model combine vectors that encode similar directions of motion in the locally generalized space. The model assumes the selectivity of traffic flows, which is based on the properties of the local field, rather than on complex and specialized interactions. Model local cells calculate the main directions of optical flow. In particular, at each position the cell has a generalized field corresponding to the main direction of movement. This field makes each cell less sensitive to deviations from its main direction of motion. The local field model summarizes data with the same preferred direction of movement in a spatial area around their center (see Fig. 4). In addition, the model forms the probability of the direction of motion. Thus, based on the summation of vectors, it is possible to generate motion maps that allow to determine the contours of a dynamic object and the types of its motion.

5   Monitoring of Dynamic Objects Motion

The general scheme for analyzing videos with dynamic objects includes five stages (see Fig. 5):

– video capture and preprocessing;
– segmentation of the video scenes and selection of cells areas;
– characteristics measurement;
– definition of laws for the formation of a general description of cell motion;
– cell state classification.

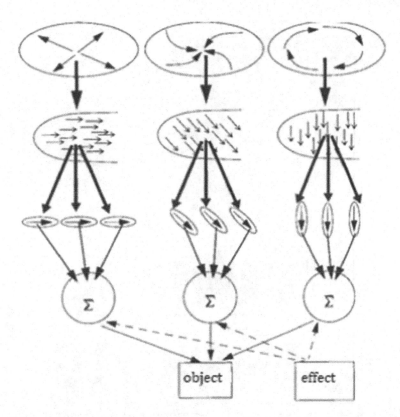

Fig. 4. Scheme of the model of building motion maps. The optical flow field is converted to a vector map. The model cells form the setting of the Gaussian direction of movement in this coordinate system. Adders determine the directions of movement based on the direction of the cells.

The most important characteristics for describing dynamic objects in microscopic images are: position characteristics (coordinates, speed of motion, direction change, trajectory), morphological characteristics (size, shape, degree of object shape change), optical characteristics (brightness, color, optical density), and also the duration of the observation.

The formalized concept of the structural model of a dynamic object is an ordered set of patterns $A = \langle A_1, A_2, ..., A_n \rangle \subseteq \Omega_n$, which corresponds to the total structural description A, if object pattern $A \in \Omega$ can be completely uniquely reconstructed by combining elements from A, which formally can change over time:

$$A = \delta(A) = A_1 \oplus A_2 \oplus ... \oplus A_n \tag{1}$$

where δ – operation of structural reconstruction of the pattern according to the structural description; $\oplus$ – operation of combining patterns from Ω, on which, in the general case, no additional conditions are imposed, except that Ω closed with respect to $\oplus$. It should be noted that the effect of blocking some objects by others, typical for

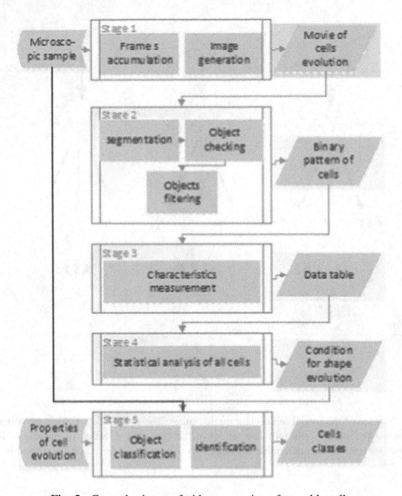

Fig. 5. General scheme of video processing of movable cells.

images in a video sequence, in contrast to many other areas of application of structural analysis, makes the order of combining elements of the visible scene fundamentally important. Therefore, the operation ⊕ in the general case cannot be either symmetric or associative, although sometimes such a restriction is nevertheless imposed.

Thus, the definition of a model of dynamic objects is performed through a changing preimage L with time-constant properties, which consists of n components:

$$L = \delta(L) = L1 \oplus L2 \oplus \ldots \oplus L_n \tag{2}$$

In this case, the types of dynamic elements are known, which are specified by the characteristic predicates like elements $M_i(L_i) \in \{0,1\}$, $i = 1,\ldots,n$. In addition, given m conditions or connections predicates $M_k(L) \in \{0,1\}$, $k = 1,\ldots,m$. Then the preimage model takes the form:

$$M(L) = M_1(L_1) \cdot \ldots \cdot M_n(L_n) \cdot M_1(L) \cdot \ldots \cdot M_m(L) \tag{3}$$

The variables n and m are considered to be time-variable parameters that are also subject to optimization, and predicates are considered as probabilistic or fuzzy, taking values by [0,1]. In this case the problem of structural segmentation of dynamic objects will correspond to the most general case of structural image analysis.

The motion description of objects system can be performed not only at the pixel level, but also at the region level. The characteristics for describing the movement at the region level are the direction of movement, the speed of movement and the intensity of movement in the region determined on its basis. The determination of motion at the region level and the corresponding motion maps are described in [10, 15].

The motion maps are used to determine the type and directions of motion in a video sequence and to determine the number of pixels moving in the selected directions. In this case, the motion is described for all nodes (hypothetical centers of motion) through which the moving pixels pass. Thus, the dynamic object model is defined as:

$$A = \delta(A) = OP \oplus OCM \oplus ICM \oplus OQ \oplus IQ \tag{4}$$

were OP, OCM, ICM, OQ, IQ are corresponding motion maps. Thus, the simple motion of a dynamic object can be described using the concepts of an algebraic field and a ring.

There are three types of dynamic objects motion: directional motion, aggregation (moving towards a common center), and scattering (moving away from the center). The signs of aggregation are: a) several objects move to one image region from other areas; b) the speed of motion of these objects is greater than the speed of chaotic motion; c) at least two predominated directions of movement can be distinguished. The signs of scattering include: a) several objects move in the direction from their com-mon center to other regions of the image; b) the speed of their motion exceeds the speed of chaotic movement; c) at least two predominated directions of movement can be distinguished.

For the last two types of motion, it is possible to define the algebraic concepts of a group and a ring based on the presence of a hypothetical center of motion. In this case, by analogy, we can define the additive operation for the group$C(q_i, \vec{v}, \vec{a})$, with the displacement operation specified on it $\{\circledast\}: C + C \to C$. Thus, it is possible to define an algebraic element as a motion towards the center, a neutral element as the absence of motion and an inverse element as a motion from the center. The associativity property is present in this case.

Thus, relative to motion, algebraic groups of events can be distinguished as simple motion and motion relative to a hypothetical center. It is allows to consider the problem of motion from an algebraic point of view with the vector as the reference concept. Pixel displacement vectors δq^i can be obtained based on the calculation of optical flows. The vectors of the integral optical flow are additionally used $\tilde{q}^i$. Therefore, the displacement vector obtained on the basis of the integral optical flux can be expressed as:

$$\tilde{q}^i = \sum \delta q^i_j \tag{5}$$

where j is frame change index in the video sequence.

6 Practical Results

As experiments, the movement of vesicles containing the GLUT4 protein onto the cell membrane was considered. GLUT4, an insulin-regulated glucose transporter protein, is predominantly found in the cytoplasm of adipose and muscle cells in the absence of insulin. Understanding the effect of insulin on the spatiotemporal regulation of intracellular GLUT4 transport is important for elucidating the pathogenesis of type 2 diabetes in humans.

The GLUT4 intracellular transport movement dataset was derived from a total internal reflection fluorescence microscopy (TIRF) image sequence. TIRF microscopy is an optical technique used to observe the fluorescence of individual molecules, based on the phenomenon of total internal reflection. Parameters such as the speed of movement of vesicles in the near-membrane region, their number and density were determined for the vesicles.

Registration of the appearance of vesicles is carried out on binary images obtained because of threshold segmentation, which is the result of calculating the difference between the brightness of the images of the vesicles and the background. Segmentation consists in the fact that the brightness value of each pixel is compared with a threshold value, which is determined based on the correspondence of its local environment to the Gaussian distribution and a predetermined user correction to deter-mine the deviation from the Gaussian distribution.

The selected dynamic objects are controlled by means of motion maps, which make it possible to form a description and conduct monitoring at the level of the graph structure.

The construction of a set of protein transport graphs in cells corresponding to a set of all vesicles isolated at the segmentation stage consists of the following steps:

1) Selection of the initial branches of the graphs in accordance with the number of vesicles.
2) Splitting the video sequence into minimum time intervals is performed for the entire video sequence. The time for each event is determined, and then the minimum time interval according to which the timeline is split.
3) Construction a set of graphs (see Fig. 6). For each node, the state of the cell is registered, according to which the number of inputs-outputs for each block is determined. The simple motion block has one input and one output, the intersection block has one input and two outputs, the membrane delivery block is the terminator of the graph branch. Thus, each branch of the graph represents a family tree for an individual vesicle.

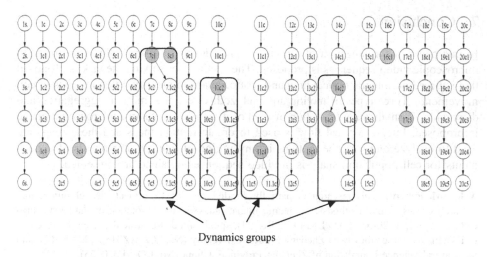

Dynamics groups

Fig. 6. A set of graphs describing the movement of individual vesicles.

The use of graphs allows tracking the stages of GLUT-4 delivery in the cell. It also reduces the analysis time based on the transformation of dynamic objects into dynamic groups on the frame of the video sequence (see Fig. 7).

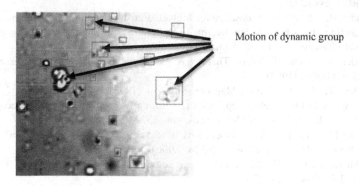

Motion of dynamic group

Fig. 7. Combining vesicle tracks into dynamic groups on a video sequence frame.

The paper formalizes the problem of the motion analysis of dynamic objects and scenes based on the algorithms and methods developed by the authors for analyzing the behavior of the cell population as a system of dynamic objects, which are based on the use of the concept of an integral optical flow. The main types of movement have been determined, which make it possible to distinguish the key moments of the movement of cells in a population and describe the stages of development and inter-action of cells. The formalization of operations on dynamic objects has been completed.

7 Conclusion

In this paper, a formalization of the task of monitoring cell population movement in microscopic video-sequences is proposed. The method for solving the task is proposed that is based on integral optical flow and motion maps to identify different types of cell movements. Three types of motion are analyzed: directional motion, aggregation and dispersion. Formalization of motion of a set of dynamic objects in a microscopic image is proposed. Integral optical flow is used to create motion maps and these maps are used to analyze and describe motions in any region of interest. The results of experiments for cell population analysis in video sequences obtained are presented.

Acknowledgment. This research is partially funded by BRFFI project "Development and research of descriptive methods of dynamic image analysis for automation of diagnostic procedures" (project: 20-57-00025/BRFFI F20R-134), special funds for basic the scientific research in Provincial Universities from Zhejiang Shuren University (No. 2021XZ018,2022XZ014), and the Natural Science Foundation of Zhejiang Province, China (No. LQ21F020025).

References

1. Sternberg, S.R.: Language and architecture for parallel image processing. In: Proceedings of the Conference on Pattern Recognition in Practice. Amsterdam, pp. 35–44 (1980)
2. Ritter, G.X., Wilson, J.N.: Handbook of Computer Vision Algorithms in Image Algebra, 2nd edn. CRC Press (2001)
3. Gurevich, B.: A class of descriptive logical transformations in problems of image understanding. In: Abstracts 5th International Seminar on Digital Image Processing and Computer Graphics, pp. 17–18. Samara (1994)
4. Grenander, U.: General Pattern Theory: A Mathematical Study of Regular Structures. Clarendon, Oxford (1993)
5. Zhuravlev, Y.: Selected Works. Magister, Moscow (1998)
6. Zhuravlev, Yu.I.: On Algebraic approach to solution of problems of pattern recognition or classification. In: Problems of Cybernetics, vol. 33. Nauka, Moscow (1996)
7. Gurevich, I.B., Yashina, V.V.: Operations of descriptive image algebras with one ring. Pattern Recogn. Image Anal. **16**, 298–328 (2006)
8. Kimbahune, V., Uke, N.: Blood cell image segmentation and counting. Int. J. Eng. Sci. Technol. **3**(3), 2448–2453 (2011)
9. Mosig, A., et al.: Tracking cells in Life Cell Imaging videos using topological alignments. Algor. Molecul. Biol. **4**(10), 4:10 (2009) https://doi.org/10.1186/1748-7188-4-10
10. Chen, Ch., Ye, S., Chen, H., Nedzvedz, O.V., Ablameyko, S.V.: Integral optical flow and its application for monitoring dynamic objects from a video sequence. J. Appl. Spectrosc. **84**(1), 120–128 (2017). https://doi.org/10.1007/s10812-017-0437-z
11. Huh, S.: Automated mitosis detection of stem cell populations in phase-contrast microscopy images. IEEE Trans. Med. Imaging **30**(3), 586–596 (2011)
12. Ascione, F.: Investigation of cell dynamics in vitro by time-lapse microscopy and image analysis. Chem. Eng. Trans. **38**, 517–522 (2014)
13. Li, K., Chen, M., Kanade, T., Miller, E., Weiss, L., Campbella, P.: Cell population tracking and lineage construction with spatiotemporal context. Med. Image Anal. **12**, 546–566 (2008)

14. Perner, P.: Tracking living cells in microscopic images and description of the kinetics of the cells. Procedia Comput. Sci. **60**, 352–361 (2015)
15. Chen, H., Ye, Sh., Nedzvedz, O., Ablameyko, S.: Image motion maps and their applications for dynamic object monitoring. Pattern Recogn. Image Anal. **29**(1), 131–143 (2019)

Predicting Events by Analyzing the Results of the Work of Predictive Models

Archil Prangishvili[1], Zurab Gasitashvili[1], Merab Pkhovelishvili[2], and Natela Archvadze[3](✉)

[1] Georgian Technical University, Kostava Street 77, 0171 Tbilisi, Georgia
`{a_prangi, zur_gas}@gtu.ge`
[2] Muskhelishvili Institute of Computational Mathematics, Georgian Technical University, Grigol Peradze, 4, 0159 Tbilisi, Georgia
`merab5@list.ru`
[3] I.Javakhishvili Tbilisi State University, Ilia Tchavtchavadze Avenue 1, 0179 Tbilisi, Georgia
`natela.archvadze@tsu.ge`

Abstract. Building much more effective new hybrid models from prediction models is discussed. The algorithm for selection of model pairs, triplets, etc. and the advantage of obtained model over any best prediction model is given. The advantage of prediction models with higher number of pairs over lower number of pairs is shown. The algorithm of taking into consideration the "approximate coincidence" of predictions is discussed when selecting pairs, triplets, etc. of models.

Keywords: Prediction models · Approximate accuracy · Probability of prediction success · Dynamic and static prediction

1 Introduction

Please note Some prediction models are based on using of "parallel data" [1–4], although it must be noted that the term "parallel data" is differently explained in each of them.

In practice, parallel data is used during prediction of various events, including natural disasters: earthquake, landslide, tsunami, mudflow, etc., for prediction economical (business, macro economy), political events (elections, positions of political forces), for effective solving of prediction tasks in the sphere of medicine and other fields.

The definition of parallel data is based on introduction of new type of dependence between the data, which is called "parallelism between the data" [1, 5–8]. Parallelism between the data is mutual dependence between those data, which are used for prediction of the same event. Various data affecting the same event may exist in different periods (parallel by time) or locations (parallel by location) and/or provide other additional information on prediction of the same event [9, 10].

The main idea of algorithms for building of prediction models is reviewed by us through parallel data and is the following: Let us assume that there are several models

© Springer Nature Switzerland AG 2022
A. V. Tuzikov et al. (Eds.): PRIP 2021, CCIS 1562, pp. 64–78, 2022.
https://doi.org/10.1007/978-3-030-98883-8_5

of prediction. From them, it is necessary to select such pairs, triplets, etc. from several models, which give much better result than a single best model from them or two models separately.

This algorithm was the following: such models were found, for which the number of coincidences of unsuccessful predictions for some given event was as low as possible, but successful predictions were necessary for them.

In this paper we first review static prediction models for natural disasters, when a result(s) of prediction should be guessed, for example, when, where and with which specifications occurred the event of interest.

Unlike static predictions, a prediction is dynamic, when for each time interval it is necessary to forecast an event of certain value. Such is, for example, a daily forecast of exchange rate, forecast of oil price, monthly subsistence level, annual income, human health condition, scope of coronavirus spread, etc.

The distinctive sign, by which the static prediction is different from the dynamic one, is its dependence on the time of prediction event. Actually it means that we should distinguish, how a result, i.e. prediction values, are declared. If it occurs continuously, with some predefined time interval, then this is dynamic prediction, but if time is one of prediction elements, then it is static prediction. For example, earthquake prediction implies declaring that date as one of the results, when earthquake is expected, therefore, it belongs to static prediction, and currency exchange rate is forecasted daily, therefore, it is dynamic prediction.

In this article we will establish lemmas for the task of static prediction and show, how the accuracy of such models is increased through our algorithm. Specific data are taken for earthquake prediction task. Each prediction model is build based on certain predecessors. For earthquake the predecessor is geophysical phenomenon (mainly), which precedes the actual earthquake. For their part, geophysical precursors are divided into the following categories: seismic, hydro geodynamic, deformation, geochemical, thermal, gravitational, electromagnetic and, precursors obtained via remote monitoring by means of satellite technologies developed recently [11].

Despite the fact that quite high number of predecessors exist, not any of them ensures high-accuracy prediction for time, place and magnitude of future earthquake. The probability of successful prediction of each predecessor (ratio of number of successful predictions to the number of all given predictions) does not exceed 0.5% [12]. One of the ways for overcoming this situation is to use several prediction predecessors simultaneously, although for each of them it is necessary to perform observation for a long time and process vast amount of data, which is not done in many models till now. "The practice of recent years show that their simultaneous use would improve the reliability and efficiency of prediction assessment, at least in medium-term (first years) prediction".

2 "Success Probability" of Prediction

Assume that we have several prediction models, which provide some predictions through their predecessors (for example, for earthquakes - when it would occur, at which location and with which magnitude). These predecessors should be "necessary predecessors" that means that if earthquake occurs, they will inevitably provide the prediction. If some predecessors do not provide prediction on actually occurred earthquake, it will be no longer considered.

We study history, let's assume that there is plenty of data and it is necessary to calculate, based on predecessors, how many times the prediction of earthquake occurrence was given and how many times actual earthquake occurred. Assume that we consider the necessary predecessors and the models created for them: $A_1, A_2, ..., A_n$, where n is the number of considered predecessors. t denotes time, during which we perform analysis and the number of actually occurred earthquakes is m. We calculated the number of earthquakes predicted by each predecessor: $p_1, p_2, ..., p_n$. For example, A_i model, which was based on i predecessor, predicted earthquake occurrence p_i - times.

For the model Ai, we call **a probability of success** as quotient obtained by division m by pi shown in %. Let's designate this as K_i:

$K_i = \frac{m}{p_i} 100\%$.

For example, if earthquake actually occurred 4 times, and we calculate $K_i = \frac{4}{20} 100\% = 20\%$ then the probability of A_i success will be 20%.

Put the sequence of model success in descending order and this sequence denote as: $k_1, k_2, ...k_n$ sequence. k_i is a model created for i-th predecessors. We get that k_1 highest value, which was determined by the prediction, the value of k_2 is less than that of k_1 and so on.

It is necessary to consider a combination of models (two, three, etc.) and assessment of the probability of their combined success. The assessment and selection of combinations is done according to the parallel probabilities [13, 14].

Lemma 1 – if such pairs of models are selected, for which the number of coincidences of unsuccessful predictions for some given event was as low as possible, but existence of successful predictions is a mandatory condition for each of them, then the success probability calculated for combination of any such best pair is always higher than or equal to the success probability of the best model from all models.

Comment: In accordance with this Lemma, if we take a best ki model and pair it with anyone, even with a model with the worst success rate kj, then their combined result (i.e. combined success) is not worse, than the success of model ki. For example, if kj gives conclusion that earthquake occurred 5 times, even if others result in values such as 10 or 7, the intersection of their successes cannot exceed 5.

Proof: Let's use the following designations - designate the set of the given prediction models P over time with - T, which combines different n models:

$$P = \{P_1, P_2, ..., P_n\} \tag{1}$$

Now consider each model: The model P_1 gives prediction on k number of occurrence of given event over the time T; the model P_2 gives prediction of l number for the same time T, etc. Similarly, the model P_n gives prediction of e number for the same time T, i.e. We have:

$$P_1 = \{p_{11}, p_{12}, \ldots, p_{1k}\}$$
$$p_2 = \{p_{21}, p_{22}, \ldots, p_{2l}\}$$

$$\cdots$$

$$p_m = \{p_{21}, p_{22}, \ldots, p_{2v}\}$$

$$\cdots$$

$$p_n = \{p_{n1}, p_{n2}, \ldots, p_{ne}\}$$

Let us assume that during the same time period T, u number of events actually occurred: $p_{real} = p_r = \{p_{r1}, p_{r2}, \ldots, p_{ru}\}$; each p_{ri}, where $i = 1 \cdots u,$, for earthquake case, is characteristics of one of the occurred earthquakes, in particular, i^{th} earthquake.

Our goal is to show that for the given predictions, there are at least two predictions, for which the probability of combined occurrence's success probability is greater than or equal to the prediction success probability (designate it as P_g) of the best model:

$\min(P_{ij}) \leq P_g$, where $i, j = 1 \ldots n$.

Graphical representation of the Lemma 1 is following (see Fig. 1):

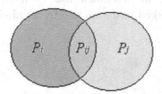

Fig. 1. Graphical representation of the Lemma 1 with Euler-Venn diagram.

Let's consider the intersections $(P_i \cap P_g)$. The intersections are less than or equal to P_i as well as P_g, in accordance with the definition of intersection. According to our designation, $P_{ij} = P_i \cap P_j$, therefore, we have $P_{ij} \subseteq P_g$. Thus, there is at least one intersection of model pairs, and the number of predictions of this intersection is less than or equal to the number of predictions of the best model, what we wanted to prove.

Lemma 2: The higher number of intersections of prediction models, the better prediction we would get. For example, the best triplet - combination of three predictions would give better result than the best pair of prediction (deuce), the best quad gives better result than the best triplet and so on.

Proof in the case of three models: Let's assume that there are given models defined by the formulas (1) and (2). Let's designate the best model among them as P_g. Let's take any three models: P_i, P_j and P_k, and consider their intersection: $P_{ijk} = (P_i \cap P_j \cap P_k)$. $P_{ijk} \subseteq P_i \cap P_j, P_{ijk} \subseteq P_i \cap P_k, P_{ijk} \subseteq P_k \cap P_j$. Therefore, we have that the intersection of any randomly selected three models is less than or equal to the intersection of the best two models, what we wanted to prove. Let's show the graphical representation of Lemma 2 (see Fig. 2), which is obtained in the case of combined use of three models:

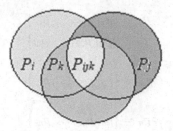

Fig. 2. Graphical representation of the Lemma 2 with Euler-Venn diagram in the case of three models.

It is possible to extrapolate Lemma 2 for number n of predictions, i.e. the probability of combined success of n number of predictions is not worse than the success probability of $n-1$ number of predictions:

$\min(P_1 \cap P_2 \cdots \cap P_n) \leq \min(P_1 \cap P_2 \cdots \cap P_{n-1})$.

This lemma is similarly proven by use of induction method. We have already proved the n = 2 case (see Lemma 1).

Figure 3 shows the case of combined use of n models, where the intersection:$(P_1 \cap P_2 \cdots \cap P_n)$ is marked in the middle by a red circle:

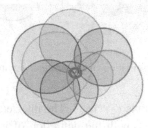

Fig. 3. The corresponding graphical representation of Lemma 2 in the case of n models. (Color figure online)

3   Selection Best Pairs

The best pair is one that does not have intersection between each, except actual, occurred predictions.

For example, we calculated the pair or k_i and k_j predictions and let's calculate, by their combined prediction, which number of coincidences we have with the actual situation (for example, coincided n times). For example, the event occurred actually m times, if we calculate success %, we get $\frac{n}{m} 100\% = 20\%$, but if it turned out that k_i and k_j jointly only two times had prediction success for the event, then it means that k_i and k_j is the best pair.

It is an interesting metamorphosis - it is possible to find such models' pair, which separately have a high rate of error, but intersection of their prediction may give the best result. To show this, let's consider the example from the problem of earthquake prediction.

In Table 1, the list of earthquakes occurred on the territory of Georgia is given, which belong to the earthquakes with moderate strength (magnitude 4–5). The information was taken from the online map of earthquakes [15], where there are maps, lists, data and information on earthquakes, and a seismic map of the world.

We took earthquake magnitude, occurrence date, time and name of epicenter as characteristics of each earthquake. The table contains earthquakes occurred in 2020–2021. UTC means the Coordinated Universal Time.

Table 1. Earthquakes occurred in Georgia in 2019–2021.

N	Magnitude	Date	Time	Epicenter
1	4.7	16.08.2021	00:49 (UTC)	Georgia, Kvemo Kartli region, Dmanisi municipality
2	4.4	15.10.2019	14:57	15 km. Southwest of Zestap'oni, Georgia
3	4.3	13.03.2021	10:00 (UTC)	Georgia, region of Racha-Lechkhumi and Kvemo-Svaneti, Onsky municipality
4	4.3	1.04.2020	05:23 (UTC)	4.2 Georgia (sak'art'velo)
5	4.2	04.11.2020	18:49 (UTC)	Georgia (sak'art'velo)
6	4.2	12.07.2020	05:01	Georgia (sak'art'velo)
7	4.1	15.08.2021	22:36 (UTC)	Georgia, region of Samtskhe-Javakheti, Ninotsminda municipality
8	4.1	17.04.2021	20:46	17 km. North-northwest of P'ot'i, Georgia
9	4.1	17.04.2021	20:07 (UTC)	Georgia, Colchis National Park
10	4.1	13.03.2021	09:46	5 km. West of Oni, Georgia
11	4.0	14.07.2021	06:35 (UTC)	Georgia, region of Samtskhe-Javakheti, Ninotsminda municipality
12	4.0	04.11.2020	16:20 (UTC)	Georgia (sak'art'velo)

Let us review several models of earthquake prediction specifically for Georgia. Designate the earthquake prediction models as $Mod_1, Mod_2, \ldots$, etc. which provide some predictions through their predecessors (for example, for when it would occur, at which location and with which magnitude). We must choose only those models from these models, which satisfy the necessary condition, i.e. intersection of the set of model predictions with the set of actual events should result in the set of actual events. We call this condition a **necessary condition** for choosing a prediction model [16]. This condition in the case of earthquake means the following: If during the time T there occurred, for example, 12 earthquakes (as in our example), only those models should be considered that predicted all these twelve earthquakes. Assume that such are the following models: $Mod_1, Mod_2, \ldots, Mod_n$. In our case it is not essential, what specifically is each model and based on which predecessors of the earthquake it makes the prediction.

The numbers of predictions, the numbers of successful and failed predictions must be calculated for each model and calculated the probability of success for each model. It is obvious in this that the sum of successful and failed predictions is equal to the total number of predictions. As for the **probability of success** [17], it is calculated for each model and determines, how many times earthquake prediction was made and how many times an actual earthquake occurred. Assume that in total for 5 models there is calculated probability success and these values are: 6.00; 6.32; 7.06; 6.12; 7.59.

Author of each model of earthquake prediction claims that their model is best and argues that their model predicted each actually occurred earthquake. Neither of them provides number of wrong predictions, and, therefore, do not calculate success probability, which is quite low values. The success probability for a model might be low, but it is possible to find another model for this model, with which a combined possibility of success ensures the best result. We will show the correctness of this for our example.

We should consider pairs of models as a next step for the algorithm. In total there will be 10 pairs: M1, M2,...,M10, ხოლო M1 $= Mod_1 \cap Mod_2$; M2 $= Mod_1 \cap Mod_3$; M3 $= Mod_1 \cap Mod_4$; M4 $= Mod_1 \cap Mod_5$; M5 $= Mod_2 \cap Mod_3$; M6 $= Mod_2 \cap Mod_4$; M7 $= Mod_2 \cap Mod_5$; M8 $= Mod_3 \cap Mod_4$; M9 $= Mod_3 \cap Mod_5$; M10 $= Mod_4 \cap Mod_5$. For each model, we should calculate the numbers of predictions made, the numbers of successful and not successful predictions and, also, calculate the success possibilities for each pair. Let us analyze the obtained table by the corresponding diagram (see Fig. 4), where we see that the best result is obtained from M9 - combination of two models Mod_3 and Mod_5. The combined probability of success for them is increased up to 75%. Despite the fact that separately these models have significantly lower rates of success: 7.06% and 6.06%, than others. For the considered examples, it is possible that two pairs of the models show the same result. In such a case, an expert should decide, which one of them should be used.

Obviously, this applies not only to prediction of earthquakes, but to prediction of any other event, including static (most often these are problems of natural disaster prediction), and dynamic prediction, such as economic problems [16].

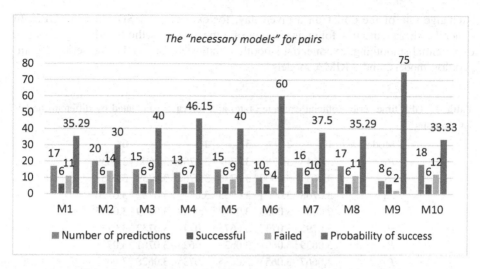

Fig. 4. The characteristics of the "necessary models" for pairs

4 The Example of Dynamic Prediction

Call prediction dynamic, when for a predetermined time interval, we must predict a certain value. For example, this applies to currency value prediction every day, prediction of subsistence minimum every month, prediction of gold price, oil price, prediction of human health, spread of influenza, etc. For example, let's consider the problem of daily prediction of currency rates, in particular, choosing the best model from the models predicting currency rate.

The algorithm of dynamic prediction described by us, can be presented in the form of 5 steps:

1. A table should be composed, where for time T it is shown prediction and actual rate obtained from model $P_1, P_2, \ldots, P_n$;
2. A table should be composed, where deviation from the rate will be shown for the same time it is shown T;
3. A list should be composed, where models will be given, which obtained correct results for each day;
4. All possible pairs of models should be composed, and number of correct predictions should be calculated for them;
5. Pair/pairs should be singled out, for which the values obtained at 4th step are maximal. This will be the best pair/pairs.

We present the implementation of all 5 steps of this algorithm with the example of currency exchange rate prediction.

Step 1:

Assume that there are prediction models $P = \{P_1, P_2, \ldots, P_n\}$ for currency rate (see Table 2). Each of them gives P_i prediction for the same period. It may be daily prediction (for each next day), or monthly, or yearly prediction.). P_{real} is the real exchange rate of the dollar on a given day, for example, 1 USD = 3.1050 GEL. In general, we can discuss following types of time series methods: Moving average, exponential smoothing, exponential smoothing adjusted for trend, time-series decomposition models, and ARIMA models.

Table 2. GEL time series (official exchange rate) and forecasts calculated by different models 6 days data.

Model/Day	1	2	3	4	5	6
P_1	3.0643	3.0781	3.0764	3.0752	3.0606	3.0639
P_2	3.0637	3.0800	3.0776	3.0766	3.0759	3.075
P_3	3.0768	3.0604	3.0753	3.08	3.0782	3.0726
P_4	3.0654	3.0655	3.0777	3.0629	3.0639	3.0695
P_5	3.0795	3.0737	3.0675	3.0744	3.0732	3.075
P_6	3.0639	3.0681	3.063	3.0623	3.0781	3.0721
P_7	3.0667	3.0653	3.0635	3.0735	3.0628	3.0698
P_8	3.0771	3.0632	3.0778	3.0641	3.0621	3.08
P_9	3.0701	3.0795	3.0663	3.068	3.08	3.0616
P_{10}	3.0647	3.07	3.0703	3.0795	3.0713	3.0647
P_{real}	**3.070**	**3.074**	**3.077**	**3.077**	**3.074**	**3.074**

Step 2:

The next step of the algorithm is counting the inaccuracies for each model of the forecast. The P_i model inaccuracies is indicated with S_i when $i = 1 \ldots n$ (Table 3):

Table 3. Calculating the inaccuracies for each predictive model.

S_1	0.00570	−0.00410	0.00060	0.00180	0.01340	0.01010
S_2	0.00630	−0.00600	−0.00060	0.00040	−0.00190	−0.00100
S_3	−0.00680	0.01360	0.00170	−0.00300	−0.00420	0.00140
S_4	0.00460	0.00850	−0.00070	0.01410	0.01010	0.00450
S_5	−0.00950	0.00030	0.00950	0.00260	0.00080	−0.00100
S_6	0.00610	0.00590	0.01400	0.01470	−0.00410	0.00190
S_7	0.00330	0.00870	0.01350	0.00350	0.01120	0.00420
S_8	−0.00710	0.01080	−0.00080	0.01290	0.01190	−0.00600
S_9	−0.00010	−0.00550	0.01070	0.00900	−0.00600	0.01240
S_{10}	0.00530	0.00400	0.00670	−0.00250	0.00270	0.00930

Step 3:

For this step, we determine a table of Boolean values, where the value True indicates that the given method made a correct prediction, and False - incorrect prediction (Table 4).

Table 4. The table of correct and incorrect predictions.

Model/Day	1	2	3	4	5	6
P_1	False	True	True	True	False	False
P_2	False	False	True	True	True	True
P_3	False	False	True	True	False	True
P_4	True	False	True	False	False	True
P_5	False	True	False	True	True	True
P_6	False	False	False	False	True	False
P_7	True	False	False	True	False	True
P_8	False	False	True	False	False	False
P_9	True	False	False	False	False	False
P_{10}	False	True	False	True	True	False

Step 4:

Select for each day those models, which made correct predictions. A conclusion can be made on which method is best (Table 5).

Table 5. Models with the correct prediction by days

Day	Model
1	P_4, P_7, P_9
2	P_1, P_5, P_{10}
3	P_1, P_2, P_3, P_4, P_8
4	$P_1, P_2, P_3, P_5, P_7, P_{10}$
5	$P_2, P_3, P_5, P_6, P_{10}$
6	$P_2, P_3, P_4, P_5, P_6, P_7$

According to calculated deviations, the methods were selected, which gave best prediction. These are: P_2 and P_7. For each column of Table 2, we chose those methods, which gave correct prediction for a given time point, and chose the best among them for a given time interval.

Step 5:

The next stage is to build all possible pairs from prediction models. In case of 10 models, the number of these pairs is 55 (see Table 6). For each P_i and P_j pair (designate it as P_{ij}) we calculate the number of successful combined predictions. A number located at the intersection of P_i row and P_j column is the number of combined successful predictions.

After this, let us choose those pair(s), for which these numbers are maximal. For our example, these are P_{23} and P_{25} (see Fig. 5). For the given time period, this pair correctly predicted 9 cases. Which one of them is to be used, should be decided by an expert. Note that the pair P_{27} of best models P_2 and P_7 itself is not the best (predicted 8 cases).

Table 6. Success of predictions in case of model pairs

$P_i \cap P_{ij}$	P_1	P_2	P_3	P_4	P_5	P_6	P_7	P_8	P_9	P_{10}
P_1		7	3	4	5	3	8	6	4	5
P_2	7		9	8	9	6	8	5	4	7
P_3	3	9		5	7	4	7	3	3	5
P_4	4	8	5		4	3	7	5	5	4
P_5	5	9	7	4		5	5	1	4	8
P_6	3	6	4	3	5		3	2	0	6
P_7	8	8	7	7	5	3		3	7	6
P_8	6	5	5	5	1	2	3		2	4
P_9	4	4	5	5	4	0	7	2		4
P_{10}	5	7	4	4	8	6	6	4	4	

After this, let us choose those pair(s), for which these numbers are maximal. For our example, these are P_{23} and P_{25} (see Fig. 5). For the given time period, this pair correctly predicted 9 cases. Which one of them is to be used, should be decided by an expert. Note that the pair P_{27} of best models P_2 and P_7 itself is not the best (predicted 8 cases).

Of course, this matrix (Table 6) is symmetric.

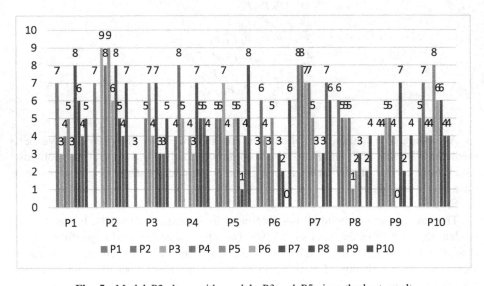

Fig. 5. Model *P2* along with models *P3* and *P5* gives the best result.

5   Updating a Prediction Model Under New Data

Geophysical conditions of environment are constantly changing, for example, an average temperature is changing every year, ocean shores are eroding with increasing rate, Earth plates are moving, etc. The question is, how to plan the change of selected scheme of prediction, from which time the pairs, triplets, etc. should be selected and recalculated?

We think that modification of prediction model, i.e. recalculation should be done from the day of last prediction event occurrence.

For consideration of relevant pairs of models, it is necessary to take corresponding figures from such a moment, when we have the aggregate of all input data. Obviously, it is possible that new prediction models may be introduced with the data of relevant predecessors, and additional regulations are required for consideration, because of search for the relevant pair. It is possible that after each actually occurred event, the selected pairs of prediction models would be changed, and other pairs would become better for prediction. Therefore, selection of each new pair should be done after occurrence of each event during static prediction, and for dynamic prediction, the process of determination of such pairs should be regulated within certain time periods. For example, if we have daily prediction data, new pairs should be selected at least once a week, according to the expert recommendation.

6   "Approximate Coincidences" of Predictions

In accordance with Lemma 2, the prediction pairs are selected. When selecting them, we determined the number of "accurate" coincidences of predictions. Now this is not sufficient and a "coincidence accuracy" should be determined. Obviously, prediction data should not directly coincide with each other, but coincide within certain intervals of time, place or other characteristics.

Hypothesis: When selecting the pairs of prediction models, an "approximate coincidence" should be taken into account.

In the nature, there is not an accurate coincidence for any parameter, neither for time, location or for other characteristics of an event. We must determine the parameters of approximate coincidence with the help of experts. It may be prediction of such period, when occurrence of given event is expected, or determination of certain radius from the epicenter. This task is faced in cases of earthquake, virus origin, start of military conflict, etc. Of course, time interval has great importance. For earthquakes, most used is short-term prediction (with interval of 24 h), short distance (within the radius of 50 km), and slight differences in magnitude (0.5 in magnitude).

7 n-Dimensional Models

If we have only 3 data and build given prediction points in the relevant 3-dimensional space: in this case, x is location, t is time and v is power. Assume, that each has its own dimension. For example: Location - plain. In this case, 4, 5 of more dimensional model will be built, depending on how much parameters are in prediction. Prediction data are presented in 3-dimensional space on Fig. 6. Here the distance between two points (predictions) is the error between their predictions. The value of "approximate coincidence" (i.e. this distance) is determined by an expert.

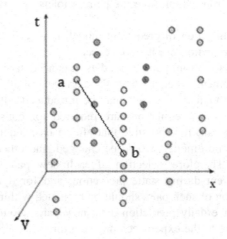

Fig. 6. Presentation of prediction data in space.

Introduction o "approximate coincidences" sharply increases the volume of calculations needed for selection of pairs of prediction models. It is necessary to utilize higher computational capacities, technical capabilities of supercomputers and use the algorithms of parallel computations and relevant programs.

If we have only 3 data and build given prediction points in the relevant 3-dimensional space: in this case, x is location, t is time and v is power. Assume, that each has its own dimension. For example: location - plain (see Pic. 6). Prediction data are presented in 3-dimensional space. Here the distance between two points (predictions) is the error between their predictions. The value of "approximate coincidence" (i.e. this distance) is determined by an expert.

If we figure the place of the event to be predicted with two or three values, not one - coordinates of the place, then instead of Pic. 6 we will have 4- or 5-dimensional space, where, like the given picture, necessary "similar" coincidences will be obtained by determining a distance between the given points. This determination should be made in accordance with the standard formula for the determination of the distance between two points in n-dimensional space, used in mathematics.

8   On the Further Development of this Theory

As it is known, not only scientists are engaged in predicting events, but also fortune-tellers, astrologers, extrasensory individuals, soothsayers, etc. Many of them use certain successors, superstitions, various omens and so on. It should be noted that they can process predictions of events similarly to scientific prediction. The main difference is that their predictions are not determined, and an area of successors is not strictly defined. But it is obvious that the formulas existing for scientific prediction, are used for their predictions and statistics of actually occurred events. For example, if some fortune-teller A gives prediction on the earthquake n, landslide m, etc., predicted to occur in a certain region, of course, we can actually calculate its prediction success, as for earthquake, as well as for landslide. By combined consideration of different predictions on similar events, it will be possible to select best pairs, triplets, etc. for predictions by the events, which will give better results, than only scientific predictions. This can be proved mathematically, as in the case of Lemma 1.

We plan to launch a site for predictions, where it will be possible to place any kind of predictions: political situations, sports results, and any other predictions, with the possibility of their further processing and finding best pairs. Data can be found from open sources, as well as by providing data from users of the site, and a result of the site's functioning will be a more accurate prediction of events through best pairs. A site for weather prediction is an example.

9 Conclusion

We considered the possibility to build much more effective new hybrid models from prediction models using parallel data. We theoretically proved the advantage of selecting model pairs over any best prediction model, and the advantage of a model obtained from n number of models, over a model obtained from $n-1$ number of models.

The best pair is one that does not have intersection between each, except actual, occurred predictions. It was recommended that recalculation of prediction model pairs should be done after each occurred event, and, at the same time, it is recommended to consider "approximate coincidence" of predictions when building a new model.

References

1. Gasitashvili, Z., Pkhovelishvili, M., Archvadze, N.: Prediction of events means of data parallelism. In: Proceedings - Mathematics and Computers in Science and Engineering, MACISE 2019, pp. 32–35, 8944725 (2019). https://ieeexplore.ieee.org/abstract/document/8944725
2. Chen, Y., Lv, Y., Wang, F.Y.: Traffic flow imputation using parallel data and generative adversarial networks. IEEE Trans. Intell. **21**(4), 1624–1630 (2019)
3. Bhimani, J., Mi, N., Leeser, M., Yang, Z.: New performance modeling methods for parallel data processing applications. ACM. Trans. Model. Comput. Simul. **29**(3), 1–24 (2019)
4. Skillicorn, D.: Strategies for parallel data mining. IEEE Concurr. **7**(4), 26–35 (1999)
5. Archvadze, N., Pkhovelishvili, M.: Prediction of events by means of data parallelism. In: Proceedings of International Conference on Matematics, Informatics and Informtional Technologies (MITI2018), pp. 120–121 (2018)
6. Gasitashvili, Z., Pkhovelishvili, M., Archvadze, N.: Usage on different types of data to solve complex mathematical problems. WSEAS Trans. Comput. **18**(7), 62–69 (2019)

7. Phkhovelishvili, M., Jorjiashvili, N., Archvadze, N.: Usage of heterogeneous data and other parallel data for prediction problems. PRIP' 2019. Pattern Recognition and Information Processing (Proceedings of 14th International Conference (21–23 May, Minsk, Belarus), pp.178–181. Minsk, Bestprint (2019)
8. Phkhovelishvili, M., Jorjiashvili, N., Archvadze, N.: Using different types data operations for solving complex mathematical tasks. computer science and information technologies. In: Proceedings of the conference (September 23–27, 2019), pp. 187–190. Yerevan, Armenia (2019)
9. Pkhovelisvili, M., Giorgobiani, M., Archvadze, N., Pkhovelishvili, G.: Modern forecasting models in economy. In: Proceedings of Materials of International Scientific Conference "Modern Tendencies of Development of Economy and Economic Science", pp. 219–224. Ivane Javakhishvili Tbilisi State University Paata Gugushvili Institute of Economics (2018)
10. Archvadze, N., Pkhovelisvili, M.: Modern Forecasting Models in Economy X International Conference of the Georgian Mathematical Union. Book of abstracts, p. 55 (2019)
11. Zav'yalov, A.D.: Prognoz zemletryaseniy: sostoyaniye problemy i puti resheniya, v zhurnale Zemlya i vselennaya, № 5, pp. 66–79 (2018) (ru)
12. Zav'yalov, A.D.: Srednesrochnyy prognoz zemletryaseniy: osnovy, metodologiya, realizatsiya. ISBN: 5-02-033946-6; Izdatel'stvo: Nauka (2006) (ru)
13. Gasitashvili, Z., Phkhovelishvili, M., Archvadze, N., Jorjiashvili, N.: An Algorithm of Improved Prediction from Existing Risk Predictions. Published by AIJR Publisher in "Abstracts of the Second Eurasian RISK-2020 Conference and Symposium" April 12–19, 2020, p. 31. Tbilisi, Georgia (2020)
14. Archvadze, N., Pkhovelishvili, M.: Reforming the Trees – C# and F# comporation. In: International Conference on "Problems of Cybernetics and Informatics" (PCI'2012), pp .93–96 (2012)
15. Earthquakes in Georgia (earthquaketrack.ru)
16. Gasitashvili, Z., Phkhovelishvili, M., Archvadze, N.: New algorithms for improvement of prediction models using data parallelism. In: 13th International Conference on Computer Science and Information Technologies CSIT 2021. Proceedings, pp. 17–20. Armenia, Yerevan, September 27 - October 1 2021
17. Gasitashvili, Z., Phkhovelishvili, M., Archvadze, N.: New algorithm for building effective model from prediction models using parallel data. Pattern Recognition and Information Processing (PRIP 2021): Proceedings of the 15th International Conference, 21–24 Sept. 2021, pp. 25–28, 246 p. UIIP NASB, Minsk, Belarus (2021). ISBN 978-985-7198-07-8

Formalization of People and Crowd Detection and Tracking for Smart Video Surveillance

Huafeng Chen[1](✉) 🆔, Rykhard Bohush[2] 🆔,
and Sergey Ablameyko[3,4] 🆔

[1] College of Computer Science and Technology, Zhejiang Shuren University,
Hangzhou, China
eric.hf.chen@zjsru.edu.cn
[2] Polotsk State University,
Blokhina Street, 29, Novopolotsk, Republic of Belarus
r.bogush@psu.by
[3] Belarusian State University, Nezavisimosti Avenue 4,
Minsk, Republic of Belarus
ablameyko@bsu.by
[4] United Institute of Informatics Problems of NASB, Surganov Street, 6,
Minsk, Republic of Belarus

Abstract. One of the promising areas of development and implementation of artificial intelligence is the automatic detection and tracking of moving objects in video sequence. The paper presents a formalization of the problem of detection and tracking of people and crowd in video. At first, we defined person, group of persons and crowd motion detection types and formalized them. For crowd, we defined three main types of its motion: direct motion, aggregation and dispersion. Then, we formalised the task of tracking for these three groups of people (single person, group of persons and crowd). Based on these formalizations, we developed algorithms for detection and tracking people and crowd in video sequences for indoor and outdoor environment. The results of experiments for video sequences obtained using a stationary and moving video camera are presented.

Keywords: Video surveillance · Moving object · Tracking by detection · Motion trajectory

1 Introduction

Detection and tracking of objects on video sequences are one of the main tasks in computer vision, which currently have a different number of technical applications and will be increasingly used for: analyzing the environment in automated systems of driving vehicles; assessing the movement of people in medicine and sports; tracking objects in industrial vision systems; recognizing the type of human activity in monitoring and security systems [1]. Unlike images, video sequences contain a much larger amount of information, which changes both in space and time. Therefore, processing and analyzing them allows to identify not only static, but also dynamic features of

© Springer Nature Switzerland AG 2022
A. V. Tuzikov et al. (Eds.): PRIP 2021, CCIS 1562, pp. 79–90, 2022.
https://doi.org/10.1007/978-3-030-98883-8_6

objects, which leads to an increase in the effectiveness of automated operation of video surveillance systems as a whole.

There are many object detection and tracking algorithms have been developed. In [2], an algorithm for tracking people on video based on the Monte Carlo method for Markov chains is proposed, in [3] - an algorithm for detecting and tracking people based on ViBe and combined HOG-SVM. Currently, algorithms based on convolutional neural networks, which are resistant to changes in illumination, dynamic background, and allow detection even in the case of significant overlaps of objects, are widely developed and used for object detection [4, 5].

Tracking a group of people is one of the most urgent tasks for video surveillance systems, but at present it is not fully solved. There are a number of approaches to solve this problem, however, due to several reasons, the effectiveness of their work is insufficient. The stage of forming an effective set of features that will be used to detect and track objects in the video sequence is one of the most difficult, since there are restrictions for it: use features that can be obtained in advance to describe objects; determine a limited set of features that will allow to get the maximum effectiveness, i.e. it is necessary to exclude uninformative features; it is possible to apply algorithms that meet the computational requirements of the developed systems.

We have developed a number of solutions that are designed to detect objects for high resolution video by using convolutional neural network [6], people tracking [7], smoke and flames detection [8]. Accordingly, we can say that the set of features used is largely related to the detection and tracking algorithms used to solve the tasks set. Therefore, in order to develop effective methods, techniques, and algorithms for detecting and tracking objects on video sequences, it is necessary to clearly formalize these tasks. It is necessary to determine the objects that will be detected and tracked, to determine the main stages of this process, as well as criteria that allow to evaluate the quality of processing and show how this is implemented in practice.

In this paper, we propose a formalization of the tasks of detecting and tracking objects (single person, group of persons and crowd) in video sequences. On the basis of the considered generalization, an algorithm for tracking a set of people and an algorithm for tracking crowd are developed. The results of experiments based on the considered criteria, allowing to evaluate the quality of the algorithms, are presented.

2 Formalization of Person Motion Detection Problem

A video sequence or video stream is a sequence of digital images (frames) $V = \{F_k\}$, k- the number of images in the sequence. The object in the image (Ob) is a local area that differs from the surrounding background and displays some of the features of the real-world object.

On each frame of the sequence obtained from a stationary video camera, as a rule, there are many objects:

$$OB_{F_k} = \left\{ Ob_q^{F_k} \right\}, q = 1, ..., Q. \tag{1}$$

According to the criterion of movement, each of them can be assigned to two main classes:

- a stationary object in a sequence of images is described by a set of features $\left(Ft^S_{Ob_q}\right)$ and its coordinates $\left(x_{Ob_q}, y_{Ob_q}\right)$, which do not change during a time interval (t). Such an object can be represented by a formal model:

$$Ob^S_q = \left(Ft^S_{Ob_q}, x_{Ob_q}, y_{Ob_q}, Ns^{F_k}_{Ob_q}\right), \tag{2}$$

where $\left(Ft_{Ob_q}, x_{Ob_q}, y_{Ob_q}\right) = const \forall F_k$, $k \in t$, $Ns^{F_k}_{Ob_q}$ - the set of possible noise effects on the object;

- a moving object in a sequence of images is characterized by a change in one or more basic parameters: shape, size, and coordinates over a time interval (t). The transformation of the shape and/or size of an object leads to a change in its features in the frames $ft^{F_k}_{Ob_q}$. Such an object can be represented by a formal model:

$$Ob^D_q = \left(ft^{F_k}_{Ob_q}, x^{F_k}_{Ob_q}, y^{F_k}_{Ob_q}, Ns^{F_k}_{Ob_q}\right), \tag{3}$$

where $x^{F_k}_{Ob_q}, y^{F_k}_{Ob_q}$ - object coordinates; $Ft^D_{Ob_q}$- a set of features of moving object, $Ft^D_{Ob_q} \supseteq ft^{F_k}_{Ob_q}$, $\forall k \in t$. Then $ft^{F_k}_{Ob_q} \cap ft^{F_{k+i}}_{Ob_q}$, that is, for the same moving object on a sequence of frames, a change in its features is characteristic.

Object detection is the determination of the location of a given object Ob^e in the image F, while its size is smaller than the size of the image, and the number of objects in the image is obviously unknown. In general, the object Ob^e detection process is implemented by comparing the features of the reference (Ft^e) and all possible fragments on the image plane using the rule-based method:

$$S\left(Ft^e, Ft^F_{Ob_q}\right) \xrightarrow[Z]{M} \max, \tag{4}$$

where S - detection accuracy; Z- a set of restrictions.

When detecting a stationary object on a sequence of images, it is necessary to consider the variability of a dynamic scene, since in addition to static ones, there are moving objects on it, and their number can change. Objects Ob^D_q can overlap a stationary object, which will cause its features to change on the sequence of frames:

$$Ft^{S,F_k}_{Ob_q} \neq Ft^{S,F_{k+1}}_{Ob_q}. \tag{5}$$

Therefore, to detect a stationary object on a sequence of images displaying a dynamic scene, it is necessary to use a method M_{STV}, that takes into account the change in features over time:

$$S\left(Ft^e, Ft_{Ob_q}^{S,F_k}\right) \xrightarrow[Z_{STV}]{M_{STV}} \max, \tag{6}$$

where Z_{STV} - a set of constraints when detecting a stationary object on a sequence of images.

Detection of moving object means to determine a location of the object Ob^D on the current frame F^k of the video sequence based on the specified F^e:

$$SD\left(Ob_{F^k}^D, Ob_{F^e}^D\right) \xrightarrow[ZD]{MD} \max, \tag{7}$$

where SD - the accuracy of detecting a moving object; MD - the method used; ZD- a set of restrictions.

3   Formalization of Crowd Motion Detection Problem

Human behaviours reflect one's emotion which can be affected by surroundings. Individual behaviours may not be reliable for indicating things happening around, but behaviours of crowd in public places are very reliable indicators.

From human nature point of view, people react rapidly to urgent events, thus their motions become fast on video. For example, when people see something dangerous, they get away from the corresponding region to prevent getting hurt. Crowds not only react to their surroundings, but they may also create emergencies. When conflict is going to happen between two groups of people, e.g., fans of two football clubs, they tend to approach each other rapidly. There are many other situations causing these crowd behaviours. That's why we have to try define types of crowd behaviour and motion.

Definition 1 (Crowd motion detection). First of all, we have to detect a crowd motion in video. It happens when many people move rapidly together in the same direction. Usually, direct crowd motion is an indicator of emergency. It may have different meanings in different situations. It can be people getting away from danger but due to limitation of walkable regions they have to go in the same direction. It can also be an organized group of people running to carry out a task, e.g., danger elimination. Three rules are proposed to identify direct crowd motion: 1) many people move from one region to another; 2) they move fast; 3) they move in one direction.

Definition 2 (Motion direction and speed). Motion direction indicates a destination where crowd move. Scientifically designed public places have reasonable planning for crowd flow. When crowd move toward unexpected positions, something abnormal may happen. In order to determine crowd motion direction in a region, we can simply divide $[0, 2\pi)$ into several intervals with equal length and count for each interval number of pixels whose motion direction is in that interval. Interval with most pixels shows main motion direction of crowd. Suppose the interval is $[2i\pi/n, 2(i+1)\pi/n)$, we can choose $(2i+1)\pi/n$ as the main motion direction θ_m. θ_m is more meaningful when crowd moves directionally, i.e., they move in the same direction.

Crowd motion directionality in region r is represented as follow:

$$md_t^{itv}(r) = \frac{n}{\left| \sum_{p \in r} (\cos \theta(p), \sin \theta(p)) \right|},$$ (8)

where n is pixel number in r, $\theta(p)$ is motion direction of pixel $I_t(p)$, $md_t^{itv} \geq 1$. The equation sign works when and only when pixels move in exactly the same direction.

Crowd motion symmetry could also be described by (8), the bigger md_t^{itv} is, the more symmetrically crowd move.

Motion speed of pixel $I_t(p)$ in time period from I_t to I_{t+itv} can be calculated as follow:

$$s_t^{itv}(p) = \frac{\left| IOF_t^{itv}(p) \right|}{itv},$$ (9)

where $IOF_t^{itv}(p)$ is displacement vector of pixel $I_t(p)$.

Thus, motion intensity in region r in the same time period is defined as flow:

$$MI_t^{itv}(r) = \frac{1}{n} \sum_{p \in r} s_t^{itv}(p),$$ (10)

where n is pixel number in r.

When determining intensive motion region, one should consider normal speed of crowd which may vary in different places and at different times. For example, people walk quickly to catch subway in the morning rush hour, but they may roam on the square after supper. After these benchmarks are determined, intensive motion region could be obtained through threshold segmentation.

Definition 3 (Crowd aggregation) Many people move rapidly toward a certain region from different directions. In typical crowd aggregation, people are from all directions symmetrically. But in real situations, that is not necessary. It depends on characteristic of the public place where people are, and at which stage the corresponding event is. For example, if two groups of people decide to attack each other after some sort of plan or emotion accumulation, aggregation in which two crowds move toward each other from opposite directions is more likely to happen. In general, three rules are proposed to identify crowd aggregation: 1) many people move toward a certain region from elsewhere; 2) they move fast; 3) there are at least two moving directions, and they are more or less symmetrical.

Definition 4 (Crowd dispersion) Many people move rapidly away from a certain region in different directions. Usually, it means something urgent or dangerous happens and people run in different directions to get away. But unless it is too crowded that people stand shoulder by shoulder, they don't necessarily move in all directions, although their motion directions are still more or less symmetrical. When two groups of people retreat from a conflict, they will cause crowd dispersion in which two crowds move away from each other in opposite directions. In general, three rules are proposed to identify crowd dispersion: 1) many people move away from a certain region to elsewhere; 2) they move fast; 3) there are at least two moving directions, and they are more or less symmetrical.

4   Formalization of Person and Crowd Tracking Problem

Object tracking can be divided into three types:

- Visual Object Tracking (VOT) - tracking of a single person;
- Multiple Object Tracking (MOT) - tracking of multiple person;
- Crowd Tracking (CT).

The first case of tracking is characterized by the fact that the object is detected and localized in the first frame, other objects are not detected.

4.1   Single Person Tracking

Tracking a moving object - determining the location of the same object on each frame of the video sequence during a time interval. This makes it possible to plot the trajectory of an object, determine its speed and acceleration. When solving practical problems, in some cases, an analysis of the trajectory of movement is required.

To perform maintenance, detection and localization procedures are required. Different ways of describing the objects of observation are used:

- a single point that characterizes the center of mass of the object or the center of the minimum possible rectangle described around the object;
- a set of key points by which the object can be uniquely identified in subsequent frames;
- a geometric primitive described around the object (most often a rectangle, less often an ellipse);
- the external contour of the object;
- a set of areas that are as stable as possible when moving, or the entire area of the object;
- invariant characteristics of the object (for example, texture, color scheme, etc.).

The trajectory of the object is a sequential display of the movement of this object on the video sequence:

$$Tr\left(Ob^{D}\right) = \left(Ob_{F_k}^{D}\right) \cdot \forall k \in t. \tag{11}$$

In physics, the trajectory of motion is called the line that a particle describes when it moves. It is obvious that for the problem to be solved, in the end, it is necessary to determine a line on the required frame of the video sequence, which will show how the observed object moved over a certain period of time.

There may be different ways to determine the coordinates of an object on the frame, but the most commonly used approach involves finding its center (one pixel per frame) with coordinates $\left(x_{Ob_q}^{F_k}, y_{Ob_q}^{F_k}\right)$. As a rule, the movement is considered in the frame coordinate system. Then the trajectory of the object on the video sequence is described by a sequence in the form of a set of coordinates of the center of the object on each frame:

$$Tr\left(Ob^D\right) = \left(Ob^D_{F_k}\right) = \left(\left(x^{F_1}_{Ob_q}, y^{F_1}_{Ob_q}\right), \left(x^{F_2}_{Ob_q}, y^{F_2}_{Ob_q}\right), \left(x^{F_3}_{Ob_q}, y^{F_3}_{Ob_q}\right), ..., \left(x^{F_n}_{Ob_q}, y^{F_n}_{Ob_q}\right)\right).$$

(12)

The trajectory Tr' of its movement can be found using method MTS and constraints ZTS:

$$STS\left(Tr'\right) \xrightarrow[ZTS]{MTS} \max,$$

(13)

where STS - the accuracy of tracking a moving single object.

Despite the development of numerous algorithms over the past decade, due to the possibility of significant visual changes in the object and illumination, background noise, occlusions, the task of tracking a single object is not fully completed.

4.2   Multiple Person Tracking

When tracking multiple objects, one need to determine the set of trajectories $TR' = \left\{Tr'_q\right\}$ of the objects in the frames, and then compare them to each other to determine the movement of objects between frames:

$$STM\left(TR, TR'\right) \xrightarrow[ZTM]{MTM} \max.$$

(14)

Several objects can be present in the frame at the same time. Moreover, objects can have almost identical visual features. Thus, it is possible to lose an object due to its intersection with a similar one, or overlap with a background element. Tracking of multiple objects is performed at long time intervals, and it is possible to predict the location on subsequent frames.

4.3   Crowd Tracking

Crowd is a large group of people with severe occlusions. Crowd tracking is to monitor state changing of crowds. Usually abnormally sudden change indicates emergency, for example, a crow splits into small groups could mean people run away from danger, two large crowds merge into one along with intensive motion could mean clash.

There may exist several crowds in one frame:

$$CR_{F_k} = \left\{Cr^{F_k}_q\right\}, q = 1, ..., Q,$$

(15)

where $Cr_q^{F_k} = \left\{ Ob_{q_i}^{F_k} \right\}, i = 1, ..., n_q$, n_q is the number of people that compose crowd $Cr_q^{F_k}$. One thing deserves to be mentioned is that crowd does not keep its composition through time, it can split, or join together with other crowds.

Because of severe occlusions, single person $Ob_{q_i}^{F_k}$ in the crowd can hardly be detected or tracked. One common way is to treat crowd as a single entity and consider imaginary particles occupy the crowd area. Along with particles moving, crowd will reshape or regroup. It is possible to track for one crowd in a certain frame where its sub-groups go in next frames:

$$Cr_q^{F_k} = \left\{ Sb_{q_i}^{F_{k+t}} \right\}, q_i = 1, ..., l_q, \tag{16}$$

where $Sb_{q_i}^{F_{k+t}}$ is a separated sub-group of $Cr_q^{F_k}$ in F_{k+t}.

It is possible to track for one crowd in a certain frame where its sub-groups came from:

$$Cr_q^{F_k} = \left\{ Sb_{q_j}^{F_{k-t}} \right\}, q_j = 1, ..., m_q, \tag{17}$$

where $Sb_{q_j}^{F_{k-t}}$ is a separated sub-group of $Cr_q^{F_k}$ in F_{k-t}.

Once sub-groups of a crowd are located in a previous frame or a posterior frame, further analysis of the crowd can be performed to determine whether certain crowd behaviour happens. Three types of behaviour are considered: direct movement; crowd aggregation; crowd dispersion.

One of the main problems for the practical use of the tracking algorithm is to ensure high accuracy with limited hardware resources and input data. In general, accurate tracking can be achieved by solving the global optimization problem, which requires the entire sequence of frames at once, which is impossible in real video surveillance systems. In the existing methods, the object tracking problem is often formulated as an optimization problem using graph algorithms [9]. Each detected object is represented as a vertex, and the transition from one vertex to another is determined by the similarity function used. Establishing an association on graphs can be solved by the method of finding the path with the minimum cost, which is most effectively solved by global optimization.

Tracking algorithms based on the selection and analysis of special points require the presence of corners in the image contours. With a small number of them, the effectiveness of tracking will be low. Methodology of detecting and tracking objects utilizing color feature and motion is considered in [10]. Probabilistic approaches use the statement that a moving object has a certain state, which is measured on each frame, and to estimate its position on the next one, it is necessary to generalize the values from the previous ones. For this purpose, methods based on the Kalman filter [11] or the particle filter [12] are used. However, objects can have a pronounced nonlinear trajectory of movement, and in this case, the assessment of the new state based on the previous ones will be determined with a high error. Therefore, different approaches are used to solve different applied problems.

5 Experimental Results

5.1 People Detection and Tracking Results

The proposed mathematical background has been tested in many real tasks that have been described in our papers [6–8]. For people tracking an effective method is based on tracking by detection. In this case, the detection stage is one of the key ones. The quality of its work largely determines the accuracy of people tracking in video. Therefore, for what follows, we will use a more accurate CNN YOLOv4, the advantages of which are indicated in [13]. After person detection in the frame, features of the selected fragment in the spatial area in the frame and in time domain in video sequence are calculated. We use features such as CNN and histogram features of H channel in HSV space when this person was last correctly detected in frame, center coordinates for selected area of a person in frame, displacement in the current frame relative to the previous one, width and height of the area in previous frame, motion trajectory, motion time. The values of the similarity function are calculated for all accompanied and detected people in the current frame. Based on these values, correspondence is established between the detected and tracked objects using Hungarian algorithm. The trajectory is created when a person is first detected. The trajectory is deleted if this person is not detected for a certain number of consecutive frames and there is no comparison for him with previous frames. Thus, in this case, we consider that he left the scene.

In real systems, object detection errors are possible. Therefore, an important task is to determine the effectiveness of tracking, taking into account the joint work of the detection and tracking stages to assess the possibility of practical use of the algorithm. Testing of the tracking algorithm for indoor surveillance and a modified algorithm for outdoor, which uses the Kalman filter, was carried out taking into account the results of human detection by CNN YOLOv4. In this case, errors in the operation of this CNN lead to a deterioration in the criteria for tracking. However, experiments reflect the real effectiveness for tracking by detection algorithms, which is very important for making a decision about their application in practice.

To evaluate the proposed approach, MOT16 metric [14] is used. Experiments for indoor video sequences were carried out on six videos from a stationary surveillance camera. Videos are taken from [14]. The total number of frames is 11890. Videos are characterized by changing in lighting, a nonlinear trajectory for people, overlap by background objects or the intersection of people trajectories, and similar characteristics.

For detection and tracking algorithm from [15] MOTA = 0.288306 is provided for all videos [14], for our proposed algorithm MOTA = 0.300860. For video sequences from a fixed indoor surveillance camera: for the algorithm from [15] MOTA = 0.8793, for our proposed algorithm MOTA = 0.9266. The experiments have confirmed that our proposed approach improves the tracking accuracy on test video sequences obtained indoors and outdoors. Example for indoor video surveillance with a changing lighting level and building trajectories of people movement is shown in Fig. 1a and b.

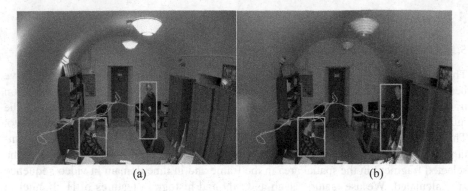

(a)   (b)

Fig. 1. Experimental results of multiple people tracking.

5.2 Crowd Motion Detection and Tracking

In the paper [16] we proposed a new method to detect crowd motion at early stage, which includes the following steps: integral optical flow computation, pixel-level motion analysis, region-level motion analysis and threshold segmentation. In the threshold segmentation step, motion intensity, quantity and motion direction are together used to describe motions and detect crowd behaviours.

We tested our method on real world videos downloaded from YouTube. Figure 2a and b show crowd tracking and behaviour detections for scenes of a Korean riot exercise. In Fig. 2a, two teams of police are moving to the centre of the scene from the right side, these teams are two sub-groups of a crowd in a posterior frame. In Fig. 2b, a group of rioters are rushing towards the police, here the two teams of police and the rioters compose a crowd, and the crowd is aggregating. Figure 2c and d show crowds' movements during an earthquake in Nepal. In Fig. 2c, people run into the street from the left corner. In a posterior frame shown as Fig. 2d, those people compose a crowd, they have just performed direct motion.

Once sub-groups of a crowd are detected in previous or posterior frames, the crowd can be tracked. Based on parameters of the movements of these sub-groups, including motion intensities, motion directions, occupied area, etc., crowd motion can be analysed, and certain behaviours can therefore be detected.

Fig. 2. Experimental results of crowd tracking and motion analysis in real word videos.

6 Conclusion

The paper presents a formalization of the problem of detecting stationary and moving objects on video sequences, taking into account their features. Three cases of tracking are considered and described: single object, multiple objects and crowds on video sequences. The approach for tracking multiple people on video sequences for indoor and outdoor video surveillance is described. The first stage requires detecting person in the input frames by YOLOv4 convolutional neural network. For solving person assignment problem, we store information about individual object in spatial domain of frames and in the time domain on a video sequence. For person description the following feature set is used: neural network and histogram features, centre coordinates of a person in the frame, offset in the current frame relative to the previous one, person width and height in the previous frame, trajectory and time of movement.

For crowd motion detection, we presented a new method to identify crowd motion at early stage. Our method mainly consists of the following steps: integral optical flow computation, pixel-level motion analysis, region-level motion analysis and threshold segmentation. The accumulative effect of integral optical flow is taken advantage to separate background and foreground and obtain intensive motion regions which are usually of interest. Pixel motion intensity, quantity and motion direction in regions are together used to describe motions and detect crowd behaviours.

Generally accepted definitions of crowd motion are not present yet, these can only be obtained through more researchers' work in computer vision and related fields. We believe that, for urgent event detection, it is important not to miss detection of related crowd motion.

References

1. Cavallaro, A., Maggio, E.: Video Tracking: Theory and Practice. Wiley, New York (2011)
2. Kuplyakov, D., Shalnov, E., Konushin, A.: Markov chain Monte Carlo based video tracking algorithm. Program. Comput. Softw. **43**(4), 224–229 (2017). https://doi.org/10.1134/S0361768817040053
3. Wang, L., Gui, J., Lu, Z.-M., Liu, C.: Fast pedestrian detection and tracking based on VIBE combined HOG-SVM scheme. Int. J. Innov. Comput. Inf. Control **15**(6), 2305–2320 (2019)
4. Mohana, H.V., Aradhya, R.: Object detection and tracking using deep learning and artificial intelligence for video surveillance applications. Int. J. Adv. Comput. Sci. Appl. **10**(12), 517–530 (2019)
5. Mane, S., Mangale, S.: Moving object detection and tracking using convolutional neural networks. In: Second International Conference on Intelligent Computing and Control Systems (ICICCS), Madurai, India, pp. 1809–1813 (2018)
6. Vorobjov, D., Zakharava, I., Bohush, R., Ablameyko, S.: An effective object detection algorithm for high resolution video by using convolutional neural network. In: Huang, T., Lv, J., Sun, C., Tuzikov, A.V. (eds.) ISNN 2018. LNCS, vol. 10878, pp. 503–510. Springer, Cham (2018). https://doi.org/10.1007/978-3-319-92537-0_58
7. Ye, S., Bohush, R.P., Chen, H., Zakharava, I.Y., Ablameyko, S.V.: Algorithm for person tracking on video sequences using face identification for indoor surveillance. Pattern Recogn. Image Anal. **30**(4), 827–837 (2020)
8. Ye, S., Zhican, B., Chen, C., Bohush, R., Ablameyko, S.: An effective algorithm to detect both smoke and flame using color and wavelet analysis Pattern Recogn. Image Anal. **27**(1), 131–138 (2017)
9. Salvi, D., Waggoner, J., Temlyakov, A., Wang, S.: A graph-based algorithm for multi-target tracking with occlusion. In: IEEE Workshop on Applications of Computer Vision (WACV), Clearwater Beach, pp. 489–496 (2013)
10. Singh, P., Deepak, B.B.V.L., Sethi, T., Murthy, M.D.P.: Real-time object detection and tracking using color feature and motion. In: International Conference on Communications and Signal Processing (ICCSP), Melmaruvathur, India, pp. 1236–1241 (2015)
11. Weng, S.-K., Kuo, C.-M., Tu, S.-K.: Video object tracking using adaptive Kalman filter. J. Vis. Commun. Image Represent. **17**(6), 1190–1208 (2006)
12. Gustafsson, F., Gunnarsson, F., Bergman, N.: Particle filters for positioning, navigation and tracking. IEEE Trans. Signal Process. **50**(2), 425–437 (2002)
13. Bochkovskiy, A., Wang, Ch.-Y. Liao, H.-Y. M.: YOLOv4: optimal speed and accuracy of object detection (2020). https://arxiv.org/abs/2004.10934. Accessed 12 June 2020
14. MOTChallenge: The Multiple Object Tracking Benchmark. https://motchallenge.net. Accessed 14 Apr 2021
15. Real-time Multi-person tracker using YOLOv3 and deep_sort with tensorflow. https://github.com/Qidian213/deep_sort_yolov3. Accessed 22 Feb 2021
16. Chen, H., Nedzvedz, O., Ye, S., Ablameyko, S.: Crowd abnormal behaviour identification based on integral optical flow in video surveillance systems. Informatica **29**(2), 211–232 (2018)

Investigation of the GAN-SSL Classifier Properties for Identification Expertise

Aleksandra Maksimova[✉] [iD]

Institute of Applied Mathematics and Mechanics, Donetsk, Ukraine
maximova.alexandra@mail.ru

Abstract. The generative adversarial nets (GANs) are investigated for classification problem. GANs for semi-supervised learning (GAN-SSL) is proposed for complex classification problem. The identification expertise problem is challenging for classification because of complex structure of classes, unbalanced samples and cross-classes. We use semi-supervised learning to solve unbalanced classes problem. Two groups of experiments were carried out. The first group of experiments for the model dataset that consist of classes of points normally distributed about vertices an eight-dimensional hypercube. The second groups of experiments for the petrol identification expertise dataset we get from laboratory of petrol quality. The experiments with good model examples get good quality more than 97%. The analysis of network parameters and generator properties is made. The classification model for petrol identification expertise was created and has 94% quality. In this work we use GAN-SSL classification on petrol identification expertise example, but this classification model can be used for diesel fuel, household chemicals items, different oils and for various other objects.

Keywords: GAN · Classification · Identification expertise · Semi-supervised learning

1 Introduction

The generative adversarial nets were proposed in 2014 by group of Jan Goodfellow [1] to generate the objects that are the same as in the training distribution of data. The GANs are two series-connected neural networks: generator G and discriminator D. The adversarial two-stage learning process is used to train this sequence of nets. The prepared train generator is used to generate examples of input data, for example, portraits of celebrities or bedroom interiors. After generator is ready the discriminator is not need more. This idea of adversarial training was later developed for classification problem by Jan Goodfellow, Tim Saliman and other in [2]. The discriminator transforms to classifier with the number of outputs corresponding to the number of classes. The advantage of this classifier is using the semi-supervised learning to train one. It is used unlabeled data for end-to-end learning of classifiers in semi-supervised learning.

The identification expertise problem in Chemistry is formally seems as a classification problem [3]. The fuzzy portrait method for identification expertise of petrol was proposed in our previous works to solve this problem [4, 5]. The quality of received

© Springer Nature Switzerland AG 2022
A. V. Tuzikov et al. (Eds.): PRIP 2021, CCIS 1562, pp. 91–103, 2022.
https://doi.org/10.1007/978-3-030-98883-8_7

models heavily dependent on available data. The specific problem for identification expertise is a very few of items for some classes, for example 15 items. If we consider objects of each class as elements of a certain probability distribution, we don't have enough items to get good classifier. The representation of samples set is not good enough. The main idea is to use semi-supervised learning to overcome our limitations with datasets using generative adversarial nets for semi-supervised learning (GAN-SSL). This work is aimed at research of novel state-of-the-art GAN-SSL classification method.

2 Related Works

GAN publications have increasingly focused on the use of class labels. The first multiclass inference strategy for GAN was developed in [6], where the number of outputs of the discriminant classifier is equal to the number of classes, and training is carried out both on unlabeled and partially labeled data. Such a network is called categorical generative adversarial network (CatGan).

The proposed in [2, 7] classification model can be used for identification expertise classification problem. The number of outputs of the discriminator corresponds to the number of real classes and one more for the fake class, produces by generator. This strategy is good working for semi-supervised learning using the GAN loss functions.

In [8] proposed novel approach to semi-supervised learning on graphs – GraphS-gan. Generator and classifier play a novel competitive game, when generator generates fake samples. This idea can help in identification expertise to find counterfeit items.

There are some papers where classical GANs architectures, like DCGAN and PGGAN using for classification [9]. The generator is training to produce realistic chest X-ray images and lymph node histology images. These images add to training data sets for classical convolutional net.

Classical GAN and GAN-SSL network it is really complicated to train. Researchers admit [1, 2] that it is difficult to understand how generator and discriminator interact with each other.

The GAN-SSL classifier is the state-of-the art approach that we investigate in this work to find it's advantages and disadvantages for identification expertise classification problem.

3 Model Framework

3.1 Problem Definition

The identification expertise is performed in quality control laboratory to identify the producer of petrol. Fuel sample parameters are measured by special instruments, for example, PetroSpec GS and as a result we have a feature vector of object. The set of producers we consider as a classes for classification problem. The training sample is tabular data where the rows correspond to the petrol samples and the columns corre-spond to the measured parameters – features.

We have in our consideration eight classes of objects grouped by producer and mark parameters. We use eight features: density, research octane number, motor octane number, volume fraction of olefinic hydrocarbons, alkane, benzene, toluene and mass fraction of methanol.

3.2 GAN-SSL Architecture

We used GAN-SSL architecture proposed in [2]. GAN architecture includes two networks: generator and discriminator neural nets. The goal of model training is to train a generator $G(z)$ that produces samples from the data distribution p_{data} by transforming vector of noise z as $x = G(z)$ $(x \sim p_g)$. The discriminator is training to distinguish real data p_{data} from the generator distribution p_g. For GAN-SSL architecture discriminator is changed to standard K-classes classifier. We do semi-supervised learning with any standard classifier by adding samples from the GAN generator to data set and add $K + 1$ class to classifier for these samples labelled like «generated fake».

Both discriminator and generator in GAN-SSL network are multilayer perceptron's. The generator takes noise z from uniform distribution on the interval [0,1] as input and outputs fake samples having the similar shape as x. Batch normalization is used in generator [10]. It is used weight normalization trick [11] before produces output layer in generator. There are three layers in the generator with tanh activation function in the output.

Discriminator consists of six linear weight norm layers based on weight normalization trick too. It is used additive Gaussian noise in every layer before output for smoothing purpose in the training mode only.

The discriminator takes in object feature vector x as input and outputs K-dimensional vector of logits $\{l_1, ..., l_K\}$. Classifier with $K + 1$ outputs is over-parameterized, so we only consider the first K outputs and assume the output for «generated fake» class. It is always 0 before softmax, because subtracting identical number from all units before softmax does not change the softmax results. We can use softmax activation function to get class probabilities $p_{model}(y = j) = \frac{\exp(l_j)}{\sum_{k=1}^{K} \exp(l_k)}$.

The number of neurons in hidden layers depends on identification expertise dataset and can be modified corresponding to velocity of problem. The discriminator must be more powerful than the generator and powerful enough for specific task. Denote the base number of neurons as N_{base} parameter for experimental result section. It means, that there are N_{base} neurons in all layers of generator and $(2N_{base}, 2N_{base}, N_{base}, N_{base}, N_{base},)$ respectively in layers of discriminator.

3.3 Learning Algorithm

There are two techniques to improve the training of GANs proposed in [2]. We use feature matching technique that addresses the instability of GANs by specifying a new objective for generator that avert it from overtraining on the current discriminator. We don't use minibatch discrimination in our work because it further improves the generator examples that is not necessary for identification expertise problem.

The loss function for discriminator consists of two components: supervised $L_{supervised}$ and unsupervised $L_{unsupervised}$ loss functions [2]

$$L_{supervised} = -\mathbf{E}_{x,y \sim p_{data}(x,y)} \log p_{model}(x, y < K + 1) \tag{1}$$

$$L_{unsupervised} = -\left\{ \mathbf{E}_{x \sim p_{data(x)}} \log[1 - p_{model}(y = K + 1|x] + \mathbf{E}_{x \sim G} \log[p_{model}(y = K + 1|x)] \right\} \tag{2}$$

where $\mathbf{E}_{x,y \sim pdata(x,y)}$ is expectation of labeled data, $\mathbf{E}_{x \sim pdata(x,y)}$ is expectation of unlabeled data, $\mathbf{E}_{z \sim noise}$ is expectation of noise.

The output of discriminator layer before softmax we denote as $f(x)$ function that uses in new objective function for generator:

$$L_{gen} = ||\mathbf{E}_{x \sim pdata(x,y)} f(x) - \mathbf{E}_{z \sim noise} f(G(z))||_{L2} \tag{3}$$

where $\mathbf{E}_{x \sim pdata(x,y)}$ and $\mathbf{E}_{z \sim noise}$ like in (2), $||f||_{L2}$ is L_2 norm.

We use minibatch stochastic **Algorithm 1** to train generator and discriminator iteratively minimizing their losses.

Algorithm 1: Minibatch stochastic gradient descent training of GAN-SSL for identification expertise.

> ***Input:*** $X^1_{unlabeled}$- identification objects dataset – shuffled unlabeled data set #1
> $X^2_{unlabeled}$- identification objects dataset – shuffled unlabeled data set #2
> $X_{labeled}$- identification objects dataset for supervised learning; y – labels of
>   classes correspond to pare (producer, mark of petrol)
>
> Make $X^1_{unlabeled}$, $X^2_{unlabeled}$, $X_{labeled}$ equal length datasets by folding $X_{labeled}$
>
> **for** *number of epochs* **do**
> > Sample minibatch from $X^1_{unlabeled}$
> > Sample minibatch from $X_{labeled}$
> > Sample minibatch from noise prior $p_g(z)$ *as* $G(z)$
> > Update the discriminator by descending gradients of losses:
> > $$L = L_{supervised} + L_{unsuprvised}$$
> > Sample minibatch from $X^2_{unlabeled}$
> > Sample minibatch from noise prior $p_g(z)$ *as* $G(z)$
> > **for** *2 steps* **do**
> > > Update the generator by descending gradients of losses:
> > > $$L = L_{gen}$$
> > **end for**
> **end for**

The gradient-based updates can be used by any standard gradient-based learning rule. We use Adam, based on adaptive estimates of lower-order moments [12].

4 GAN-SSL Experimental Research

To analyze properties of GAN-SSL neural network for classification problems we solve identification expertise classification and synthetical model classification problems both with the same number of features and classes: eight features and eight classes.

We investigate the influence of N_{base} parameter on quality of classification. The synthetic model data is much simpler for classification. We use Adam learning algorithm with learning rate parameter that is investigate too.

The properties of generator are investigated too.

4.1 Classification for Model Data

The model data set consist of classes of points normally distributed about vertices of eight-dimensional hypercube. These data have the same objects in every class and are easy to classify. The total number of objects are 7104. In the experiments we had 40 objects as labeled data, 4736 as unlabeled data and 2368 left-off examples data for testing (30% of examples from every class). All classes are normally distributed, the 1% of object is outliers. In Fig. 1 we can see the examples of feature values for synthetical model data by projection on pare of features 1 and 4.

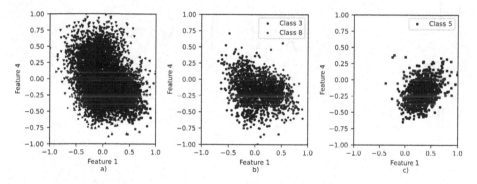

Fig. 1. Examples of feature values for synthetical model data by projection on pare of features 1 and 4. a) the examples for all classes; b) the examples of class 3 and 8; c) the examples of class 5

Figure 1 illustrates the special structure of classification synthetical problem. The input data are 8-dimentional table, so the 2-dimentional projection on feature 1 and 4 are presented. In the Fig. 1 and Fig. 5a) there are all examples of classes. The Fig. 1b) demonstrate the example of strong intersection of classes. The two-cluster structure of class 5 is shown on Fig. 1c). All data are scaled to range $[-1, 1]$.

The group of experiments are performed for different parameter N_{base} to adjust the best structure of neural network for classification. In Fig. 2 the accuracy dependencies on the N_{base} parameter is presented. The best quality of classification achieved on $N_{base} \in [200, 305]$. Accuracy is 97% on test data. The visualization of training process is presented in Fig. 3 and Fig. 7. The x-axis shows the number of epochs. Increasing the parameter N_{base} tends $L_{supervised}$ loss function to zero. The loss function of generator tends to increasing during the training.

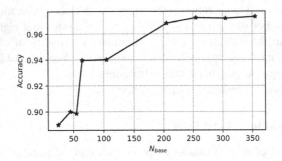

Fig. 2. The accuracy dependencies on the N_{base} parameter

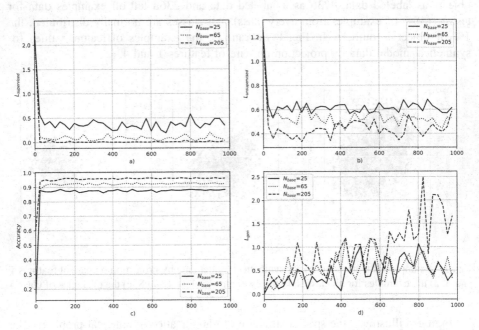

Fig. 3. Training proccess for different N_{base} parameter for synthetic model data: a) supervised loss (1), b) unsupervised loss (2), c) validation of model with respect to testing data, d) generator loss (3)

We used learning rate equal to 0.001 for this problem. The Adam stochastic optimization algorithm converges faster for $lr = 0.001$ and $lr = 0.00001$ is already too high. The Fig. 4 shows training process learning parameters for different learning rates ($N_{base} = 205$). A smaller learning rate leads to smoother changes in loss functions, but ultimately to a worse learning quality: 0.97 for lr = 0.001 and 0.95 for lr = 0.00001.

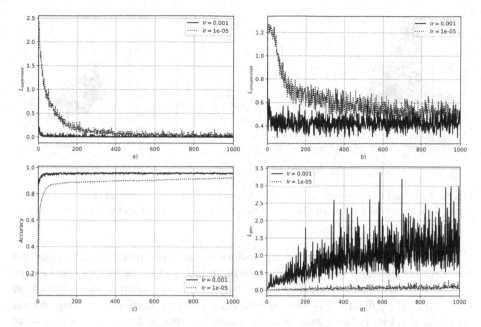

Fig. 4. Training proccess for different learning rate parameter for model synthetic problem: a) supervised loss (1), b) unsupervised loss (2), c) validation of model with respect to testing data, d) generator loss (3)

4.2 Classification for Petrol Identification Expertise

The petrol identification expertise data we received from quality control laboratory. There are different number of objects for every producer so the classes are very unbalanced. The smallest class consist of 37 examples but the most popular – of 671. We use semi-supervised learning to solve this problem. The total number of examples are 2001. We have generated samples with labels where every class have the same number of objects corresponding to length of smallest class. The rest of examples we use as unlabeled examples with repeated one for small classes in training process. In the experiments we had 48 objects as labeled data, 4032 as unlabeled data and 498 left-off examples data for testing (25% of examples from every class).

In Fig. 5 is illustrated the special structure of classes we have in consideration. The input data are 8-dimentional table, so the 2-dimensional projection on feature 1 and 4 are presented. On the Fig. 5a) there are all examples of classes. The Fig. 5b) shows the example of strong intersection of classes. The two-cluster structure of class 5 is shown on Fig. 5c). All data are scaled to range [−1, 1].

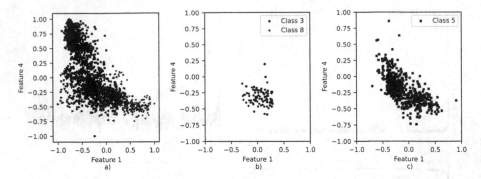

Fig. 5. Examples of feature values for indentification expertise by projection on pare of features 1 and 4. a) the examples for all classes; b) the examples of class 3 and 8; c)the examples of biggest class 5

The group of experiments are performed for different parameter N_{base} to adjust the best structure of neural network for classification. In Fig. 5 the accuracy dependencies on the N_{base} parameter is presented. The best quality of classification achieved on $N_{base} \in [65, 105]$. Accuracy is 94% on train data. The visualization of training process is presented in Fig. 7. The x-axis shows the number of epochs. Increasing the parameter N_{base} tends $L_{supervised}$ loss function to zero. The loss function of generator tends to increasing during the training.

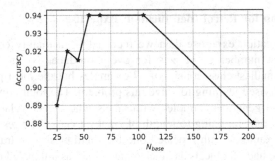

Fig. 6. The accuracy dependencies on the N_{base} parameter

4.3   Properties of Generator

The main idea of generative adversarial nets is using generator to create the examples like in the distribution of p_{data}. The uniform distribution noise z from unit square is getting to the input of generator. The output of generator has the same dimension like feature vector. In the process of training the generator starts to produce data the same data as input. ($p_g = p_{data}$). This property of GAN is stored for GAN-SSL classifier. We can see that data from the generator corresponds to input data and lie in the similar area. The confirmation is in Fig. 8 demonstrated on two-dimensional feature projections. In the Fig. 8a) the grey points are not trained generator outputs but in the Fig. 8b) these distribution p_g transformed into p_{data} distribution: the aria covered by grey points practically coincides with the aria covered with input data. We observe a similar result for the synthetic model data (Fig. 9). The image of outputs of generator corresponds to the best structure of neural network ($N_{base} = 65$ for identification expertise problem, $N_{base}= 205$ for synthetic model problem).

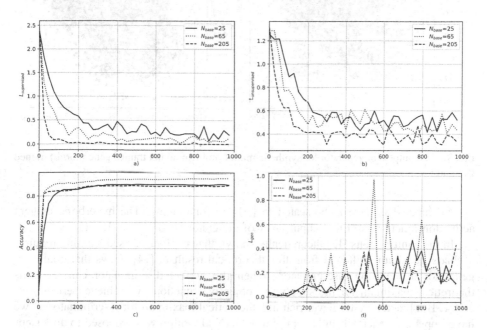

Fig. 7. Training proccess for different N_{base} parameter for identification expertise: a) supervised loss (1), b) unsupervised loss (2), c) validation of model with respect to testing data, d) generator loss (3)

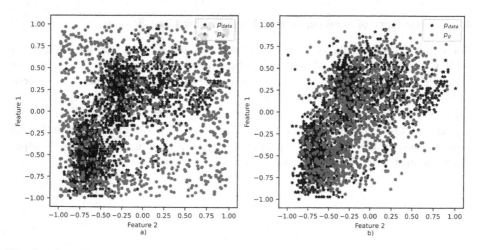

Fig. 8. The outputs of generator for identefication expertise problem: a) not trained generator; b) trained generator

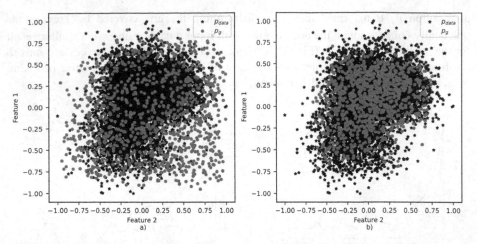

Fig. 9. The outputs of generator for synthetic model problem: a) not trained generator; b) trained generator

All input data have to be scaled to $[-1, 1]$ for training. The hyperbolic tangent activation function is in the output layer of generator so $G(z) \in [-1, -1]$.

In the contributions [13] theoretically shown that semi-supervised learning requires a «bad» generator. Different from this theoretical result in [14] shows that quality of generator depends on discriminator. When the perfect discriminator can reach its theoretical maximum for the supervised objective function, we achieve perfect generator. But practically we never rich this theoretical maximum for discriminator so we have imperfect generator. In [1] in training GAN algorithm was proposed to do k steps for discriminator training but this is computationally expensive and we didn't use this recommendation. If we will optimize the discriminator till convergence on every step of two-stage training algorithm we can achieve perfect generator.

4.4   Advantages of Semi-supervised Learning for Classification

The number of labeled data can be 10% of the total and it is can be small amount but we can have a big amount of other unlabeled objects. This one can help to get better classifier by generating the p_{data} area to point the classification boundary in a more correct position. We have very small number of examples to get a good quality classifier. Figure 10 shows the classification result for simple two-dimensional binary classification task where it was used only «stars» objects with labels to train. In this case, we assume that the marked-up examples are not more important or some especially common ones, it's just that we could not get others.

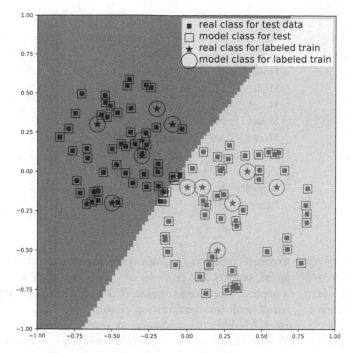

Fig. 10. The advantages of semi-supervised learning

5   Conclusion

Theoretical investigation of GAN-model are usually complicated task and propositions are general and didn't work on practice very often. The properties of the obtained models can often depend on the structure of the input data, so the resulting neural network model may differ in its characteristics from those expected in theory. There-fore, it is an interesting task to study the properties of the obtained models for different input data and compare these results with the parameters of the models that we expect to obtain on the basis of theoretical work.

In this paper we investigated the GAN-SSL performance for identification expertise classification problem. This work has showed that GAN-SSL classifiers converge quickly and have good quality for model data with good normal distributed classes with the same number of examples. The classification model for petrol identification expertise was created and has 94% quality. The number of neurons N_{base} needs to be adjusted.

The training was performed for a different base number of neurons N_{base} and learning rate parameters. The power of the generator and the discriminator must be selected to be the best for the problem of a given dimension, since it can be seen that an overly complex neural network can train unstable. The base neuron parameter for petrol identification problem is selected as 65 neurons but for model problem as 200 neurons. The best accuracy is 0.94 and 0.97 correspondingly.

The part of experimental result shows in Table 1.

Table 1. Experiments results.

Problem	N_base	lr	Accuracy
Model	35	0.00001	0.91
Model	45	0.00001	0.89
Model	25	0.001	0.89
Model	45	0.001	0.91
Model	**205**	**0.001**	**0.97**
Model	**305**	**0.001**	**0.97**
Expertise	35	0.00001	0.92
Expertise	**65**	**0.0001**	**0.94**
Expertise	105	0.0001	0.94
Expertise	205	0.00001	0.89

The identification expertise problem is challenging for classification because of complex structure of classes, outliers and cross-classes. In future work we plan to use the "generated fake" examples to generate missing data to reconstruct certain probability distribution p_{data} of difficult for classification classes.

In this work we use GAN-SSL classification on petrol identification expertise example, but this classification model can be used for diesel fuel, household chemicals items, different oils and for various other objects.

References

1. Goodfellow, I., et al.: Generative adversarial nets. In: 27th Annual Conference on Advances in Neural Information Processing Systems 27, pp. 2672–2680. Curran Associates, Inc., Red Hook (2014)
2. Salimans, T., Goodfellow, I., Zaremba, W., Cheung, W., Radford, A., Chen, X.: Improved techniques for training GAN. In: Advances in Neural Information Processing Systems, pp. 2234–2242 (2016)
3. Maksimova, A.: Formal statement of the problem of identification expertise. In: Donetsk Readings 2017: Russian World as a Civilizational Basis for Scientific, pp. 69–70. Educational and Cultural Development of Donbass, Donetsk (2017). (in Russian)
4. Maksimova, A.: The approach to the construction of information automated systems of identification examination based on machine learning methods. In: International Scientific and Technical Congress Intelligent Systems and Information Technologies, vol. 1, pp. 438–443, Taganrog (2017). (in Russian)
5. Maksimova, A.: Fuzzy approach to solve pattern recognition problem for automatisation system for identification expertise (example for petrol identification). In. International Scientific Conference Computer Science and Information Technology, Saratov, pp. 256–258 (2016). (in Russian)
6. Springenberg, J.: Unsupervised and semi-supervised learning with categorical generative adversarial networks (2016). https://arxiv.org/abs/1511.06390

7. Kingma, D., Rezende, D., Mohamed, S., Welling, M.: Semi-supervised learning with deep generative models. In: Proceedings of the International Conference on Machine Learning, pp. 3581–3589 (2014)
8. Ding, M., Tang, J., Zhang, J.: Semi-supervised learning on graph with generative adversarial nets. In. Proceedings of the 27th ACM International Conference on Information and Knowledge Management, pp. 913–922 (2018)
9. Kovalev, V., Kazlouski, S.: Examining the capability of GANs to replace real biomedical images in classification models training (2019). https://arxiv.org/ftp/arxiv/papers/1904/1904.08688.pdf
10. Ioffe, S., Shegedy, Ch.: Batch normalisation: accelerating deep network training by redusing interval covariance shift. In: ICML 2015, pp. 448–456 (2015)
11. Saliman, T., Kigma, D.: Weight normalisation: a simple reparametrization to accelerate training of deep neural networks. In: NIPS 2016, pp. 901–909 (2016)
12. Kigma, D.P., Ba, J.: Adam: a method for stochastic optimization. CoRR **abs/1412.6980** (2015). https://arxiv.org/pdf/1412.6980.pdf
13. Dai, Zh., Yang, Zh., Yang, F., Cohen, W., Salakhutdiov, R.: Good semi-supervised learning that requires a bad GAN. In: 31st Conference on Neural Information Processing Systems (NIPS 2017), Long Beach, CA, USA (2017)
14. Liu, X., Xiang, X.: How does GAN-based semi-supervised learning work? (2020). https://arxiv.org/abs/1809.00130

Comparing the Performance of Classical and Deep Learning Methods on Small Image Datasets

Vassili Kovalev[✉]

United Institute of Informatics Problems, Belarus National Academy of Sciences,
Surganova Street, 6, 220012 Minsk, Belarus
vassili.kovalev@gmail.com

Abstract. In this work, we present the results of an experimental study of the problem of image classification under the condition of small image datasets. The performance of both traditional and CNN-based methods is examined and compared based on two benchmark image datasets. The first dataset consisted of 12,000 routine hematoxylin-eosin stained histological images depicting normal and tumor areas of breast cancer. The second dataset includes 10,800 axial 2D slices of CT images representing 3 characteristic anatomical classes. Color co-occurrence matrices of an adaptive 32-color palette were used in the case of the traditional approach of histology image classification whereas CT image co-occurrence utilized suitably scaled Hounsfield CT image intensities. The classification itself was done using commonly known SVM, Random Forests, and kNN classifiers. The Deep Learning approach employs 5 Convolutional Neural Networks including a simple 3-layer VGG-like one as well as NASNet Mobile, MobileNet v3, EfficientNet-B2, and reasonably heavy BiT-S R50×1. Classification of CT images was performed using some testing framework resembling the Content-Based Image Retrieval scenario with the Top N = 24 most similar images. As a result, it was found that traditional methods outperform the CNN-based image classification technique on the training sets comprised of less than 840 images. Also, among the 5 examined CNN architectures, the BiT-S R50x1 neural network provides the best and the most consistent results.

Keywords: Image classification · Small datasets · Convolutional networks · Histology · Computed tomography

1 Introduction

1.1 The Motivation

Nowadays, the Convolutional Neural Networks (CNNs) and Deep Learning (DL) techniques are widely used for solving various image processing, filtration, segmentation, classification, clustering, and even realistic image generation problems. These methods have demonstrated tremendous promises in different application domains including medical image analysis, classification, and computerized disease diagnosis [1, 2]. However, training of CNNs with recent architectures requires large

© Springer Nature Switzerland AG 2022
A. V. Tuzikov et al. (Eds.): PRIP 2021, CCIS 1562, pp. 104–119, 2022.
https://doi.org/10.1007/978-3-030-98883-8_8

amounts of professionally labeled medical images of different classes that could be difficult to collect, laborious to label, and costly.

Presently, it is commonly understood that the classification results always depend on the degree of representativeness of images used at the training stage. Therefore, it is highly desirable that these images should be as "representative" as possible for the classification problem we are dealing with. In terms of the feature space, this means that the training image samples should cover well the regions of feature space that could be potentially populated by the image classes we considering. Such a problem is directly relevant to the following two major factors:

- the size of the training set and,
- the variability of images inherent to the classes.

The influence of the size and the variability of image sets are studied by way of gradual reduction of training set sizes as well as by varying the specific list of images included in every class of the training set.

1.2   The Context of Test Images

Both factors, the training set size and its variability were assessed using two different types of medical images including histopathological and computed tomography (CT) image data. In order to make the results more general, the traditional, as well as modern methods that capitalize on Convolutional Neural Networks (CNNs), are examined and compared on exactly the same image datasets in the context of typical classification tasks.

The histopathology image analysis based on light microscopy has long been recognized as a gold standard in cancer diagnosis. Modern digital pathology which includes whole slide imaging (WSI) scanners and automated image analysis solutions provides a more efficient and cost-effective way of handling, visualization, and analysis of the pathology image data [3]. Although the conventional methods of WSI image analysis based on the extraction of color and morphological features are still in use [4], the new DL approaches often demonstrate better performance and higher tolerance to image variability caused by a number of different factors [5, 6]. In [6] authors have isolated, carefully enumerated, and characterized 10 major challenges of DL in digital pathology which we are currently facing. The challenges that are most relevant to the present study include lack of labeled data, pervasive variability, and so-called realism of DL which is associated here with the available computational power [6]. In this particular study, we will be using routine hematoxylin-eosin stained color histopathological images depicting normal and tumor areas of breast cancer. All the images were collected by way of partitioning original WSIs to the fragments (image "tiles") of 256×256 pixels in size.

Contrary to the histopathological images, which provide comprehensive information on the micro-level based on soft tissue biopsy, the CT imaging scanners are operating on the macro-level. They convey valuable visual data about the anatomy and functions of different organs and systems of patients [7]. In this work, the CT image dataset consisted of 2D slices of chest CT images of lung tuberculosis patients. It represented 3 characteristic anatomical classes and was used as a second benchmark.

Thus, in this paper, we are trying to contribute towards the investigation of the problems of small image training sets and image variability. The experiments are performed on two typical medical image datasets that are widely used in oncology, pulmonology, and phthisiology. In order to make the results more general, both traditional and CNN-based methods are examined on the same benchmark image datasets.

2   Materials

2.1   Histopathology Images

Patients and Whole Slide Images. The original WSI histopathological images were acquired from biopsy samples of 90 different patients suspicious for breast cancer and used as the source of histological image data. These WSIs represent a sub-sample of hematoxylin-eosin stained images of lymph node sections used in the Grand Challenge [5]. The challenge was aimed at discovering the best methods and algorithms for detecting breast cancer metastases.

A total of 76 WSI images contained metastases of different sizes whereas the other 14 did not present any pathological changes and were considered to be the norm. An example fragment of a WSI image, as well as the high-resolution picture of its inhomogeneous region, are shown in Fig. 1. It should be noted that histological WSI images of biopsy samples may contain both normal and tumor regions simultaneously. This is clearly demonstrated by the presence of two different regions in Fig. 1.

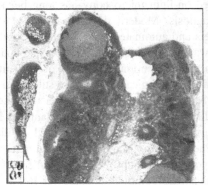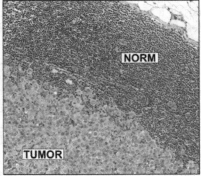

Fig. 1. Example fragment of whole slide histological image and its characteristic region

Image Datasets. Original professionally-labeled WSI images were partitioned into non-overlapping image sections (image tiles) of 256×256 pixels in size at the highest resolution level that corresponds to the $\times 40$ optical microscope magnification. A total of 12,000 tiles including 6,000 tiles of the norm and 6,000 tiles of tumor were randomly sub-sampled from the resultant set of tiles. Examples of the two image classes are given in Fig. 2.

The well-balanced train and test image datasets were created following the 70/30 percent proportion. This has resulted in 8,400 image tiles included in the training set (4,200 tiles of norm plus 4,200 tiles representing the tumor) and 3,600 images (1,800 of norm regions and 1,800 of tumor) used for testing. In a similar study [4], we experimentally confirmed that WSI tissue images of each particular patient are holding certain characteristic image patterns (features) that make them somewhat different from any others. As a result, including image tiles of one single WSI to both training and test sets creates a bias that resulted in an artificial increase of classification accuracy. With this in mind, here, image tiles of any given patient were included in the training or test set only and never in both simultaneously.

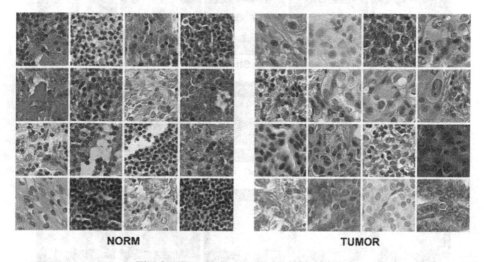

NORM   **TUMOR**

Fig. 2. Example image tiles of two classes

For the computational experiments involving the deep learning techniques the image training set was further subdivided into the 5,880 training images as such and 2,520 validation ones. Again, these particular datasets were well balanced containing exactly 50% of the norm and 50% of images representing tumor regions. The random sub-sampling was preferred on all the occasions where possible.

2.2 Computed Tomography Images

Patients and Original CT Images. A total of 414 3D chest CT scans acquired from 414 different patients suffering from lung tuberculosis were used as the source of the test CT image dataset for benchmarking. All C images were downloaded from the large international Tuberculosis Portal [8]. The original 3D scans were split into 53,677 axial 2D image slices of 512 × 512 pixels in size each. Original Hounsfield 3D CT image intensities ranged from −1000 to +1100 were re-scaled down to 0–255 grayscale intensity units of 2D image slices. Image slices were saved separately in ordinary lossless PNG format.

Image Classes. Finally, from the source set of 53,677 image slices by an experienced radiologist, there were selected 3 non-overlapping anatomical classes conditionally called "shoulders", "heart", and "liver" (see Fig. 3). Each class consisted of 3,600 images what is amounted to a total of 10,800 2D image slices. From each class, there were randomly selected 3,000 images that were included in the train set whereas the remaining 600 images were placed into the test set. Thus, the train and test sets consisted of 9,000 and 1,800 images respectively.

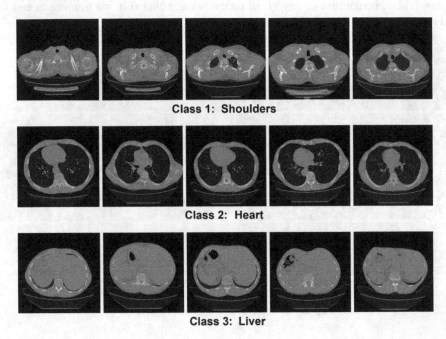

Fig. 3. Examples of 3 anatomical classes of axial CT image slices

3 Traditional Methods

3.1 Traditional Methods of Histology Image Classification

It is commonly accepted that the traditional (conventional) methods of image classification include feature extraction and classification stages. In this study, we have chosen to use the color co-occurrence matrices as basic image features as described in [9].

Feature Extraction Stage. As argued in the original paper [9], in general, any image can be considered as a composition of suitable "elementary structures". The elements of those structures (pixels) carry visual attributes (e.g., colors) and possess certain relations (e.g., distances between them). Consequently, the image content can be characterized by an appropriate co-occurrence matrix where attributes and relationships are represented by the different matrix axes. Thus, in a simple case, a 2D color image can be sufficiently represented by a 3D co-occurrence matrix (3D array) of (color 1, color 2, distance) type, the elements of which represents the frequency of spatial occurrence of pairs of certain colors at given distance spacing.

It is clear that such raw 3D arrays could potentially be of very large size due to the possibly large number of distinctive image colors. However, given that the hematoxylin-eosin stained histological images are reasonably poor in colors, the original RGB color space was reduced down to the palette of the most common 32 colors. This was accomplished with the help of an adaptive algorithm of reducing color space based on k-means clustering as implemented in the commonly known Python PIL library. The inter-pixel spacings were selected to be 1, 2, and 4 pixels. As a result, the original co-occurrence image descriptors had the form of 3D arrays with the dimensionality of $32 \times 32 \times 3$.

Next, due to the spatial interdependence of image regions and high autocorrelation (say, deviation of present image patterns from white noise), the elements of color co-occurrence arrays are highly correlated. This particularly means that they are still too redundant to be utilized as image features directly. In order to avoid unnecessary redundancy, the co-occurrence features were reduced further using the Principal Component Analysis method. Finally, the limited set of principal components is actually used as image features. The advantage of such features is that they are compact, linear, and mutually uncorrelated.

Classification Stage. The image features were inputted into the Support Vector Machine (SVM) and Random Forests (RF) classifiers. These classifiers were selected because they typically provide competitive results and their software implementations are available broadly. The relatively low computational expenses required by the classifiers allow to subsample given amount of image data from the whole dataset of 8400 training images and independently repeat the (subsampling-training-prediction) loop 100 times for the assessment of the image variability factor discussed above as well as for obtaining reliable estimates of classification accuracy.

3.2 Traditional Methods of CT Image Classification

Feature Extraction Stage. In general, the feature extraction of grayscale 2D CT image slices was done in a way similar to the extraction features of histological images described above. However, in this case, we used a variant of generalized grayscale co-occurrence matrices that were originally introduced in [10] for 3D images and suitably adapted them to properly describe the content of 2D images.

The classical co-occurrence matrices perform well for characterization and discrimination of general, typically very distinct textural image classes such as reptile skin, leaves, brick walls, etc. Since the medical image textures (structures) are typically not so salient, we need to increase the sensitivity and specificity of co-occurrence features. This is because we need to enable detection and separation of rather faint and not well-defined textural differences to distinguish certain dissimilarities associated with anatomical and structural variabilities, normal appearance vs. patterns of pathological changes, etc.

In order to increase the sensitivity and specificity, we can proceed in two different ways [10]. First, increasing the co-occurrence matrix dimensionality (number of axes) by combining elementary image features of different sorts such as the intensities of pixel pair, local gradient magnitude, mutual orientations of gradient vectors, etc. Alternatively, we can consider the spatial occurrence of more than two image pixels simultaneously. In this work, we have chosen the second option and used 3-pixel co-occurrence, i.e., the co-occurrence of intensities of pixels situated in the corners of equilateral triangles. In terms of work [10], for every fixed inter-pixel distance such raw 4D co-occurrence features of the (intensity1, intensity2, intensity3, distance) type can be abbreviated as *IIID*.

The original image intensities were quantized down to 32 intensity bins. The inter-pixel spacings were selected to be 1, 2, and 4 pixels. Thus, the raw IIID co-occurrence image descriptors had the form of 4D arrays with the dimensionality of $32 \times 32 \times 32 \times 3$. Note that in both occasions including histology and CT raw co-occurrence image descriptors there is one more way to reduce their size. This can be simply done by sorting all the indices of 2D square-shaped sub-matrices in descending order which makes them lower triangular. Given that this is a nested procedure with triangle-of-triangle-of-triangle structures, such a technique reduces the number of co-occurrence elements dramatically. We do not consider here this trick in detail because it is one of the typical instruments of experienced software engineers.

The remaining step of converting the raw co-occurrence image descriptors using the PCA method is identical to the one described above.

Classification Stage. At the preliminary experimentation step, it was found that conventional methods of feature extraction followed by SVM and RF classification of CT image slices provide nearly 100% of classification accuracy for all 3 classes except Class 1. Moreover, all CNNs involved in the experiment demonstrate 100% of classification accuracy or slightly lower. Most likely this is because the 3 anatomical classes created based on CT scans of 414 patients are relatively distinct and the power of both conventional and CNN-based methods is high. In these circumstances, the natural decision was to restrict the testing conditions further and to consider a more difficult task which, nevertheless, will be disclosing the structure of feature space of the CT image classification task on a deeper level and will be useful for the main goals of the study.

The goal of the corresponding experiment was to compare classes of nearest neighbors of each of 1,800 images of the test set in the feature space and to document the results of such comparison in a compact form. This task is very similar to the Content-Based Image Retrieval scenario which is often used in computer-assisted medical diagnosis. In the essence, it also resembles the kNN classifier.

Thus, the experiment is performed in the loop consisting of the following steps:

- select the next single image I_k as one of 600 query examples of given class of the test set consisting of 1,800 images,
  - calculate the distance in feature space from image I_k to each of other 1,799 ones,
  - sort out the 1,799 distances in descending order and select the N nearest neighbors,

- count the number of correct (same class as the query image) and wrong (another class) images among the N nearest neighbors,
- add the classification results for every Top-i position separately for i running from 1 to N,

• report the cumulative number of correct images for every i-th position of Top-N.

The number N of Top-N images most similar to the given query was chosen to be 24. The distance metrics being used everywhere is $L1$ norm.

4   CNN-Based Methods

4.1   CNN-Based Methods of Histology Image Classification

A total of 5 CNN with different architectures were examined in order to get a comprehensive picture of the dependence of the quality of image classification on the training set size and the specific contents of training images, i.e., the degree of coverage of "clouds" corresponding to different image classes in the feature space.

At the first, exploratory step we start with the simple, VGG-like CNN architecture that consisted of only 3 convolutional + *MaxPooling* layers with 16, 32, and 64 filters respectively (Fig. 4). This is because the assessment of the use of limited image training sets was particularly targeted in this study. In addition, such a decision enables other researchers to easily reproduce results of the computational experiments reported in this paper. The convolutional part of CNN was followed by a fully connected neural network with 512 intermediate nodes.

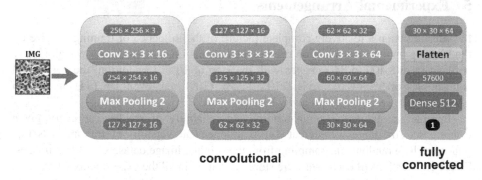

Fig. 4. Simple convolutional neural network

Note that despite the simple architecture, under condition of 256 × 256 pixels of input image size the CNN contains 29,515,809 trainable parameters (weights). It was found that the use of *GlobalMaxPooling* instead of a straightforward *Flattening* of the output of the convolutional part of the neural network reduces the number of trainable parameters down to 57,377 with no accountable reduction of the classification accuracy.

At the further steps the well-known CNNs with more sophisticated architectures were tested. They included NASNet Mobile, MobileNet v3, EfficientNet-B2, and reasonably heavy BiT-S R50×1. The number of trainable parameters of each CNN is given in Table 1.

4.2   CNN-Based Methods of CT Image Classification

The CT image slice classification task using CNNs was accomplished in the same way as this was done in the case of histological images. As it was already stated earlier, all CNNs involved in the experiment have demonstrated 100% of classification accuracy or slightly lower. Therefore, here the CNNs were used as image feature extractors and the classification itself was done using conventional methods as described in Sect. 3.2 above.

Table 1. Number of parameters in CNNs

CNN architecture	Number of parameters	Number of trainable parameters
Simple 3 layers	57,377	57,377
MobileNet v3	1,532,018	1,519,906
NasNet Mobile	4,271,830	4,235,092
EfficientNet B2	7,771,380	7,703,812
BiT-S R50×1	23,504,450	23,504,450

5   Experimental Arrangements

In order to obtain a relatively complete picture of the influence of training set size on the histology image classification results, the original image training set was gradually reduced from 8,400 to 840 images with the step of 10%. In addition, the very small sub-samples of 5% (420), 2.5% (210), 1.25% (105), and even 1% (84) of original image dataset were also examined where possible.

In order to guarantee comparability and reliability of results, for every given training set size there were created 100 independent versions of training sets that generated by a random sup-sampling from the original image datasets of 8,400 images. These 100 versions of each size were stored and used in all the experiments all over the study presented in the paper for repetition of the same experiments 100 times each. On all the occasions the test set was kept exactly the same and consisted of 3600 images including 1,800 images of norm and 1,800 images of tumor.

The pipeline of computational experiments included the major steps given below.

1. Initial preparations. They included converting original color RGB images into the reduced paletted representation with 32 colors as well as calculation of color co-occurrence matrices for each of 12000 images.
2. Creating a data table by way of storing vectorized versions of co-occurrence matrices into 12000 different rows. Performing PCA on the resultant data table for

obtaining a concise feature representation of every image involved in the experiments.

3. Splitting the whole image dataset into the train and test subsets by 70/30 rule. In the case of CNN-based classification (not applicable to conventional SVM and RF) the train set was further split by the same rule into the part used for training as such and the validation.

4. Cary out the conventional part of classification experiments in 14 steps by way of step-by-step reduction of training set size from the original 8400 images down to 84 ones as described above. At every classification step except for the first one, the training plus prediction procedure repeated 100 times on varying versions of image training sets. As a result, the total number of training and prediction steps was amounted up to 13 * 100 + 1 = 1301. This was to account for the inhomogeneity of original image classes as well as for the variability of images the training set is made of.

5. The CNN-based experiments were done in a similar manner. However, in this case, one more key parameter came into the way what is the number of training epochs that need to be performed. Also, due to known fluctuations of the training process, the exact measurement of classification accuracy often includes performing a safe, i.e., over-rated number of epochs in order to identify the best one.

6. There are some additional control parameters such as random seeds different values of which may lead to slightly different results. These parameters increase potential computational expenses even further. For estimation purposes let us simply suppose that we need only 10 additional exploratory runs due to these factors specific for CNNs. Then the number of repetition loops of type (sub-sampling, training, prediction, adjusting control parameters) increases up to approximately 13,000 which is going beyond the reason.

6 Results

6.1 Results of Histology Image Classification

Results of histology image classification experiments using conventional methods are summarized below. They are partly itemized for reasons of clarity.

- Color co-occurrence matrices were computed using a fast algorithm based on indexing arrays that implemented in R language. The elements below the leading diagonal of square-shaped (color-color slices) of resultant 3D arrays were summed up to the corresponding elements situated below the leading diagonal to avoid dependence of results on the rotation and reflection of original images as described in [9].

- The image features, i.e., principal components were selected using values of 0.9, 0.95, and 0.98 as thresholds for cumulative variance. These resulted in 21, 221, and 370 principal components respectively. After corresponding local experimentations, the value of 0.95 was finally selected as the basic one and used in all the computational experiments.

- In CNN-based classification with 14 different training set sizes the images for training and validation were selected at random by 70/30 proportion. The amounts of norm and tumor images were kept equivalent in both subsets.

Results of image classification using conventional methods are summarized in Fig. 5. As it can be seen from the top panel of Fig. 5, the difference between the mean accuracy values provided by SVM and RF classifiers is reasonably low with a maximum mutual deviation of about 1%.

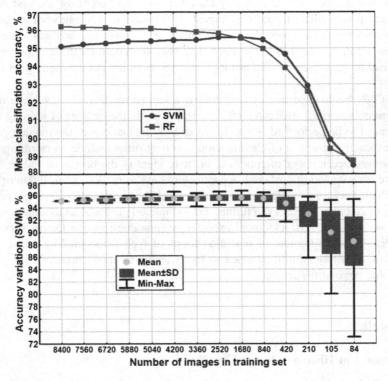

Fig. 5. The mean classification accuracy achieved across 100 replications by SVM and RF methods (top) and its STD, Min, and Max values in case of SVM (bottom)

Next, the shape of plots suggests that the mean accuracy is keeping almost constant for all training set sizes reduced from 8,400 down to 840 images. Then it drops quickly from 95.1% (SVM) and 96.2% (RF) down to 88.5% and 88.8% respectively when reaches the smallest training set of 84 images.

Interestingly, in case of SVM (bottom panel of Fig. 5) the most fortunate version of very small training set consisted of only 84 images provides as high as 95.3% of the classification accuracy. This is even slightly better than the results achieved on the whole training set consisted of 8,400 images (see corresponding whiskers of the box-and-whiskers plots of Fig. 5).

The pattern of variability of SVM classification results even more important for practical tasks. While the training sets remain relatively large, the standard deviation keeping small and ranged from STD = 0.172% of classification accuracy for 7560 images and going up to STD = 0.545% for 840 images. Then it increases significantly and achieves STD = 3.946% in the case of 84 images randomly chosen for training. The extreme values ranged more substantially. For instance, in case of SVM and 84 training images, the classification accuracy varied in 100 repetitions from 73.1% to 95.3%. The described behavior can be explained by the following two reasons:

- the large portions of training images represent better the whole population (general regularity),
- the histological images used in this study are very heterogeneous (see Fig. 2) and vary significantly depending on the patient, biopsy techniques, sample preparation and staining protocols, image acquisition devices used in different hospitals, and some other factors.

Results of classification achieved by classification using Simple CNN are given in Fig. 6. From a first glance, it becomes clear that results produced by Simple CNN are generally comparable with the ones obtained using color co-occurrence features followed by SVM and RF (see bars for 8400, 420, and 840 images in the training set). However, once the training set is reduced further, the popular nowadays DL-based approach starts to lose completely against classical methods. This is especially obvious when the Simple CNN results are compared to the ones produced by SVM. For making this fact easier to capture, the bottom panel of Fig. 6 provides two plots that compare results produced by Simple CNN and the maximum accuracy achieved either by SVM or RF classifiers for each step of the experiments.

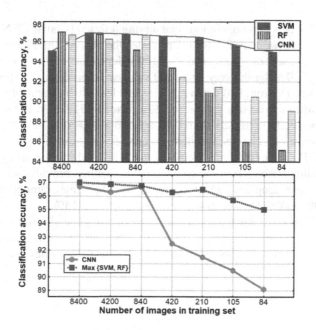

Fig. 6. The best classification accuracy achieved on large (8400−840) and small (420−84) training sets by SVM, RF, and simple CNN

It is clear that due to the low computational expenses both SVM and RF methods can be comfortably run in parallel and the best result can be taken as the final solution. Note that such results are not surprising at all because it is commonly known that CNNs are hardly usable in the circumstances when only a few tens or hundreds of images are available for training. The use of possible benefits provided by augmentation and other similar techniques should be discussed separately.

Results of histology image classification by different CNNs trained on small training sets are shown in Fig. 7.

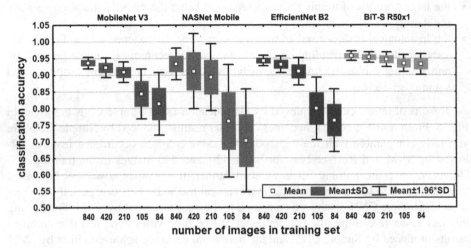

Fig. 7. Results of histology image classification by CNNs trained on small training sets

From Fig. 7 it is becoming obvious that among 4 tested popular CNN architectures the convolutional network BiT-S R50x1 provides the best results in terms of both the mean classification accuracy computed over 100 independent replications with different training sets as well as by the very small STD values. In particular, 10-times reduction of the training set size from 840 down to 84 images leads to a reasonably small drop of the mean classification accuracy from 95.7% down to 93.3%. At the same time, the STD value moderately increased from 0.72% up to 1.60% only. In case of the worst results demonstrated by NasNet Mobile the mean accuracy drops from 93.4% down to 70.3% while STD increases from 2.40% up to 7.90%. More interestingly, the SVM classifier operating on conventional co-occurrence features provides well competitive results in the mean accuracy, which decreases for the same training set sizes from 95.5% to 90.0% and STD increases from just 0.55% to 3.13%.

The results reported above allow concluding that in general, on the small training sets traditional methods outperform all tested CNN architectures except for BiT-S R50x1, which has been demonstrated surprisingly consistent behavior.

6.2   Results of CT Image Classification

The task of CT slice image classification/retrieval was implemented by way of a subsequent comparison of the class of each of 600 images of given class with classes of remaining $(1,800 - 1)$ images from the test set in their 24-neighborhood. The results are reported in form of the cumulative number of correct classes, i.e. classes identical to the current image in feature space. Both conventional co-occurrence features and features generated by convolutional parts of CNNs are examined. It should be pointed out once more that such a classification setup is similar to the query-by-example scenario of content-based image retrieval used as one of the supporting tools in recent computerized disease diagnosis. It also has several points with the kNN classifier in common.

As a result of a series of corresponding classification experiments with 3 classes of CT images considered with this study, it was found that all tested CNNs provide feature vectors of good quality that resulted in 100% of classification accuracy (see Fig. 8 as an example). This means that all the most similar images from 24-neighborhood of each of 1,800 query image examples are retrieved correctly.

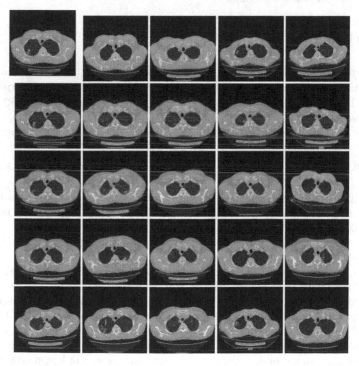

Fig. 8. Example of CT image slice retrieval using features produced by CNN BiT-S R50x1 (query image example is given on the top-left corner)

It was also found that the co-occurrence features provide 100% of image classification/retrieval accuracy for Class 2 (heart) and 3 (liver). However, it was not the case with retrieval of Class 1 (shoulder). More detailed results of retrieving Class 1 are presented in Fig. 9. Note that the "ideal" plot would be the straight horizontal line.

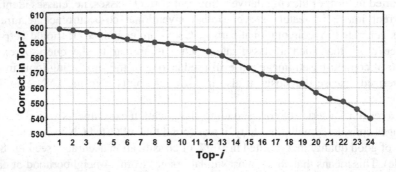

Fig. 9. Number of correct CT slice images of Class 1 (shoulders) in Top-24 most similar when using co-occurrence image descriptors

7 Conclusions

From the results reported with this study we may conclude that traditional methods outperform the CNN-based image classification on the training sets comprised of less than 840 images. Also, among the 5 CNN architectures, the BiT-S R50x1 neural network provides the best and the most consistent results.

References

1. Zhou, S.K., et al.: A review of deep learning in medical imaging: imaging traits, technology trends, case studies with progress highlights, and future promises. Proc. IEEE **109**(5), 820–838 (2021)
2. Litjens, G., et al.: A survey on deep learning in medical image analysis. Med. Image Anal. **42**, 60–88 (2017)
3. Aeffner, F., et al.: Introduction to digital image analysis in whole-slide imaging: a white paper from the digital pathology association. J. Pathol. Inform. **10**(1), 1–17 (2019)
4. Veta, M., Heng, J.Y., Stathonikos, N., Bejnordi, E.B., Beca, F., et al.: Predicting breast tumor proliferation from whole-slide images: The TUPAC16 challenge. Med. Image Anal. **54**, 111–121 (2019)
5. Bejnordi, B.E., Veta, M., van Diest, P.J., van Ginneken, B., Karssemeijer, P.J.N., et al.: Diagnostic assessment of deep learning algorithms for detection of lymph node metas-tases in women with breast cancer. J. Am. Med. Assoc. **318**(22), 2199–2210 (2017)
6. Tizhoosh, H.R., Pantanowitz, L.: Artificial intelligence and digital pathology: Challenges and opportunities. J. Pathol. Inform. **9**(38), 1–6 (2018)
7. Hsieh, J., Flohr, T.: Computed tomography recent history and future perspectives. J. Med. Imaging **8**(5), 052109, 1–24 (2021). https://doi.org/10.1117/1.JMI.8.5.052109

8. Rosenthal, A., et al.: The TB portals: an open-access, web-based platform for global drug-resistant-tuberculosis data sharing and analysis. J. Clin. Microbiol. **55**(11), 3267–3282 (2017). https://doi.org/10.1128/JCM.01013-17
9. Kovalev, V., Volmer, S.: Color co-occurrence descriptors for querying-by-example. In: International Conference on Multimedia Modelling, pp. 32–38, IEEE Comp. Society Press, Lausanne (1998)
10. Kovalev, V.A., Kruggel, F., Gertz, H.-J., von Cramon, D.Y.: Three-dimensional texture analysis of MRI brain datasets. IEEE Trans. Med. Imaging **20**(5), 424–433 (2001)

Generative Autoencoders for Designing Novel Small-Molecule Compounds as Potential SARS-CoV-2 Main Protease Inhibitors

Mikita A. Shuldau[1,2], Artsemi M. Yushkevich[1], Ivan P. Bosko[1], Alexander V. Tuzikov[1], and Alexander M. Andrianov[3(✉)]

[1] United Institute of Informatics Problems, National Academy of Sciences of Belarus, Minsk, Republic of Belarus
[2] EPAM Systems, Minsk Office, Minsk, Republic of Belarus
[3] Institute of Bioorganic Chemistry, National Academy of Sciences of Belarus, Minsk, Republic of Belarus
alexande.andriano@yandex.ru

Abstract. Two generative autoencoder models for designing novel drug-like compounds able to block the catalytic site of the SARS-CoV-2 main protease (M^{Pro}) critical for mediating viral replication and transcription were developed using deep learning methods. To do this, the following steps were performed: (i) architectures of two neural networks were constructed; (ii) a virtual compound library of potential anti-SARS-CoV-2 M^{Pro} agents for training two neural networks was formed; (iii) molecular docking of all compounds from this library with M^{Pro} was made and calculations of the values of binding free energy were carried out; (iv) two neural networks were trained followed by estimation of the learning outcomes and work of two autoencoders involving several generation modes. Validation of autoencoders and their comparison revealed the best combination of the neural network architecture with the generation mode, which allows one to generate good chemical scaffold for the design of novel antiviral drugs with suitable pharmaceutical properties.

Keywords: SARS-CoV-2 · Main protease · Deep learning · Generative autoencoder · Semi-supervised learning · Virtual screening · Molecular docking · Binding free energy calculations · Anti-SARS-CoV-2 drugs

1 Introduction

To date, computer-aided drug design has become an important tool allowing one to significantly reduce the time and costs required for developing novel therapeutic agents. In recent years, computer-assisted mathematical and statistical models, such as machine learning, are increasingly being used for drug design and discovery. Despite these methods becoming more common in cheminformatics, their potential in this field is yet to be revealed.

Generative models have proven to be promising in tasks of text [1] and image [2] generation, including generation of medical images like X-ray ones. Despite the traditional similarity-based virtual screening of chemical databases, such as PubChem

© Springer Nature Switzerland AG 2022
A. V. Tuzikov et al. (Eds.): PRIP 2021, CCIS 1562, pp. 120–136, 2022.
https://doi.org/10.1007/978-3-030-98883-8_9

[3, 4], provide wide possibilities for identification of novel potential drugs, it has certain disadvantages compared to generative statistical models. One of the major incentives to use generative models is a better exploration of a molecular feature space. Similarity-based search provides exploration of focused chemical space, limited by search space diversity of compounds at disposal, while generative statistical models allow one to cover molecular feature space of much wider chemical diversity. The second reason for generative model superiority is conditional sampling. Generation of new molecules from a chemical space is not the only option: predicted binding free energy could be used as an additional dimension, which allows one to generate molecules from a subset of investigated chemical space with a preset binding affinity.

The SARS-CoV-2 coronavirus genome is positive-sense, single-stranded RNA and consists of $\sim 30,000$ nucleotides, and its replicase gene encodes two overlapping polyproteins, pp1a and pp1ab, required for virus replication and transcription [5]. These polyproteins undergo extensive proteolytic processing by two cysteine proteases, namely papain-like protease PLpro and 3-chymotrypsin-like protease 3CLpro (also known as the main protease M^{Pro}) which is essential for mediating viral replication and transcription [6, 7]. The main protease digests polyprotein at no less than 11 conserved sites, starting with the autolytic cleavage of this enzyme itself from pp1a and pp1ab [8]. This indicates the extremely important role of M^{Pro} in the life virus cycle and makes this enzyme one of the most attractive targets for the development of effective antiviral drugs [9].

SARS-CoV-2 M^{Pro} has been used as a target for screening clinically approved drugs as potential virus inhibitors in the hope of identifying drugs that are effective against COVID-19 (reviewed in [10]). Since the safety profiles of these drugs are well-documented, such an approach combining the structural design of drugs with virtual screening and molecular modeling methods can significantly facilitate and accelerate the detection of antiviral compounds with clinical potential in order to re-profile them for the treatment of patients infected with a new type of coronavirus. A literature analysis also showed that the natural M^{Pro} inhibitors currently under studies are mainly derived from plants, marine organisms and microorganisms [10]. In addition, covalently binding peptidomimetics and small molecules are investigated and various compounds show antiviral activity in infected human cells [11]. However, taking into account SARS-CoV-2 mutations [12–15], studies on the development of novel antiviral compounds capable of blocking the functionally important sites of the viral proteins are also extremely significant.

This research is devoted to the development of the generative autoencoder based on a linear molecule representation in the Simplified Molecular Input Line Entry System (SMILES) format [16] to design novel drug-like molecules as potential SARS-CoV-2 M^{Pro} inhibitors. One of the core ideas behind using SMILES, or more precisely, vectorized SMILES for model training was the recovery capabilities of such data. Generative models were shown to provide a decent ground for screening results enrichment, however the use of descriptors similar to fingerprints may complicate the recovery of the chemical structures themselves [17]. In contrast, SMILES-based vectorization is supposed to be a good alternative to using fingerprints in deep learning cheminformatics approaches when the ability to restore the structure of chemical compounds is important. That is why the SMILES format was selected in this study as the architectural basement for the constructed generative autoencoder to generate potential inhibitors of the selected protein target.

2 Methods

2.1 Training Set Preparation

The developed generative autoencoder is built to be specific for a target protein, and, therefore, the training dataset should include compounds potentially active towards the target of interest. As noted above, the autoencoder developed in this study was adopted for generation of potential SARS-CoV-2 M^{pro} inhibitors, and, accordingly, a virtual compound library of possible high-affinity ligands of this enzyme was formed for preparation of a training dataset.

Pharmacophore-Based Virtual Screening. To identify small-molecule compounds potentially active against SARS-CoV-2 M^{pro}, the pharmacophore-based virtual screening was performed by a web-oriented platform Pharmit [18] allowing one to search for small molecules based on their structural and chemical similarity to another small molecule [19]. Seventeen pharmacophore models were generated based on six peptidomimetics and ten small-molecule inhibitors of SARS-CoV [9], the predecessor of SARS-CoV-2, using the PharmaGist web-server [20]. Virtual screening was performed in the nine Pharmit molecular libraries containing over 213.5 million chemical structures, resulting in a set of 711 102 compounds that satisfied one of the seventeen constructed pharmacophore models. PubChemPy [21] which provides a way to interact with PubChem in Python [22] was used to additionally enrich the screened dataset with potential inhibitors based on the compounds selected from PubChem by the molecular similarity search with a Tanimoto coefficient of 0.8.

Molecular Docking. Compounds identified by the pharmacophore-based virtual screening and molecular similarity search in PubChem were subject to the preliminary molecular docking with the unliganded SARS-CoV-2 M^{Pro} structure (PDB ID: 6Y84) [23]. These compounds were then filtered based on the values of the docking scoring function with the energy threshold of –7 kcal/mol, which corresponds to the standard activity threshold of 10 µM commonly used *in vitro* screening. The dataset of 353 467 potentially active compounds was subject to the refining molecular docking with the SARS-CoV-2 M^{Pro} structure. Analysis of the distribution of scoring function values after the refining docking resulted in the filtration of successfully docked compounds that exhibited the values of binding free energy lower than the selected binding free energy threshold of –6 kcal/mol.

SMILES Space Revision and Vectorization. Based on a linear SMILES notation, the dataset of selected compounds was cleared from those containing non-recognizable atoms, non-abundant isotopes, other than druglike (H, C, N, O, P, S, F, Cl, Br, I) atoms or those which molecular weight was above the selected threshold of 1000 Da. Structure representations of the prepared compounds in the linear notation SMILES were obtained by Python 3 using the RDKit module [24]. Based on the frequency distribution of SMILES elements in the prepared dataset, compounds possessing at least one SMILES element with frequency less than 0.001 were filtered out. Finally, distribution of SMILES lengths was investigated and compounds with SMILES representation longer than 120 characters were eliminated (Fig. 1A). After all the filters applied, the dataset consisted of 342 102 distinct ligands and corresponding SMILES. The SMILES were vectorized into a matrix according to the maximum length and symbols vocabulary size (Fig. 1B), with the added start and end symbols represented by "!" and "E".

The obtained 342 102 compounds combined with the corresponding values of molecular docking scoring function formed the dataset which was split into the training, validation, and test sets comprising 70%, 15% and 15% of the original dataset, respectively. When forming the subsets, a stratified split was used to preserve equal energy distributions within all 3 sets. The validation set was used to evaluate the model's ability to reconstruct the input SMILES during training, while test SMILES were used to sample new compounds from by adding distortion to their latent representation. Thus, the corresponding datasets for model training, validation and generation of new molecules were prepared.

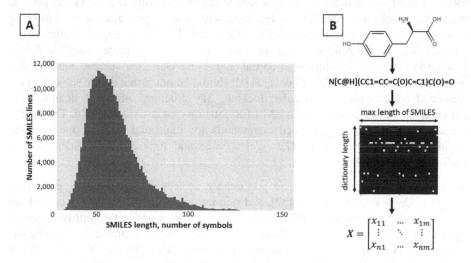

Fig. 1. SMILES space revision and vectorization: (A) SMILES length distribution for the training set; (B) Vectorization procedure of an example molecule.

2.2 3D Structures Generation for Generated Molecules

To evaluate the ability of deep learning model to generate novel compounds active towards the target protein, molecular docking of these molecules should be performed. In doing so, 3D structures of the generated molecules are required. To obtain these 3D structures from a linear notation SMILES, a script was developed in Python 3 using the RDKit module. The generation pipeline included the following steps: SMILES input, SMILES validity check, 2D coordinates generation, 3D coordinates generation, optimization of the structure in the MMFF94 force field, addition of hydrogen atoms, and re-optimization in the MMFF94 force field [25, 26]. Generation of 3D structure coordinates was performed using the ETKDGv3 [27] algorithm.

2.3   Molecular Docking

Preparation of Protein Structure. The crystal structure of the unliganded SARS-CoV-2 M^{pro} was taken from the Protein Data Bank (PDB ID: 6Y84) [23]. This SARS-CoV-2 M^{pro} structure was prepared by adding hydrogen atoms and annotating atoms with partial charges by Gasteiger scheme [28] followed by the structure optimization in the UFF force field [29] using the OpenBabel software [30]. The structure of SARS-CoV-2 M^{pro} prepared in this way was used for the preliminary and refining molecular docking both during the dataset preparation and molecular docking of the generated compounds.

Preparation of Ligand Structures. Prior to the preliminary docking, preparation of the ligand structures was the same as described for the SARS-CoV-2 M^{pro} structure. This procedure was performed using OpenBabel but included an additional step of rotatable bonds identification which is auto-made by this software. However, prior to the refining molecular docking, the ligand structures were prepared via the following two steps: i) optimization in the MMFF94 force field [25, 26] to remove steric clashes and addition of hydrogen atoms that are absent in the initial structures using the RDKit module in Python 3, ii) addition of partial charges by Gasteiger scheme and rotatable bonds identification using MGLTools [31]. It should be noted that before subjecting the generated compounds to molecular docking, 3D structures of novel ligands were obtained from the generated linear SMILES notations, as described above. The further preparation steps of the generated compounds for molecular docking included the addition of partial charges by Gasteiger scheme and rotatable bonds identification performed by MGLTools.

Molecular Docking Settings. The preliminary molecular docking was performed using the QuickVina 2 program [32], and refining molecular docking was carried out by AutoDock Vina software [33]. The calculations were made in the approximation of rigid receptor and flexible ligands. In both cases, the grid box included the catalytic site of SARS-CoV-2 M^{pro} with the following parameters: $\Delta X = 19$ Å, $\Delta Y = 21$ Å, $\Delta Z = 23$ Å centered at $X = -20$ Å, $Y = 19$ Å, $Z = -26$ Å. Thus, the grid box volume was $19 \times 21 \times 23 = 9177$ Å^3. The value of the exhaustiveness parameter defining the number of individual sample "runs" was set to 10 and 50 for preliminary and refining docking, respectively.

2.4   Deep Learning

Models Architectures. Two deep learning models have been developed, namely an unsupervised SMILES-based Long Short-Term Memory (LSTM) [34] autoencoder (the embeddings model) and a semi-supervised SMILES-based LSTM autoencoder (the energy model). In the energy model, the value of binding free energy was used both as an additional dimension in the latent space for learning based on information from previously docked compounds and as an approximate value in the generation mode. The high-level architectures representing both of the models were combined into one scheme which is shown in Fig. 2.

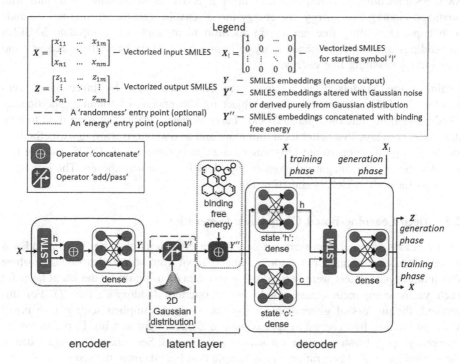

Fig. 2. High-level architecture of molecular autoencoder models.

The embeddings model is composed of the encoder part, 2D Gaussian noise entry point on the latent layer and the decoder part. This model receives vectorized SMILES matrix as input which follows through the LSTM layer. The peculiarity of this model is defined by the fact that LSTM output itself is not used, instead the hidden and cell states vectors are derived, which are concatenated together and then put through a dense layer. The output of this dense layer serves as a latent vector or SMILES embeddings in the context of the autoencoder. The embeddings are fed to two dense layers in parallel, creating initial hidden and cell state inputs for the LSTM layer in the decoder part. There is also the decoder input layer used as input for the decoder LSTM, which in the training mode receives the same vectorized SMILES matrix X as the encoder input, and, as a conventional LSTM generative model, it predicts the next symbol. However, in the generation mode, decoder input starts the generation process with a start symbol '!' only, embeddings are used to predict the initial states of decoder LSTM and they basically define which kind of SMILES will be generated.

The energy model differs from the embeddings model in the additional neuron located on the latent layer of the model and responsible for the value of binding free energy. While the embeddings model allows one to generate molecules from random SMILES embeddings as well as adding noise to SMILES embeddings of ligands with predicted binding free energy, the energy model enables one to generate new ligands with a preset binding free energy, in addition to attempts to manipulate SMILES embeddings of the given ligands to try to improve their structures after decoding and thus increase binding free energy.

Training the Models. Both models were composed layer by layer using TensorFlow 2.1 [35]. The models were subject to 150 epochs of training, additionally "Reduce learning rate on a plateau" and "Early stopping" callbacks were used to help the model converge to a better local minimum and also avoid overfitting. A method for stochastic optimization Adam [36] was used as an optimizer with 0.005 learning rate initial value and the categorical cross-entropy loss function was chosen. The loss score progress for both models is shown in Fig. 3.

2.5   Deep Learning-Based Compounds Generation

Two methods of generation were subjects of our consideration. The first method was based on the generation from random numbers drawn from normal distributions, where distributions parameters were derived using test data distribution on the latent layer for each vector component ('pass' mode in the operator 'add/pass', Fig. 2). For this method, the process of generation for the energy model implied setting an *a priori* value of binding free energy to approximate generated ligands with. Experiments for different energy thresholds were carried out (see Results, Sect. 3.3). The major idea of the second method of generation was to sample best ligands from the test set, and to try to add noise to their SMILES embeddings ('add' mode in the operator 'add/pass', Fig. 2). This approach was supposed to change the reconstructed ligand, and, in the case of the energy model, also improve the binding free energy, forcing the generation of more promising ligands. The combinations of two autoencoder models and two generation methods are summarized in Table 1.

Table 1. Description of the investigated combinations of generative LSTM autoencoder models and generation methods.

Model	Generation starting point description	Generation process description
Unsupervised (embeddings model)	Random number vectors drawn from fitted normal distributions	Random numbers are used as embeddings and fed to the decoder
Unsupervised (embeddings model)	Compounds with binding free energy less than −8 kcal/mol, sampled from the test set	Embeddings for these compounds are calculated, distortion is then added and updated embeddings are fed to the decoder

(continued)

Table 1. (*continued*)

Model	Generation starting point description	Generation process description
Semi-supervised (energy model)	Random number vectors drawn from fitted normal distributions and a preset binding free energy value	Random vectors are used as embeddings and are passed as latent layer inputs along with a preset binding free energy value
Semi-supervised (energy model)	Compounds with binding free energy less than −8 kcal/mol, sampled from the test set and improved binding free energy values	Embeddings for these compounds are calculated, then distortion is added and updated embeddings along with improved binding free energy values are passed to the decoder

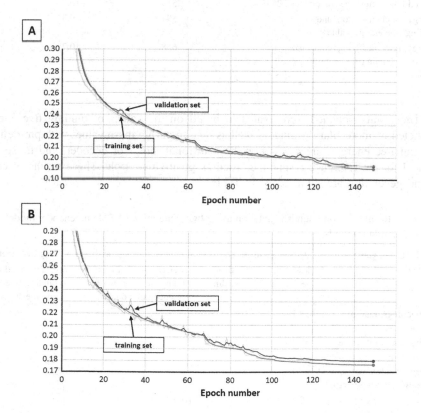

Fig. 3. Train and validation losses for autoencoder model: (A) Unsupervised (embeddings) model; (B) Semi-supervised (energy) model.

3 Results

3.1 Overview of General Results

As noted above, both models were tested using each of two generation methods. The number of generated compounds as well as the lowest values of binding free energy obtained using two models and two generation methods are provided in Table 2.

Table 2. Number of generated compounds and the lowest values of binding free energies obtained using two generative LSTM autoencoder models and two generation methods.

Model name, generation method	Number of valid compounds from generated	Number of successfully docked compounds	Lowest predicted binding free energy, kcal/mol
Embeddings, random vectors	1000	986	−10.6
Embeddings, reference compounds	2543	2518	−10.3
Energy, random vectors and binding free energy value	600	594	−9.3
Energy, reference compounds and improved binding free energy values	662	658	−10.2

The results obtained were evaluated based on the values of binding free energy predicted by molecular docking, as well as by comparing these values with pre-defined binding free energy values given as the additional input for decoder, and those calculated for the reference compounds used as positive controls. These results of compound generation are summarized in Table 3.

Table 3. Results of compounds generation using two generative LSTM autoencoder models and two generation methods.

Model name, generation method	Percentage of generated compounds with the predicted binding free energy			
	less than −8 kcal/mol	less than −9 kcal/mol	lower compared to the binding free energy of reference compounds	lower compared to the binding free energy threshold
Embeddings, random vectors	28.1%	6.0%	-	-
Embeddings, reference compounds	38.4%	8.6%	7.1%	-
Energy, random vectors and binding free energy value	25.4%	1.4%	-	8.3%
Energy, reference compounds and improved binding free energy values	40.4%	16.1%	10.0%	2.0%

3.2 Results of Experiments by Models and Generation Modes

Embeddings Model, Random Vectors Generator. Although this model does not utilize reference compounds or values of binding free energy for generation, it is capable of generating new potential inhibitors of the selected target only by generating compounds from the embedding's distributions inferred from the training data. In the set of generated compounds, the share of molecules with the predicted values of binding free energy less than –9 kcal/mol was 6%, which exceeds the same share in the training dataset (1.8%) by almost 4 times.

Embeddings Model, Test Set Compounds are used to Generate New Compounds from. This generation method utilizes compounds available and tries to generate new potential inhibitors from them. The share of generated compounds with high binding affinity is considerably larger, with 38.4% of compounds exhibiting the predicted values of binding free energy less than –8 kcal/mol and 8.6% of compounds showing the predicted values less than –9 kcal/mol.

Energy Model, Generation from Random Numbers with Several Preset Values of Binding Free Energy. The semi-supervised model utilizes a version of "style and content" disentanglement for molecular data. According to the results obtained, 31% and 64% of generated compounds showed the values of binding energy within the deviations from the pre-defined binding free energy value equal to 1 kcal/mol and 2 kcal/mol, respectively.

Energy Model, Test Set Compounds Used as Starting Points to Generate More Compounds, Preset Binding Free Energy Values are Shifted Towards Lower Values by 0.5 and 1.0 kcal/mol Steps Relative to Corresponding Test Compounds. This combination of the model and generation method proved to generate the top compounds throughout four already presented modes of generation. 52% of generated compounds are located within 1 kcal/mol deviation from the reference compounds, while 16.1% of generated compounds have the values of binding free energy lower than –9 kcal/mol.

3.3 An Experiment with Setting Different Binding Free Energy Thresholds

The energy model, where compounds were generated from Gaussian noise, was tested for the suggested ability to force generation of compounds exhibiting lower binding free energies as lower binding free energy thresholds are passed to the 'energy' neuron. In doing so, several experiments were conducted, generating compounds with the preset binding free energies from –7 kcal/mol to –11 kcal/mol with a step of –1 kcal/mol. The results of these experiments are shown in Fig. 4.

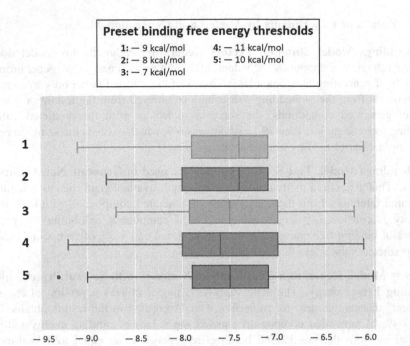

Preset binding free energy thresholds

1: — 9 kcal/mol   4: — 11 kcal/mol
2: — 8 kcal/mol   5: — 10 kcal/mol
3: — 7 kcal/mol

VINA binding free energy, kcal/mol

Fig. 4. Box-and-whisker plots describing distribution of results of experiments with setting different binding free energy thresholds from –7 kcal/mol to –11 kcal/mol with the step of –1 kcal/mol. Box-and-whisker plots were constructed in a standard way: lines in the middle of boxes are medians, faces of boxes are correspondingly first (Q1) and third (Q3) quartiles, whiskers have a length of 1.5 times interquartile range IQR = Q3 – Q1.

In order to test whether the differences of the mean values of binding free energy between distributions representing the conducted experiments are of statistical significance, a two-sided t-test was used, with the null hypothesis H_0 being that distribution mean values are the same. We performed the t-test between all the pairs of energy distributions for different thresholds (Table 4), and none of the calculated p-values were below a chosen significance level of 0.05 to be able to reject the H_0. Namely, the lowest p-value of 0.22 (> 0.05) was observed between distributions for the binding free energy thresholds of –11 kcal/mol and –9 kcal/mol. Thus, one can assume that the distributions actually have the same mean values of binding free energy.

Table 4. A two-sided t-test results for H_0 of equal distribution means using significance level of 0.05 for experiments with setting different binding free energy thresholds on the 'energy' neuron from −7 kcal/mol to −11 kcal/mol with the step of −1 kcal/mol.

Binding free energy threshold N 1, kcal/mol	Binding free energy threshold N 2, kcal/mol	p-value
−11.0	−10.0	0.76
−11.0	−9.0	0.22
−11.0	−8.0	0.50
−11.0	−7.0	0.34
−10.0	−9.0	0.32
−10.0	−8.0	0.62
−10.0	−7.0	0.43
−9.0	−8.0	0.81
−8.0	−7.0	0.99
−8.0	−7.0	0.83

3.4 Experiment with Gaussian Noise Utilization

Another experiment aimed to check if generating from reference compounds using the 'energy' neuron benefits from adding noise was performed. To do this, new compounds were generated using source compounds, where embeddings of reference compounds were altered with Gaussian noise of mean 0, and the binding free energy values passed to the 'energy' neuron were set lower than those of reference compounds. Then the reference compounds were again used to generate new molecules, however, in this case, no Gaussian noise was added, only the value of binding free energy passed to the 'energy' neuron was set to lower values compared to reference compounds. This was done to check whether the model would be able to improve and restructure compounds given an 'updated' binding free energy value only, or whether additional alteration is required to help the model. The results of these experiments are shown in Fig. 5.

A two-sided t-test was used to compare the means of two distributions shown on the plot, with the null hypothesis H_0 being that distribution means are the same. The p-value of 0.00068 obtained was below the significance level of 0.05 chosen. This provides enough evidence to reject the null hypothesis H_0 and actually suggest, that the observed differences between distribution means are of statistical significance. Hence, the distribution of compounds generated purely based on the improvements of binding free energy have a better mean value of binding free energy. This result suggests that adding extra noise is only confusing the energy model when trying to capitalize on binding free energy change.

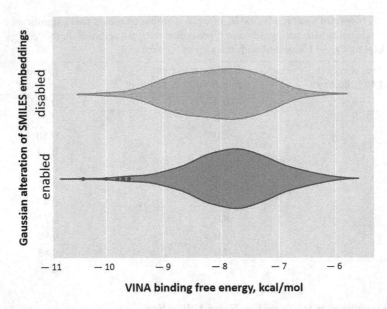

Fig. 5. Violin plots describing distributions of experiments with and without Gaussian noise alteration of SMILES embeddings for generation from reference compounds using the 'energy' model.

3.5   Models and Generation Modes Comparison

To visualize comparison between all models and generation modes, the cumulative binding free energy distribution was plotted for all the models (Fig. 6). This comparison method allows one to observe the general quality of samples generated, disregarding their number as it takes into account distributions as a whole. Due to the very low number of generated compounds exhibiting the values of binding free energy above –6 kcal/mol (less than 2.8% of all generated compounds), the generation results were filtered using this threshold which was also used earlier for preparation of the training dataset.

In order for the results to be comparable, certain generations modes had to be chosen. For the embeddings model, all compounds generated from Gaussian noise (experiment I) and all compounds generated using reference compounds embeddings that were altered with Gaussian noise (experiment II) were selected. The latter generation mode included reference compounds exhibiting the values of binding free energy lower than –9 kcal/mol. Using the energy model, three additional experiments were used. The first one (experiment III) generated compounds from Gaussian noise using the preset values of binding free energy of –9 kcal/mol and lower which were passed to the 'energy' neuron. The second experiment (experiment IV) involved reference compounds where the corresponding embeddings were altered with Gaussian noise, while the preset values of binding free energy passed to the 'energy' neuron were improved with a step of 0.5 kcal/mol and 1.0 kcal/mol compared to the docking results for the corresponding reference compounds. Finally, the last experiment (experiment V) also involved reference compounds, but no Gaussian alteration was applied, instead only an improved value of binding free energy was passed to the 'energy' neuron.

As evident from the plot of cumulative binding free energy distribution (Fig. 6), models from experiments II, IV and V generated more compounds with lower values of binding free energy, since their respective lines are located lower than those of the other experiments. In general, right-side shift of a cumulative curve relative to the others for every fixed dataset fraction f means that the rest dataset fraction of 1-f for the right shifted curve contains more compounds with lower values of binding free energy. For example, assuming $f = 0.8$, one can observe that for experiments I and III the top 20% of all generated compounds demonstrating the values of binding free energy above -8.0 kcal/mol, while for experiments II and IV the corresponding values are slightly lower than -8.0 kcal/mol, with the results of experiment V being much closer to -8.5 kcal/mol.

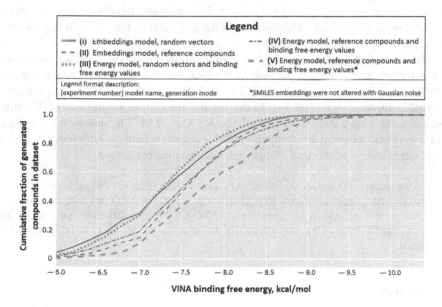

Fig. 6. Cumulative binding free energy distributions.

3.6   Results Discussion

The model comparison proved that the attempt to generate new compounds based on already existing ones outperforms sampling new compounds from random noise (Table 3 and Fig. 6). In addition, the energy model seems to have managed to utilize the introduced 'energy' neuron and also produces more compounds with lower values of binding free energy than the pure embeddings model (Fig. 6). Moreover, the Gaussian noise alteration seems to diminish the benefits of 'energy' neuron usage (Fig. 5). Unfortunately, setting lower binding free energy threshold passed to the 'energy' neuron does not statistically significant resulting in generation of more promising compounds (Fig. 4).

Summarizing all the data obtained, one can conclude that the architecture of the molecular autoencoder model used in experiment V is the most promising of all the options reviewed.

4 Conclusion

Two generative autoencoder models for prediction of effective drugs against SARS-CoV-2 M^{Pro} were developed to identify novel potential inhibitors able to block the catalytic site of the enzyme. The designed generative models combined with molecular docking proved their great potential to enrich screening pipelines with new compounds exhibiting satisfying binding properties. The generative power of the designed models is confirmed by the fact that out of 4805 successfully generated compounds only one compound was found in the original dataset. This indicates the richness of unexplored chemical space and proves an importance of development and application of generative models in drug design and discovery.

The developed autoencoder models combined with traditional methods of molecular modeling may provide a productive platform for identification of promising anti-COVID-19 agents that target the SARS-CoV-2 main protease critically important for the viral replication cycle [10, 11]. In this regard, the further progression of this study assumes generating a wide set of potential SARS-CoV-2 M^{Pro} ligands by the developed neural network followed by computer-aided evaluation of their antiviral potency, *in silico* identification of the lead compounds and biomedical assays.

Acknowledgments. This study was financed by grants of the Belarusian Republican Foundation for Fundamental Research (projects F21COVID-002 and F21ARMG-001) with the support of the Alliance of International Organizations (ANSO-CR-PP-2021-04). The authors are also grateful to the PRIP2021 Conference team for the selection of this study to be supported for publication.

References

1. Iqbal, T., Qureshi, S.: The survey: text generation models in deep learning. J. King Saud Univ. Comput. Inf. Sci. (2020). https://doi.org/10.1016/j.jksuci.2020.04.001
2. Sorin, V., Barash, Y., Konen, E., Klang, E.: Creating artificial images for radiology applications using generative adversarial networks (GANs) – A systematic review. Acad. Radiol. **27**(8), 1175–1185 (2020). https://doi.org/10.1016/j.acra.2019.12.024
3. Kim, S., et al.: PubChem in 2021: new data content and improved web interfaces. Nucleic Acids Res. **49**(D1), D1388–D1395 (2021). https://doi.org/10.1093/nar/gkaa971
4. PubChem Homepage. https://pubchem.ncbi.nlm.nih.gov/. Accessed 10 Dec 2021
5. Chen, Y., Liu, Q., Guo, D.: Coronaviruses: genome structure, replication, and pathogenesis. J. Med. Virol. **92**(4), 418–423 (2020). https://doi.org/10.1002/jmv.25681

6. Anand, K., Palm, G.J., Mesters, J.R., Siddell, S.G., Ziebuhr, J., Hilgenfeld, R.: Structure of coronavirus main proteinase reveals combination of a chymotrypsin fold with an extra α-helical domain. EMBO J. **21**(13), 3213–3224 (2002). https://doi.org/10.1093/emboj/cdf327

7. Yang, H., et al.: The crystal structures of severe acute respiratory syndrome virus main protease and its complex with an inhibitor. PNAS USA **100**(23), 13190–13195 (2003). https://doi.org/10.1073/pnas.1835675100

8. Hegyi, A., Ziebuhr, J.: Conservation of substrate specificities among coronavirus main proteases. J. Gen. Virol. **83**(3), 595–599 (2002). https://doi.org/10.1099/0022-1317-83-3-595

9. Pillaiyar, T., Manickam, M., Namasivayam, V., Hayashi, Y., Jung, S.H.: An overview of severe acute respiratory syndrome-coronavirus (SARS-CoV) 3CL protease inhibitors: peptidomimetics and small molecule chemotherapy. J. Med. Chem. **59**(14), 6595–6628 (2016). https://doi.org/10.1021/acs.jmedchem.5b01461

10. Yan, F., Gao, F.: An overview of potential inhibitors targeting non-structural proteins 3 (PL^{pro} and Mac1) and 5 (3CL^{pro}/M^{pro}) of SARS-CoV-2. Comp. Struct. Biotechnol. J. **19**, 4868–4883 (2021). https://doi.org/10.1016/j.csbj.2021.08.036

11. Ullrich, S., Nitsche, C.: The SARS-CoV-2 main protease as drug target. Bioorganic Med. Chem. Lett. **30**(17), 127377 (2020). https://doi.org/10.1016/j.bmcl.2020.127377

12. Forster, P., Forster, L., Renfrew, C., Forster, M.: Phylogenetic network analysis of SARS-CoV-2 genomes. PNAS USA **117**(17), 9241–9243 (2020). https://doi.org/10.1073/pnas.2004999117

13. Pachetti, M., et al.: Emerging SARS-CoV-2 mutation hot spots include a novel RNA-dependent-RNA polymerase variant. J. Transl. Med. **18**, 179 (2020). https://doi.org/10.1186/s12967-020-02344-6

14. Yao, H., et al.: Patient-derived SARS-CoV-2 mutations impact viral replication dynamics and infectivity in vitro and with clinical implications in vivo. Cell Discov. **6**, 76 (2020). https://doi.org/10.1038/s41421-020-00226-1

15. Khailany, R.A., Safdar, M., Ozaslan, M.: Genomic characterization of a novel SARS-CoV-2. Gene Rep. **19**, 100682 (2020). https://doi.org/10.1016/j.genrep.2020.100682

16. Weininger, D.: SMILES, a chemical language and information system. 1. Introduction to methodology and encoding rules. J. Chem. Inf. Model. **28**(1), 31–36 (1988). https://doi.org/10.1021/ci00057a005

17. Andrianov, A.M., Nikolaev, G.I., Shuldov, N.A., Bosko, I.P., Anischenko, A.I., Tuzikov, A. V.: Application of deep learning and molecular modeling to identify small drug-like compounds as potential HIV-1 entry inhibitors. J. Biomol. Struct. Dyn. 1–19 (2021). https://doi.org/10.1080/07391102.2021.1905559

18. Pharmit Homepage. http://pharmit.csb.pitt.edu. Accessed 10 Dec 2021

19. Sunseri, J., Koes, D.R.: Pharmit: interactive exploration of chemical space. Nucleic Acids Res. **44**(W1), W442–W448 (2016). https://doi.org/10.1093/nar/gkw287

20. Schneidman-Duhovny, D., Dror, O., Inbar, Y., Nussinov, R., Wolfson, H.J.: Deterministic pharmacophore detection via multiple flexible alignment of drug-like molecules. J. Comput. Biol. **15**(7), 737–754 (2008). https://doi.org/10.1089/cmb.2007.0130

21. PubChemPy Homepage. https://pubchempy.readthedocs.io/. Accessed 10 Dec 2021

22. Python Homepage. https://www.python.org/. Accessed 10 Dec 2021

23. RCSB PDB Homepage. https://www.rcsb.org/pdb/. Accessed 10 Dec 2021

24. RDKit Homepage. http://www.rdkit.org/. Accessed 10 Dec 2021

25. Halgren, T.A.: Merck molecular force field. I. Basis, form, scope, parameterization, and performance of MMFF94. J. Comput. Chem. **17**(5–6), 490–519 (1996). https://doi.org/10.1002/(SICI)1096-987X(199604)17:5/6<490::AID-JCC1>3.0.CO;2-P

26. Tosco, P., Stiefl, N., Landrum, G.: Bringing the MMFF force field to the RDKit: implementation and validation. J. Cheminformatics **6**(1), 1–4 (2014). https://doi.org/10. 1186/s13321-014-0037-3
27. Wang, S., Witek, J., Landrum, G.A., Riniker, S.: Improving conformer generation for small rings and macrocycles based on distance geometry and experimental torsional-angle preferences. J. Chem. Inf. Model. **60**(4), 2044–2058 (2020). https://doi.org/10.1021/acs. jcim.0c00025
28. Gasteiger, J., Marsili, M.: A new model for calculating atomic charges in molecules. Tetrahedron Lett. **19**(34), 3181–3184 (1978). https://doi.org/10.1016/S0040-4039(01) 94977-9
29. Rappe, A.K., Casewit, C.J., Colwell, K.S., Goddard, W.A., Skiff, W.M.: UFF, a full periodic table force field for molecular mechanics and molecular dynamics simulations. J. Am. Chem. Soc. **114**(25), 10024–10035 (1992). https://doi.org/10.1021/ja00051a040
30. O'Boyle, N.M., Banck, M., James, C.A., Morley, C., Vandermeersch, T., Hutchison, G.R.: Open babel: an open chemical toolbox. J. Cheminformatics **3**(1), 33 (2011). https://doi.org/ 10.1186/1758-2946-3-33
31. MGLTools Homepage. http://mgltools.scripps.edu/. Accessed 10 Dec 2021
32. Alhossary, A., Handoko, S.D., Mu, Y., Kwoh, C.-K.: Fast, accurate, and reliable molecular docking with QuickVina 2. Bioinformatics **31**(13), 2214–2216 (2015). https://doi.org/10. 1093/bioinformatics/btv082
33. Trott, O., Olson, A.J.: AutoDock Vina: improving the speed and accuracy of docking with a new scoring function, efficient optimization, and multithreading. J. Comput. Chem. **31**(2), 455–461 (2010). https://doi.org/10.1002/jcc.21334
34. Hochreiter, S., Schmidhuber, J.: Long short-term memory. Neural Comput. **9**(8), 1735–1780 (1997). https://doi.org/10.1162/neco.1997.9.8.1735
35. TensorFlow Homepage. https://www.tensorflow.org/. Accessed 10 Dec 2021
36. Kingma, D.P., Ba, J.: Adam: a method for stochastic optimization. In: Proceedings of the 3rd International Conference on Learning Representations (ICLR), San Diego (2015)

Mask R-CNN-Based System for Automated Reindeer Recognition and Counting from Aerial Photographs

Vladimir Valentinovich Mikhailov[1]([⊠]) [iD],
Vladislav Alekseevich Sobolevskii[1] [iD],
and Leonid Aleksandrovich Kolpaschikov[2] [iD]

[1] St. Petersburg Federal Research Center of the Russian Academy of Sciences,
39, 14th line V.O., 199178 Saint-Petersburg, Russia
`mwwcari@gmail.com, arguzd@yandex.ru`
[2] Directorate of Taimyr Nature Reserves, Talnakhskaia, 22, Entrance 2,
663300 Norilsk, Russian Federation

Abstract. The complexity of recognition and counting of reindeer in the natural environment from photographs is determined by the variability of recognition factors. The aim of the study is to develop a methodology and software implementation, which can solve the problem of recognition and counting of reindeer as high variability objects. To date, there exist two main approaches: feature-based recognition based on a binary pixel classification and reference-based recognition using convolutional neural networks (CNN). In this case, solving the problem of feature space recognition by pixels requires a lot of specialists' time to analyze the images, select the features and criteria for separating images and background, and choose efficient algorithms for pixel classification and deer counting. In contrast, CNN solves the task of classification directly from images, using learned neural network architectures, without any manual processing. Therefore, CNN was used to solve the task. The methodology and recognition programs have been developed using CNN of the Mask R-CNN architecture. In this case, first the network is trained to recognize animals as a class from an array of MS COCO dataset images and then re-trained on an array of aerial photographs of reindeer herds. On average, in the test sample, 82% of reindeer were recognized. At the same time, there were no false positives at all. A software prototype of the recognition system based on the CNN with a web interface has now been created, and the software is operated with limited functionality.

Keywords: Recognition · Convolutional neural networks · Aerial images · Reindeer

1 Introduction

The complexity of solving the task of automatic recognition of reindeer in aerial photographs depends on the presence and degree of variability of factors associated with recognition. Such factors include:

© Springer Nature Switzerland AG 2022
A. V. Tuzikov et al. (Eds.): PRIP 2021, CCIS 1562, pp. 137–151, 2022.
https://doi.org/10.1007/978-3-030-98883-8_10

- The variety of reindeer images as objects of recognition, which can differ significantly in color, size and shape.
- Artifacts in the photo that are similar in some respects to the objects of the class being recognized.
- Backgrounds in the image, uniform or heterogeneous in color, may vary significantly in different images.
- Light conditions. Subjects may be in the sun or shade, photos may be taken at different times of day. All this leads to changes in brightness and color characteristics of objects and the background.
- The location of objects in the image. Reindeer can be positioned at different distances and angles to the camera. The images of animals can overlap and be partially obscured by background elements.

The complexity of a recognition task depends on the dimensionality of the factor space (the number of factors) and on the number of distinguishable values of each factor in the image. In the beginning, complexity can be estimated by the number of factors with variability. The highest complexity level corresponds to problems in which all factors have variability. The lowest complexity level corresponds to tasks with fixed values of recognition factors. Partitioning the original set of images into subsets in order to capture the values of any factors simplifies the task of recognition on each subset of the data, but increases the amount of manual work involved in analyzing and grouping the imagery.

The methodologies currently used for counting the numbers of wild reindeer in tundra populations (Taimyr, Yakutia, and Chukotka reindeer, as well as migrating herds of reindeer - Canadian and Alaskan caribou) are based on ecological characteristics of the species. In hot weather, during the flight of blood-sucking insects, reindeer gather in crowds of thousands in a limited area in the northern part of the summer range [1, 2]. The clusters are photographed from an aircraft and the animals in the clusters are counted manually by operators for each photo. A single photo can contain anywhere from a few hundred to 1000 or more reindeer. The largest herd that was captured in one photo and counted "by head" contained about 35000 animals (Taimyr, Upper Taimyr River area, 28.07.2017). The total number of the shots of herds in aerial counts can be as high as several thousand. As a result, the bulk of reindeer in a population is counted by direct count. The number of animals not included in the aggregations is estimated by approximation by area [3].

Manual processing of survey results by biologists takes approximately three months. However, for the purposes of ecologically sound management of population dynamics, rational use of species' biological resources and the determination of harvesting rates for reindeer, calculated data should be available 10–15 days after the end of the aerial survey. These reasons determine the relevance of setting the task of image processing automation. However, modern neural network architectures oriented at the recognition of objects from their images, as well as the original data arrays containing archived aerial photographs of reindeer herds, taken during aerial counts, are now available. All of this is sufficient to implement an automated reindeer herd counting system based on aerial photographs.

2 Principles and Approaches to Recognition of Natural Objects

The task of recognizing wildlife objects has a great theoretical value. The solution of this task makes it possible to see wildlife diversity, to identify specific objects according to external features, to find out their species, to find their scientific names and, if desired, – their properties, place and role in the ecosystem. From a scientific point of view, the process of recognition and registration reveals the species composition of the ecosystem and the dynamics of its components. In conservation work, such information is the basis for choosing conservation measures for populations and ecosystems and for assessing their effectiveness. For commercially important species, regular population counts are essential for determining harvesting limits to ensure the sustainable use of biological resources.

Historically, the task of recognition of biological objects was solved by creating identifiers that allow establishing the place of a given object in the general system of biological classification, that is, the species, genus, family and other classification levels. Methodologically, the problem is solved in the determinants using two fundamentally different approaches. The first one is recognition by features. The developers of such determinants are specialists in biological systematics and classification. They define attributes that allow objects to be grouped together at some level of classification and features by which objects move into different groups at a lower level of classification and are already differentiated in them. The result is a tree with branching along the key features. Object recognition is reduced to movement along the tree from the root (or some other level of classification) to the branches with the selection of the direction at the branch points in accordance with the values of the attributes. The second approach is pattern matching. The identifier contains a set of reference images of different types of objects. The method of recognition consists in the comparison of the object sought with the samples to select the most "similar" one. The user here acts as an expert who evaluates the degree of similarity of the images. Accordingly, the recognition error will depend on the expert's experience, knowledge and his/her personal features of visual perception of objects. This approach can be very effective for recognition at the species level, since it is based on comparing and contrasting holistic visual images, which is a natural routine task of the human visual system. In many cases, feature identifiers are supplemented with a set of reference images, and a person, when assessing "similarity", mentally highlights similar and different features of objects.

Computer-based wildlife recognition systems are also built using these two approaches. However, when recognizing objects by their features in the natural environment, new tasks arise. This is related to the search for features that distinguish the image of an object from the background and noise, similar in some characteristics to the desired object. In this case, the determination of species is often not relevant, because the type of recognition object is known in advance. An important cognitive property of feature-based recognition system is "transparency" regarding the composition of the used features of the recognition object, methods, technological chain of image transformations and results, including intermediate ones. However, during the recognition of objects with high variability in a non-stationary environment, difficulties arise due to the need for pre-classification of images, search and expansion of the composition of the features, changing methods and image processing algorithms. [4] suggests that it is impossible to formalize completely the processes of object recognition in such circumstances and stresses the need to move from an automatic to an interactive image processing technology.

In one of the first works on recognition and counting of reindeer [5], differences in values of their spectral brightness were taken as a sign of separation of reindeer and the underlying surface. Based on the results of the experiments, a color pair was chosen - green (background) and blue (recognizable object). The inequation by which the pixels of the object differ from the pixels of the background was made up afterwards. The segment assignment to the deer image was performed by analyzing the area and elongation of the segmented area. The test showed a very high recognition and counting accuracy of reindeer in the artificially generated "simple" images (green background, no interference and no overlapping of objects with each other). The counting error was about 2%. However, when working with real images the error rate increased sharply due to the high variability of recognized objects and survey conditions.

Different methods of binarization and segmentation are discussed in [6] and the results of their use in recognition of reindeer by features on samples of images with similar characteristics of background and coloration of reindeer are analyzed. The comparison of experimental results with manual deer counting data showed that the closest match (±15–20%) is given by binarization by color tone thresholds and saturation. The presence of artifacts on the image that are close in brightness characteristics, shape and area to deer images leads to an unacceptable increase in error.

The experimental results have shown that the system of recognition and counting of reindeer in aerial photographs based on the features should be based on the following principles: the detailed analysis and classification of images, collection of statistical data on the characteristics of pixels relating to reindeer images, definition of the most informative features and selection of effective algorithms of pixel classification and counting of reindeer. The system must have sufficient intelligence for the combination of methods for recognizing reindeer in the submitted image.

On the other hand, in modern reference recognition systems artificial neural networks (ANNs) are widely used as recognition subjects [7, 8]. In such systems, an ANN is trained on a set of images in which recognition objects (benchmarks) are marked in advance. After that the trained ANN is used to recognize the objects of a given class in a real environment, on stills and video frames. The logic of object recognition is encapsulated in the ANN itself and does not need to be developed explicitly. On the other hand, due to the complexity of ANN structures, the interpretation of their results is often difficult. The process of "learning" such structures is mostly empirical. There are very few well-established methods for creating ANNs, and even they are not suitable for many applications. Most often, they present only general recommendations and reflect developers' empirical experience in solving a particular class of problems.

The systems of recognition and counting of objects from photographs that are known from literature sources are mainly focused on humans as observational objects.

To a lesser extent this applies to other living organisms. Let us consider some of such systems.

Article [9] presents a program for recognition of animals and their behavior in the wild from photographs taken from 225 camera traps of the Serengeti Reserve (Tanzania). The reason for developing the system was that, due to limited human resources, only a fraction of the information stored on the servers was actually used. The recognition software was developed jointly at the universities of Wyoming, Minnesota, Auburn, Harvard, Oxford and at Uber AI. The work used the deep learning method of various CNN architectures [10]. 1.5 million images were used in the work, of which 1.4 million served for network training and 0.1 million - for testing. According to the test results, the probability of detecting animals with a yes/no binary response was about 96%. Animal species out of 48 possible choices were recognized with 99% probability. However, counting animals in clusters 1, 2,... 10, 11–50, >50 was performed by the software with an accuracy of only 63%. This indicates the difficulty of fixing a single animal in the image under the conditions of possible overlapping of images of animals, their partial overlapping by foreign objects and other distortions.

CNNs were also used to recognize elephants in satellite images [11]. Archived images from Worldview-3 and Worldview-4 satellites at 31 cm resolution, taken between 2014 and 2019 in a national park in the Republic of South Africa, Addo Elephant, were used to train the network. The area covers over 1,600 km and is home to more than 600 savannah elephants. Addo Elephant has a heterogeneous landscape, with bushland, lowland forest, open grassland and water bodies. During the day, elephants move about the area and sometimes douse themselves in mud to get protection from the heat. All this makes them difficult to spot.

The developers tested the system on an independent sample of images of Kenya territories and compared its accuracy with the results of 51 volunteers who identified elephants manually. Machine learning experts, scientists and national park staff took part in the experiment. The likelihood of finding elephants in a heterogeneous area using CNN was 78%, and humans finding elephants - 77%. For a homogeneous area, the results were 73% and 80%, respectively.

The website [12] presents material on the development and testing of an automatic recognition, segmentation and enumeration system for harbor seals, developed as part of the Kaggle Data Science platform's online competition. The problem statement is related to the monitoring of the Western Aleutian Islands seals population, carried out by drones. The processing of the obtained photos is done manually, which takes about 4 months each year. Seals are counted according to five sex and age classes. An array of 948 marked photographs was generated for the development of the automatic system, and a further 18,641 images were submitted for testing the system. The images were taken from different heights and scales. There are interferences similar to animal images, and no clear visual distinctions between some classes of seals. These reasons complicate the task of automatic recognition and counting of seals in aerial photographs. The solution proposed in this paper is based on the basic architecture of Inception-Resnet-V2 CNN, which is extended by adding a 256-neuron FC layer + Dropout + a final FC layer of 5 neurons. The project is ranked 4th out of 385 participants. The peculiarity of this article is that it not only describes a particular system, but also looks in detail into the whole process of its development with an analysis of right and wrong decisions when selecting the architecture and parameters of the neural network.

The website [13] presents the Seek iNaturalist recognition software for nature lovers. The software uses SSD (Singl-Shot Multy Box Detector) based on CNN. This architecture makes it possible to use miniaturized mobile devices for real-time photo and video image analysis.

A few remarks can be made regarding the construction of automatic animal recognition systems based on the existing understanding of the classification problem and available software developments:

- the animal in the natural environment is a complex object to recognize. The variability of images on photographs, their overlapping and the presence of noise leads to recognition errors made both by humans and automatic systems;
- the CNN apparatus is currently the most suitable one for recognition of images of natural objects;
- the recognition process accuracy can be improved by increasing the volume of the training sample or by shifting to the interactive mode of image processing with human participation;
- modern CNN architectures make it possible to create mobile applications for working in the field directly during survey operations.

The evaluation of existing projects aimed at recognition of animals in their natural habitat has shown that the system for recognizing and counting reindeer in aerial images must be based on a detailed analysis and classification of images, determining the most informative features and selecting efficient algorithms for recognizing, segmenting and counting reindeer. The system must have sufficient intelligence for combining the methods of recognizing reindeer in the submitted image.

3   Recognition of Animals in Aerial Images from Reference Images Using Artificial Neural Networks

3.1   Convergent Neural Networks as an Image Recognition Tool

Nowadays ANNs are widely used to solve the problem of wildlife objects recognition by learning from their reference images [14]. This class of ANN architectures is a highly specialized tool, suitable primarily for images and other data that can be represented in matrix form.

Since images store all information in the form of two-dimensional matrices (i.e., pixels), when dealing with them it is necessary to consider not only the values coming from the neurons themselves, but also the values from the group of nearest neurons. To this end, besides neurons there is another type of elements in convolutional layers of CNN that apply certain linear operations to all input data of each neuron of the convolutional layer - the convolutional core. This core is a grid which "sweeps" across the image (or the convolutional layer of the previous layer), and searches patterns in the data. If it finds a part of the image that matches a core pattern, it passes a large positive value to the current layer's computational neuron. If there is no match, the core will transmit a small value or zero.

Due to the fact that the convolution core is applied to every position in the image, the convolution layer of CNN is extremely effective in image processing tasks because features or patterns in the images can appear anywhere in these images. That is, unlike other ANNs, CNN is able to analyze context-dependent data.

However, since CNNs are composed of multiple convolutional layers, each successive layer receives data from the previous convolutional layer as its input layer. This happens because the convolutional layer itself is also a two-dimensional array and its output value vector can be represented as an image. In this case, each subsequent convolutional layer will be able to find increasingly complex patterns and patterns of the original input array.

The Mask Regions with Convolution Neural Networks (MRCNN) architecture [15] was chosen for this task. This architecture is a subset of the classical CNN. Due to its complexity it is more successful in the task of semantic and object segmentation of images [16, 17]. A generalized scheme of MRCNN is shown in Fig. 1.

A key feature of this architecture is the combination of a CNN architecture such as Faster R-CNN, which is responsible for the classification task, with the Mask Head module, which is responsible for the image segmentation task. The result of MRCNN is the combined response of the two described components.

FRCNN is a CNN, which searches the image of objects, and then additionally makes a classification of the found object. The output of this CNN is a bounding rectangle for each object (i.e., a rectangular bounding box that constrains the found object) and a class label of the found object with a confidence rating.

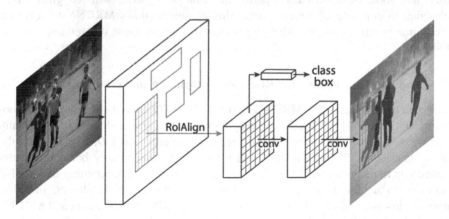

Fig. 1. Generalized MRCNN scheme (from [15]).

The first phase of FRCNN consists of running two enabled CNNs simultaneously: a backbone network (ResNet, VGG, Inception, or similar) and a regional positioning network. These networks process each image arriving at the FRCNN input and provide an output of a three-dimensional array - an array of suggested two dimensional regions. These two-dimensional regions are the excised portion of the image in which the backbone CNN has detected an object. The size of these parts is not fixed and depends on the size of the recognized object.

In the second step, FRCNN predicts the coordinates of the bounding rectangles and object classes for each of the proposed areas obtained in the first step. Each proposed region may have a different size, but since convolutional layers in CNN always require a fixed size vector for prediction, this step also scales the found regions. The size of the regions is scaled using either the RoI algorithm or the RoIAlign method.

MRCNN in turn is an extended version of FRCNN, augmented with a branch to predict segmentation masks for each region of interest. The second phase of MRCNN already uses only RoIAlign, which helps to preserve the original spatial coordinates that are offset when RoI is used. This is necessary to combine RoIAlign output with the data from the first phase, and a mask can be generated for each RoIAlign response using the Mask Head module (which in turn is also implemented using convolutional layers). Such masks represent a two-dimensional matrix, which for every pixel within a region boundary object determines whether that pixel belongs to the searched object or not.

This approach, on the one hand, allows defining more precisely the boundaries of the searched object. Ideally, MRCNN can accurately calculate all the pixels in the image that represent the searched object. On the other hand, during training, the data from the Mask Head module is used for additional training of the backbone CNN. This also improves the accuracy of the main CNN.

The Mask Head module performs semantic segmentation only of the current object being searched for, since it uses the results of the main CNN calculation for the pixel-by-pixel search. That is, even if two objects of the same class are located next to each other, the Mask Head on each separate iteration of its work will recognize pixels belonging to only one of these objects. This approach allows MRCNN to solve the recognition problem correctly when the objects it seeks are close or even overlap each other.

3.2   Training the Network for Reindeer Recognition in Aerial Images

The basic training array for MRCNN is the MS COCO dataset (Microsoft Common Objects in Context) [18]. This dataset is by far the largest one used for training machine learning models to solve detection and segmentation problems [19, 20]. To date, this dataset consists of 328,000 images. All image data have already been tagged and formed into training samples. Therefore, using this array for basic training of MRCNN allows us to set for it all the basic concepts of different object classes, including animals. However, reindeer images are not part of the MS COCO dataset and MRCNN by default is not able to distinguish them from a number of other animals (sheep, gazelles, cows, horses).

Figure 2 shows the results of recognizing reindeer in an aerial photo using a basic MRCNN trained on MS COCO dataset. In the image, correctly recognized reindeer images are marked green and there are 4 such images. The objects mistaken for reindeer are marked red and there are 32 of them.

Fig. 2. Reindeer recognition result using basic MRCNN trained on MS COCO dataset.

The specifics of aerial photographs are that herds are photographed from different distances, in different landscapes, under different lighting conditions, animals in the images have different colors and may be positioned at different angles to the camera, sometimes overlapping each other. These peculiarities of aerial photos create additional difficulties in solving the task of reindeer recognition.

The task of reindeer recognition from aerial photography is not trivial. Therefore, a two-stage MRCNN training procedure has been proposed to solve it. Initial training on the MS COCO dataset, which includes images of other animals, is necessary for the network to learn to recognize animals as an object class. In a second step, MRCNN is further trained on an array of aerial photographs of reindeer herds. This approach is known as transfer learning [21] and is currently used in many tasks for which it is impossible, for one reason or another, to collect an array of training data for the specific situation in question. Therefore, the model is first trained on a large array of similar situations, and after that it is further trained on target examples.

Therefore, an input array of case studies was prepared, containing a training sample of 100 aerial images of herds with all animals marked, and a test sample of 30 original images of herds that were not included in the training sample.

The model was trained with the following MRCNN parameters: 20 training epochs; 60 training steps per epoch; learning rate 0.0058 (dimensionless); detection miss threshold 0.7 (dimensionless). Since CNNs are generally black boxes, it is not possible to explicitly describe the effect of specific parameter values on the performance of the trained network. The values have been determined from experience with CNN and empirical observations in the training process.

Figure 3 shows the result of reindeer recognition by a model that has been retrained from aerial photographs of reindeer herds. In the same photo as the one shown in Fig. 6, the model correctly recognized 70 reindeer out of 93 (75% accuracy) and made not a single mistake of the second kind, i.e., it did not recognize an object that was not a reindeer. On average, the model correctly recognized 82% of the reindeer in the entire training dataset.

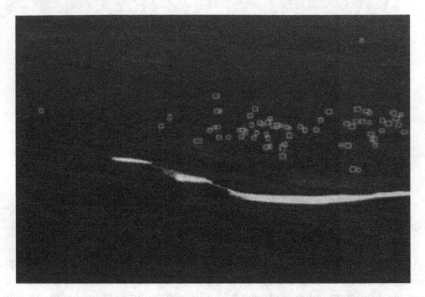

Fig. 3. Reindeer recognition result using the retrained MRCNN.

3.3   The Web Interface of the System and the Results of Its Validation on an Independent Data Set

So far, a software package with a web interface has been created for the developed network and the software itself has been put into limited operation. As the system has been developed using a service-oriented architecture (SOA) [22], this package can be used either permanently or remotely via the Internet. In order to work with the system, a user has to upload JPEG (.jpg) or GIF (.gif) images to their computer.

The system interface contains a set of window forms for:

- loading aerial photographs from the user's computer for processing,
- launching the software for reindeer identification and counting in the images,
- presentation of the program operation results displaying on the screen the still with marked reindeer images recognized by the system and the total number of counted animals,
- downloading the results to the user's computer.

After viewing the marked image, if the user is not satisfied with the accuracy of the software complex, he/she can continue processing the image manually using the program for manual image processing (Sect. 2) or in any graphic editor that supports the. jpg file extension.

A view of the graphical interface of the deer identification and counting system is shown in Fig. 4.

Fig. 4. System interface window, "Program successfully completed work" mode.

The software was tested on an independent array of 10 aerial images. Figure 5 shows a photograph of a small herd of reindeer. There were 4 recognition errors - 2 reindeer were recognized twice and 2 calves were not recognized. In total out of 41 reindeer, 35 were recognized correctly. However, the error of counting the number of animals in the herd was only 10%, which is quite high for automatic wildlife recognition systems. The reason for this, in this case, is the high image quality and the high resolution of the reindeer themselves, as well as the strong contrast of the background with the recognition objects.

Fig. 5. Deer recognition in a homogeneous field.

The image (Fig. 6) shows that MRCNN works well with large herds. It can be seen in the image that the network recognized reindeer at different distances from the camera with equal efficiency. The network is therefore not bound to a specific resolution and is able to work with a distorted perspective. The recognition error was around 3%.

Fig. 6. Recognizing and counting deer in a large herd on a homogeneous background.

A herd of reindeer in a typical heterogeneous tundra landscape is shown in Fig. 7. It can be seen from the marking of reindeer images that MRCNN can handle images that are obscured by background objects such as puddles, lakes, hillocks, etc. Background objects have never been mistaken for reindeer images by the recognition system. It is also noticeable that the network works well with herds, in which reindeer gather in very dense groups. The recognition error was around 17%.

Fig. 7. Large herd against a heterogeneous background.

4 Conclusion

The researches have shown that the development of the automatic system of recognition and counting of reindeer in the attribute space demands a lot of experts' time for the analysis of images, selection of features and criteria of separation of images of animals from the background, carrying out different kinds of test computer experiments [6]. In contrast, CNN learns to perform the task of classification directly from images without prior manual feature selection. The presence of ready-made CNN architectures, trained to recognize different kinds of objects in images, makes it possible by additional training to effectively create applications aimed at the recognition of specific species of animals. In this way the authors created a software system for recognition and counting of reindeer from aerial photographs. Let us enumerate some promising directions of the development of the complex.

- Decreasing the errors of recognition. It is necessary to increase the volume of the training sampling, especially for the highly "noisy" and multi-scale images of animals. However, the relationship between the error rate and sample size is exponentially decaying, and an excessive increase in the sample size can lead to overtraining the model. Therefore, the number of images that would need to be added to the training sample cannot be estimated in advance. In addition, when counting animals in clusters, a situation may always arise that an automatic recognition system cannot cope with. In this case, the recognition system can work interactively in conjunction with an image processing program.
- Porting the software complex to high performance servers. The specifics of computing, when using MRCNN, imposes a number of requirements on hardware. The commercial use of a software system requires parallel operation of a software

complex by several users, which can significantly burden the system. Despite the parallelism of the software system architecture, additional research and stress testing is required to determine requirements to hardware.

- Video image analysis. At present, the MRCNN architecture is used in video image processing in a number of projects [23]. Software libraries are available which allow integrating this architecture into software packages dealing with video streaming. This makes it possible to modify the presented development for recognition and counting of deer in the video stream. Such an approach will speed up the process of obtaining the counting results, as it eliminates the image editing procedure required in discrete photographing of reindeer herds.
- Counting other species of animals and birds. The basic array for the initial training of the MRCNN is the MS COCO dataset (Microsoft Common Objects in Context) image array. Reindeer images serve the purpose of pre-training the CNN. Similarly, without changing the CNN architecture and interface organization, the system can be retrained to recognize and count flocks of saigas, flocks of geese during the molting period or some species of polar gulls.

Acknowledgements. This work was supported by World-Wide Fund for Nature - Contract № BBF003107, RFBR Grant № 19-37-90112 and Budget Subject № 0073- 2019-0004.

References

1. Zirjanov, V. A., Pavlov, B. M., Jakushkin, G. D.: Ecological basics of counting the number of hunting animals in the tundra zone of Taimyr. Problems of Hunting Krasnoyarsk Region, pp. 70–72 (1971). (in Russian)
2. Kolpashikov, L.A., Mikhailov, V.V., Russell, D.E.: The role of harvest, predators, and socio-political environment in the dynamics of the Taimyr wild reindeer herd with some lessons for North America. Ecol. Soc. **20**(1), 9 (2015)
3. Chelintsev, N.G.: Mathematical basis of animal counting. GU Tsentrohotkontrol, Moscow (2000). (in Russian)
4. Soloviev, N.V., Sergeev, M.B.: Image recognition of a set of homogeneous objects with high variability. In: Scientific session of SUAE: collection of reports: in 3 parts, part 2, pp. 427–430. SUAE, Saint Petersburg (2019). (in Russian)
5. Mikhailov, V.V., Harin, J.V.: On the construction of a system for recognizing and counting animals from aerial photographs. Inf. Control Syst. **2**, 22–28 (2011). (in Russian)
6. Mikhailov, V.V., Kolpaschikov, L.A., Sobolevskii, V.A., Soloviev, N.V., Yakushev, G.K.: Methodological approaches and algorithms for recognising and counting animals in aerial photographs. Inf. Control Syst. **5**, 20–32 (2021). (in Russian)
7. Simon, J.D.: Prince Computer Vision: Models, Learning, and Inference. Cambridge University Press, Cambridge (2012)
8. Ayyadevara, K., Reddy, Y.: Modern Computer Vision with PyTorch: Explore Deep Learning Concepts and Implement over 50 Real-World Image Applications. Packt Publishing, Birmingham (2020)
9. Norouzzadeh, M.S., et al.: Automated animal identification using deep learning techniques. Proc. Nat. Acad. Sci. USA **115**(25), 5716–5725 (2018)

10. LeCun, Y., et al.: Backpropagation applied to handwritten zip code recognition. Neural Comput. **1**(4), 541–551 (1989)
11. Duporse, J., Isupova, O., Reece, S., Macdonald, D., Way, T.: Using very high-resolution satellite imagery and deep learning to detect and count African elephants in heterogeneous landscapes. Remote Sens. Ecol. Conserv. **7**(3), 369–381 (2021)
12. Kaggle: how our nets counted sea lions in the Aleutian Islands. https://habr.com/ru/company/ods/blog/337548/. Accessed 27 Dec 2021
13. iNaturalist Homepage. https://www.inaturalist.org/pages/seek_app. Accessed 27 Dec 2021
14. LeCun, Y., Haffner, P., Bottou, L., Bengio, Y.: Object recognition with gradient-based learning. In: Shape, Contour and Grouping in Computer Vision. LNCS, vol. 1681, pp. 319-345. Springer, Heidelberg. https://doi.org/10.1007/3-540-46805-6_19
15. He, K., Gkioxari, G., Dollar, P., Girshick, R.: Mask R-CNN. In: CVPR: Computer Vision and Pattern Recognition 2017 (2017)
16. Ganesh, P., Volle, K., Burks, T.F., Mehta, S.S.: Deep orange: mask R-CNN-based orange detection and segmentation. IFAC PapersOnLine **52**(30), 70–75 (2019)
17. Zhao, G., Hu, J., Xiao, W., Zou, J.: A mask R-CNN based method for inspecting cable brackets in aircraft. Chin. J. Aeronaut. **34**(12), 214–226 (2021). https://doi.org/10.1016/j.cja.2020.09.024
18. Lin, T.-Y., et al.: Microsoft COCO: common objects in context. In: Fleet, D., Pajdla, T., Schiele, B., Tuytelaars, T. (eds.) ECCV 2014. LNCS, vol. 8693, pp. 740–755. Springer, Cham (2014). https://doi.org/10.1007/978-3-319-10602-1_48
19. Patterson, G., Hays, J.: COCO attributes: attributes for people, animals, and objects. In: Leibe, B., Matas, J., Sebe, N., Welling, M. (eds.) ECCV 2016. LNCS, vol. 9910, pp. 85–100. Springer, Cham (2016). https://doi.org/10.1007/978-3-319-46466-4_6
20. Srivastava, S., Divekar, A.V., Anilkumar, C., Naik, I., Kulkarni, V., Pattabiraman, V.: Comparative analysis of deep learning image detection algorithms. J. Big Data **8**(1), 1–27 (2021). https://doi.org/10.1186/s40537-021-00434-w
21. Weiss, K., Khoshgoftaar, T.M., Wang, D.D.: A survey of transfer learning. J. Big Data **3**, Article 9 (2016)
22. Niknejad, N., Ismail, W., Ghani, I., Nazari, B., Bahari, M., Che Hussin, A.R.B.: Understanding service-oriented architecture (SOA): a systematic literature review and directions for further investigation. Inf. Syst. **91**, Article 101491 (2020)
23. Yang, L., Fan, Y., Xu, N.: Video instance segmentation. In: 2019 IEEE/CVF International Conference on Computer Vision (ICCV), pp. 5188–5197 (2019)

Retinal Image Analysis Approach for Diabetic Retinopathy Grading

Yuliya Golub[1] , Marina Lukashevich[2(✉)] ,
and Valery Starovoitov[1]

[1] Joint Institute of Informatics Problems, The National Academy
of Science of Belarus, Surganova Street, 6, Minsk, Belarus
[2] Belarusian State University of Informatics and Radioelectronics,
Platonova Street, 39, Minsk, Belarus
lukashevich@bsuir.by

Abstract. The eye is a complex organ that performs many functions. One of its components is the retina. One of the important properties of the retina is the reflection of the visible signs of a number of diseases. Diabetic retinopathy is the most common complication and the main cause of vision loss in diabetic patients. The retina also shows signs of other diseases that strongly affect visual impairment, such as cataracts, glaucoma, and macular degeneration. All of these diseases begin asymptomatically. Therefore, it is important to detect them at the very beginning of the disease and prescribe treatment. Advances in artificial intelligence (AI), especially in deep learning, are improving pathological image analysis in daily clinical practice. We have developed an approach for identifying and classifying diabetic retinopathy. It includes a universal method for segmentation of the retinal region for arbitrary fundus images and an assessment of the quality of the original image. Low quality images are excluded from further analysis.

Keywords: Diabetic retinopathy · Retina image analysis · Image preprocessing · Machine learning · Convolution Neural Network

1 Introduction

There are many different types of eye disease and they can affect people at all ages. The most common eye diseases are age-related conditions such as presbyopia and cataracts, but there are also many serious eye diseases such as glaucoma and macular degeneration. Some of the most common eye diseases are those affecting the retina. This means that doctors require a wide range of diagnostic tools to confirm a diagnosis, as well as to determine the severity of an eye disease. The fund's image analysis is used to detect different stages of the 3 main diabetes-based eye diseases, i.e. Diabetic Retinopathy, Diabetic Macular Edema, and Glaucoma. One of the most common is diabetic retinopathy.

In our research, we have considered Diabetic Retinopathy because it causes blindness (the most severe consequences). Also known as diabetic eye disease, diabetic retinopathy is a disorder of the retina that is seen in patients with diabetes. Diabetic

© Springer Nature Switzerland AG 2022
A. V. Tuzikov et al. (Eds.): PRIP 2021, CCIS 1562, pp. 152–165, 2022.
https://doi.org/10.1007/978-3-030-98883-8_11

retinopathy can develop at any stage of diabetes, but is most often seen in people who have had the disease for at least five years and have shown little improvement in their vision despite treatment. It is a leading cause of blindness. Diabetic retinopathy affects up to 80% of those who have had diabetes for 20 years or more. Diabetic retinopathy often has no early warning signs. Digital pathology nowadays plays an increasingly important role in basic, translational, and clinical pathology research and in routine clinical practice. Retinal (fundus) photography with manual interpretation has largely been replaced by digital image analysis, which is faster, cheaper, and more objective.

The clinical signs of DR include (3) multiple cotton wool spots (accumulations of axoplasmic debris within adjacent bundles of ganglion cell axons); (2) venous beading and/or looping; (1) microaneurysms (deep round and blot haemorrhages); (4) hard exudates (lipid deposits); and (5) intraretinal microvascular abnormalities (dilated preexisting capillaries), Fig. 1.

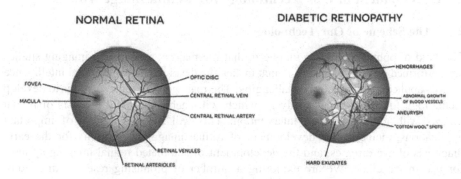

Fig. 1. The clinical signs of DR [1]

The application of Deep learning (DL) in general and Convolution Neural Networks (CNN) in pathology has been particularly useful for the examination of medical images. Today, digital image processing and machine learning are widely applied to the pathological image analysis, which provides significant support for medical research and clinical practice. Machine learning algorithms can be used for a variety of image analysis, including the detection of disease, the measurement of tissue characteristics, and the reconstruction of images. The application of AI in retina image analysis has been particularly useful [2, 3].

These previous studies demonstrated that CNN is effective in classifying DR images. In [4] reported that most of the studies, almost 70%, classified the fundus images using binary classifiers such as DR or non-DR, while only 27% classified the input to one or more stages, as shown in Fig. 2.

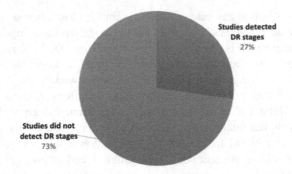

Fig. 2. The ratio of studies that classified the DR stages [4]

2 Development of Our Technology for Retina Image Analysis

2.1 The Scheme of Our Technology

The field of ophthalmology is unique in that the majority of medical imaging studies are performed on retinal images, which makes the development of artificial intelligence for this application particularly challenging. The main goal of our research is to develop technology for retina image analysis, which will enable the rapid analysis of retinal images with minimal human intervention. This will have a number of important applications, including the development of retinal imaging algorithms for the early diagnosis of eye diseases, and the development of automated retinal imaging systems for use in the clinic. We are exploring a number of promising research directions, including image quality analysis and deep learning.

The technology includes the next stages. *Collecting dataset of retina images* from public datasets. One of the goals of the project is to collect a dataset of retina images obtained in different conditions and using different equipment. Thanks to this it is possible to develop new technology, but not a new method or approach suitable for limited amount of images. *Quality image analysis.* This stage will allow to select images for the next stages of processing and decision making. It will increase the quality of decision making in the framework of retinal imaging. It will also improve the quality and the quantity of the results in the future stages of the pipeline. *Image preprocessing.* The main goal of image preprocessing is to improve the quality of images, so that they can be used for training and testing. The image preprocessing can be done using different methods. The purpose of preprocessing is not to alter the content of the image, but it is to enhance the images for better quality. Some pre-processing methods include image filtering, brightness correction, mask cropping, and circle (mask) cropping. *Machine learning model development* for decision making (image classification). At this stage the main direction for our future research is a neural network approach (deep learning). And the promising approach is using the convo-lution neural network. *Model evaluation* using different classic metrics. The vast majority of retina image dataset is unbalanced. It needs to find a suitable metric for unbalanced classes [5].

The scheme of our technology development for retina image analysis is presented on Fig. 3. We have marked those stages that were explored during the first preliminary stage of our project. Also the next stages and directions of scientific researches are presented in this scheme.

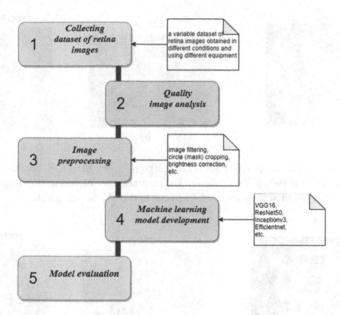

Fig. 3. The scheme of new technology development for retina image analysis

2.2 Quality Image Analysis

Poor quality images can reduce recognition accuracy. According to the Deep Mining division of Google, one in ten patients suffers from misinterpretation of medical information [6]. Also, automatic evaluation of digital image quality allows: saving the time spent by a human expert on visual assessment; saving storage space for data and time on the operation of automated systems.

The authors of this paper having summarized the results of their research propose the following algorithm for retinal image quality evaluation which consists of several successive stages performed for each analyzed image. The quality evaluation is performed for the central part of the image, since the FOV area can occupy from 44 to 99% of the image area.

The algorithm of retinal image quality evaluation consists of the next stages.

1. from a grayscale retinal image, cut out the central portion, stepping back ¼ of the height and width from the edge of the image: crop (Fig. 4 and 5).
2. scale the crop fragment to a size of 512 × 512 pixels (Fig. 4 and 5).
3. calculate local quality estimates for the square crop fragment and build a histogram of their distribution.

4. approximate histogram of local estimates by distributions of random variables and calculate parameters: mean (normal distribution parameter), scale and form (Weibull distribution parameters).

Fig. 4. Results for the image 20170413112017305.jpg from the DDR database [7]: a) the original image (2460 × 1904 px) with the marked central fragment; b) the crop fragment (953 × 1231 px); c) the result of scaling the crop fragment to the 512 × 512 px size

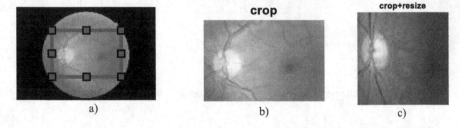

Fig. 5. Results for the image 10162_left.jpeg from the Kaggle database [8]: a) the original image (4752 × 3168 px) with the central crop fragment marked; b) the crop fragment (1585 × 2377 px); c) the result of scaling the crop fragment to the 512 × 512 px size

It is suggested to use the G (green) image channel for on-line analysis of the image quality, as it is the most contrasting one. The second step of the algorithm is necessary because the initial retinal images are formed by different cameras (for example, Topcon D7000, Topcon TRC NW48, Nikon D5200, etc.), so they differ greatly (for example, the DRR dataset images have sizes from 702 × 717 pc to 5184 × 3456 pc). In the third step of the algorithm 26 quality scores were used: ACMO, BEGH, BISH, BREN, CMO, CONT, CURV, EBCM, FFT, FISH, FUS, GORD, HELM, JNBM, KURT, LAPD, LAPL, LAPM, LOCC, LOEN, MLV2, PSIS, SHAR, SVDB, WAVS described in [9–11]. The parameters mean, scale, and form were tested as global image estimates.

In Tables 1 and 2 we have selected scores which allow to divide retinal images into two classes (satisfactory and unsatisfactory quality). Experiments have shown that it is difficult to select a single quality score for retinal images from different datasets.

Table 1. Quality thresholds for images from DRIMDB dataset

Measure	BREN	EBCM	FISH	LAPD	SHAR	WAVS
Parameter	scale	form	mean; scale	mean, scale	mean; scale	mean; scale
Threshold	0,92	0,35	0,79; 0,8	0,4; 0,88	0,35; 0,7	0,45; 0,55

Table 2. Quality thresholds for images from DDR dataset

Measure	BREN	EBCM	PSIS	SVDB
Parameter	scale	scale	mean; scale	form
Threshold	0,79	0,045	0,6; 0,67	0,4

2.3 Image Preprocessing

As we mentioned above retina images contain different types of noises and artefacts. That is why the first stage of the proposed method is image preprocessing. Improvement of the quality of input data can improve the performance of machine learning model. This stage includes reducing lighting-condition effects and cropping uninformative area. The registrations of digital retina images were conducted with many lighting conditions. Some images are very dark and difficult for visualization.

Image smoothing techniques help in reducing the noise. Using different image prospecting libraries, image smoothing (also called blurring) could be done in many ways. In this method, we have performed image smoothing using the Gaussian filter with sigma parameter equal 10. Gaussian filters have the properties of having no overshoot to a step function input while minimizing the rise and fall time. In terms of image processing, any sharp edges in images are smoothed while minimizing too much blur [12].

An approach to brightness preprocessing is also proposed. The technology proposes to perform image preprocessing using the CLAHE algorithm for the green channel or the L channel from the Lab color model. The Fig. 6 shows the entropy of the transformed images. Visually, the difference is insignificant, so you can use the standard set of CLAHE transformation parameters.

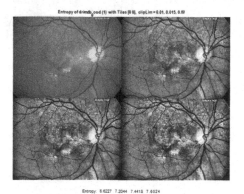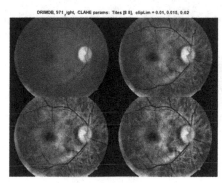

Fig. 6. Top-left are original G images, next after CLAHE. Entropy increases after the transformation

Cropping is a quite typical step for such kind of images. To solve our case, one method would be to look for rows and columns that have at least one pixel along rows and columns that is greater than some lower limit or threshold as a pixel value. So, if we are sure that the black areas are absolute zeros, we can set that fix threshold.

We have proposed new algorithm for retina image cropping based on the next steps. On the first stage we build a histogram for R image channel. Than calculate the leftmost peak (this is the background), calculate the average brightness for R channel, and between the peak and the average brightness look for min on the histogram. It indicates the threshold of binarization. The next step is binarization. The R image channels, the binarization results based on our algorithm and the results based on Otsu algorithm are presented in Figs. 7, 8, 9, 10, 11, 12 and 13.

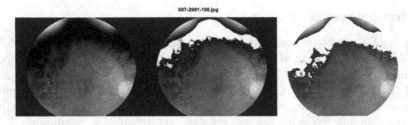

Fig. 7. The example #1. The R image channel (left), global thresholding by R(T < 2) = 255 (middle), global thresholding by R(T < 25) = 255 (right)

Fig. 8. The example #2. The R image channel, the binarization result based on our algorithm and the result based on Otsu algorithm

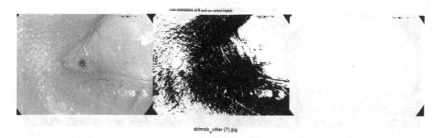

drimdb_utler (7).jpg

Fig. 9. The example #3. The R image channel, the binarization result based on our algorithm and the result based on Otsu algorithm

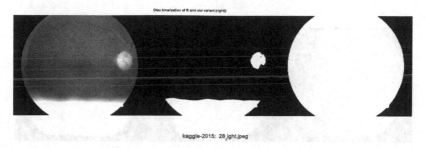

kaggle-2015: 28_ight.jpeg

Fig. 10. The example #4. The R image channel, the binarization result based on our algorithm and the result based on Otsu algorithm

kaggle-2019: 0a262e8b2a5a.png

Fig. 11. The example #5. The R image channel, the binarization result based on our algorithm and the result based on Otsu algorithm

The Fig. 14 shows the examples of R channels from HRF dataset and their binary masks constructed by Otsu's method (middle row) and the proposed algorithm (bottom row). The correlation of the bottom row masks is 0.999997, which confirms the individuality of all masks.

Fig. 12. The example #6. The R image channel, the binarization result based on our algorithm and the result based on Otsu algorithm

Fig. 13. The example #7. The R image channel, the binarization result based on our algorithm and the result based on Otsu algorithm

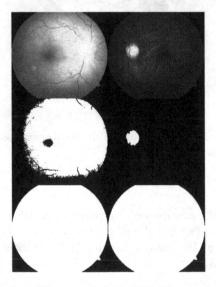

Fig. 14. The examples of R channels from HRF dataset and their binary masks

3   Experimental Environment

The goal of our research on this stage was to develop machine learning model for classifying samples from retina image dataset into 5 classes (0 – No DR, 1 – Mild, 2 – Moderate, 3 – Severe, 4 – Proliferative DR). There are two main approaches in image analysis and classification: traditional approach and deep learning approach. In the framework of traditional approach we perform feature extractions and decision making [13]. In deep leaning neural network extracts features and makes decision themselves. Deep neural networks consist of a large number of layers, have complex and difficult for interpretation. But it is a good variant for large datasets with variable samples. We have selected deep learning approach for this research, because it is promising direction for variable data.

We obtained images for training, validation and testing from a Kaggle competition [14]. It provides a large set of retina images, taken using funds photography under a variety of imaging conditions. A clinic has rated each image for the severity of diabetic retinopathy on a scale of 0 to 4 (0 – No DR, 1 – Mild, 2 – Moderate, 3 – Severe, 4 – Proliferative DR). Like any real-world data set, noise is presented in both the images and labels. Images may contain artifacts, be out of focus, underexposed, or overexposed. The images were gathered from multiple clinics using a variety of cameras over an extended period of time, which will introduce further variation. The examples of the images from this dataset are shown on Fig. 15.

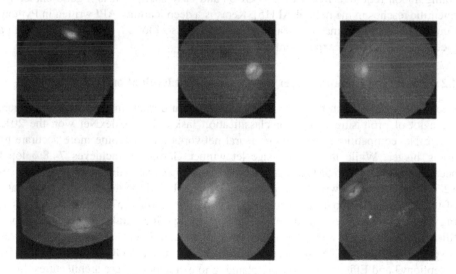

Fig. 15. Examples of the images from exanimated dataset

The dataset is highly imbalanced, with many samples for level 0, and very little for the rest of the levels. It was divided into two parts for training and testing machine learning model, Fig. 16.

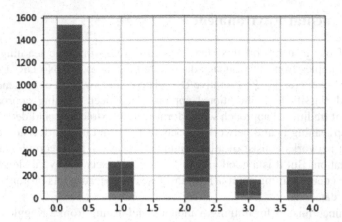

Fig. 16. The amount of samples from each classes (5 classes)

4 Methodology of Experiments

4.1 Experimental Details

Colaboratory from Google and Keras framework were used for experiments. Colaboratory, or "Colab" for short, allows to write and execute Python in browser, with zero configuration required, free access to GPUs and easy sharing. It is a good choice for scientific reaches in the field of AI [15]. Keras is a deep learning API written in Python, running on top of the machine learning platform TensorFlow. It was developed with a focus on enabling fast experimentation.

4.2 Machine Learning Model Development and Evaluation

Deep learning approach has become more popular in digital image processing. There are a lot of promising model for classification tasks. Since AlexNet won the 2012 Image Net competition, convolution neural networks have become more accurate by going bigger. While the 2014 ImageNet winner GoogleNet achieves 74.8% top-1 accuracy with about 6.8M parameters, the 2017 ImageNet winner SENet (achieves 82.7% top-1 accuracy with 145M parameters. Recently, GPipe further pushes the state-of-the-art ImageNet top-1 validation accuracy to 84.3% using 557M parameters: it is so big that it can only be trained with a specialized pipeline parallelism library by partitioning the network and spreading each part to a different accelerator. There are several state-of-art CNN models suitable for our task: VGG16 [16], ResNet50, Inceptionv3 and EfficientNet. We are planning to exam all of these architectures. In the framework of our preliminary stage we have built machine learning model using VGG16.

The ImageNet Large Scale Visual Recognition Challenge (ILSVRC) is an annual computer vision competition [17]. Each year, teams competed on two tasks. The first is to detect objects within an image coming from *200* classes (object localization). The second is to classify images, each labeled with one of *1000* categories (image classification). This model won the 1st and 2nd place on the above categories in 2014 ILSVRC challenge. This model achieves *92.7% top-5* test accuracy on ImageNet dataset which contains *14* million images belonging to 1000 classes. VGG-16 architecture map is presented on Fig. 17.

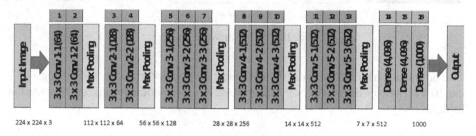

Fig. 17. VGG-16 architecture map

The input to the network is image of dimensions *(224, 224, 3)*. The first two layers have *64* channels of *3 * 3* filter size and same padding. Then after a max pool layer of stride *(2, 2)*, two layers which have convolution layers of 256 filter size and filter size *(3, 3)*. This followed by a max pooling layer of stride *(2, 2)* which is same as previous layer. Then there are *2* convolution layers of filter size *(3, 3)* and *256* filter. After that there are *2* sets of *3* convolution layer and a max pool layer. Each has *512* filters of *(3, 3)* size with same padding. This image is then passed to the stack of two convolution layers. In these convolution and max pooling layers, the filters use filters with the size *(3, 3)*. In some of the layers, it also uses *(1, 1)* pixel which is used to manipulate the number of input channels. There is a padding of *1-pixel* (same padding) done after each convolution layer to prevent the spatial feature of the image.

After the stack of convolution and max-pooling layer, there is a *(7, 7, 512)* feature map. We flatten this output to make it a *(1, 25088)* feature vector. After this there are *3 fully* connected layer, the first layer takes input from the last feature vector and outputs a *(1, 4096)* vector, second layer also outputs a vector of size *(1, 4096)* but the third layer output a *number of* classes. Then after the output of 3rd fully connected layer is passed to softmax layer in order to normalize the classification vector. All the hidden layers use ReLU as its activation function. ReLU is more computationally efficient because it results in faster learning and it also decreases the likelihood of vanishing gradient problem [18].

The pre-trained model was trained on ImageNet and not on medical images. In experiments all layers for image feature extraction are used. The decision making layers of pre-trained model were deleted. Batch normalization, flatten and dense layers were added in a new model, Fig. 18.

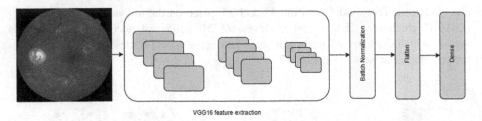

VGG16 feature extraction

Fig. 18. Neural network model

The initial image dataset was divided into two sets for training, and testing (70% and 30%). The validation set consists of 100 images. Numerical results are presented in Table 3.

Table 3. Type styles

Model	Pre-trained dataset	Precision	Recall
VGG16	ImageNet	0.9230	0.8763

5 Discussions

We have obtained preliminary acceptable results from the first phase of the study. It is obvious that the deep learning approach is a priority in computer vision in general and in our applied problem in particular. The neural network architecture used is not the best, but it allows you to get preliminary results and understand the range of problems. It is also necessary to carefully implement the stages of image preprocessing (noise reduction), since this may impair the classification results.

6 Conclusions

The method for retina image analysis has been developed, based on image preprocessing stage and deep neural network as machine learning model. This is the preliminary results of big projects for retina image analysis. The main focus was done for diabetic retina images. Also the scheme of new technology for retina image analysis was presented.

Acknowledgements. The study was supported in part by the Belarusian Republican Foundation for Fundamental Research under Grant F21PACG-001.

References

1. Diabetic Retinopathy Elmhurst. https://www.kovacheye.com/retina-elmhurst/diabetic-retinopathy/
2. Gulshan, V., et al.: Development and validation of a deep learning algorithm for detection of diabetic retinopathy in retinal fundus photographs. JAMA **316**(22), 2402 (2016). https://doi.org/10.1001/jama.2016.17216
3. Gargeya, R., Leng, T.: Automated identification of diabetic retinopathy using deep learning. Ophthalmology **124**(7), 962–969 (2017). https://doi.org/10.1016/j.ophtha.2017.02.008
4. Alyoubi, W.L., Shalash, W.M., Abulkhair, M.F.: Diabetic retinopathy detection through deep learning technique: a review. Inform. Med. Unlocked **20**, 1–11 (2020)
5. Starovoitov, V.V., Golub, Y.I.: New function for estimating imbalanced data classification results. Pattern Recogn. Image Anal. **30**(3), 295–302 (2020). https://doi.org/10.1134/S105466182003027X
6. DeepMind Technologies Limited. https://deepmind.com
7. Li, T., et al.: Diagnostic assessment of deep learning algorithms for diabetic retinopathy screening. Inf. Sci. **501**, 511–522 (2019). https://doi.org/10.1016/j.ins.2019.06.011
8. Kaggle EyePACS. https://paperswithcode.com/dataset/kaggle-eyepacs
9. Pertuz, S.: Analysis of focus measure operators for shape-from-focus. Pattern Recogn. **46**(5), 1415–1432 (2013)
10. Starovoitov, F.V., Starovoitov, V.V.: Parameters of the curve of local estimate distribution as image quality measures. Syst. Anal. Appl. Inf. Sci. **3**, 26–41 (2018)
11. Golub, Y.I., Starovoitov, F.V., Starovoitov, V.V.: Comparative analysis of no-reference measures for digital image sharpness assessment. Doklady BGUIR **7**(125), 113–120 (2019)
12. Shapiro, L.G., Stockman, G.C: Computer Vision. Prentice Hall, Hoboken (2001)
13. Haloi, M., Dandapat, S., Sinha, R.: A Gaussian scale space approach for exudates detection, classification and severity prediction. arXiv preprint arXiv:1505.00737 (2015)
14. Kaggle: APTOS 2019 Blindness Detection (Data) (2019). https://www.kaggle.com/c/aptos2019-blindness-detection
15. Welcome To Colaboratory - Google Research. https://research.google.com/colaboratory/
16. Simonyan, K., Zisserman, A.: Very deep convolutional networks for large-scale image recognition. arXiv preprint arXiv:1409.1556 (2014)
17. The ImageNet Large Scale Visual Recognition Challenge (ILSVRC). https://www.image-net.org/challenges/LSVRC/
18. Abien Fred Agarap: Deep Learning using Rectified Linear Units (ReLU). arXiv preprint arXiv:1803.08375 (2018)

Comparison of Deep Learning Preprocessing Algorithms of Nuclei Segmentation on Fluorescence Immunohistology Images of Cancer Cells

Silun Xu and Victor Skakun[✉]

Belarusian State University, Minsk, Belarus
skakun@bsu.by

Abstract. Immunohistology fluorescence image analysis is an important method for cancer diagnosis. With the widespread application of convolutional neural networks in computer vision, segmentation of images of cancer cells has become an important topic in medical image analysis. Although there are many publications describing the success in application of deep learning models for segmentation of different kind of histology images, the universal model and algorithm of its application is still not developed. Since the histological images of cancer cells are very different, it is usually difficult to get a training set of a large size consisting of images of desired similarity with the studied ones. The image preprocessing consisting in splitting input images in smaller parts and its normalization plays an important role in deep learning especially when the training set is of a limited size. In this study, we compared several approaches to create the training set of a sufficient size while having a very limited number of labeled whole slide immunohistology fluorescence images of cancer cells. In addition, we compared different normalization methods and evaluated their influence on histological image segmentation.

Keywords: CNN · Medical image analysis · Image preprocessing · Image segmentation · Nucleus of cancer cell · U-Net

1 Introduction

Immunohistology fluorescence image analysis is an important method for cancer diagnosis. Cancer tissue slice, stained with fluorescent agents accordingly to a certain protocol, is observed by the fluorescence confocal microscopy to obtain a three-channel digital color picture. Then the attempt to segment cells (also nuclei and cytoplasm) on these images is made for a subsequent quantitative and qualitative pathological analysis [1, 2]. The correct segmentation of these objects supports the correct diagnosis. The segmentation of objects like nucleus or cytoplasm on biomedical images is a pixelwise binary classification problem. The goal is to assign each pixel either to the class of pixels that forms the nuclei area or not. The artificial neural networks and especially convolutional neural networks (CNN) is the primary tool to solve the classification problem nowadays.

© Springer Nature Switzerland AG 2022
A. V. Tuzikov et al. (Eds.): PRIP 2021, CCIS 1562, pp. 166–177, 2022.
https://doi.org/10.1007/978-3-030-98883-8_12

Convolutional neural networks have gradually begun to be applied in the field of image analysis since they achieved a huge breakthrough in the field of handwritten font recognition [3]. The outstanding performance of CNN in the ImageNet competition shows that it has great potential in image analysis fields such as image feature extraction and image classification. At present, CNN has widely been applied also in medical image segmentation. The U-Net [4] architecture, specially developed to segment objects like cell nucleus on biomedical images, is widely used in medical image segmentation. The skip connections introduced in U-Net helps to merge the features of different scales that enhances its performance. For example, Neha Todewale successfully applied U-Net to perform segmentation of mammogram images [5]. Mobeen Rehman et al. tried segmentation of the brain tumor images using U-Net in their research [6]. Adnan Saood et al. realized COVID-19 lung CT image segmentation and comparative analysis also using U-Net [7]. Other CNN models, such as VGGNet [8], ResNet [9], FCN [10], Inception [11], all based on ideas of deep learning, were developed in the past ten years for image segmentation. Most of them has been successfully applied also in a field of biomedical image segmentation and classification [12].

As a step of image segmentation using neural networks, the data preprocessing has a significant impact on the segmentation results. The main purpose of image preprocessing is to eliminate irrelevant information and enhance the detectability of useful information (represented by the pixels or features in the CNN terms) to the greatest extent, thereby improving the accuracy of cell segmentation [13]. For biomedical images segmentation, preprocessing steps usually require cropping, splitting in smaller parts, regularization, intensity enhancement and normalizing to the range [0, 1] and so on [14]. Among them, due to the uneven distribution of cells in biological tissues, preprocessing steps such as the selection of cell nucleus regions also affects the ability to obtain correct segmentation results.

In the cancer pathology analysis, one usually works with samples of relatively small sizes. High diversity of cancer cases does not allow to get a large set of histological images of desired similarity. Another problem is a labeling of target objects on images. When the task is a segmentation of cells or nuclei on images, the person who does labeling must be an expert in both the cancer diagnosis and in the microscopy. Fortunately, each whole slide immunohistology image contains hundreds of cells (target objects for the segmentation). It opens the perspective for enhancing the training set by splitting the input images into a number of small images (patches). Simple splitting images into not overlapped patches, splitting with overlap (sliding), random extraction of patches are ways to enhance the training set [12].

To fulfil this task one question is naturally arising, what size of a patch is optimal for the segmentation of nuclei of cancer cells of a certain average size? Also, it is interesting to examine different strategies of the patch extraction in order to increase the size of the training set. One has to take into account that it is impossible to increase the size of the training set infinitively by a simple extraction more and more overlapped patches. Even in a case of using abundant data augmentation the segmentation will suffer from overfitting. In addition, it is interesting to know how the image preprocessing, like normalization and standardization, influences the segmentation results.

Therefore, the goal of this study is to find the most effective algorithm of preprocessing of immunohistology fluorescence images in the task of segmentation of nuclei of cancer cells. Although there are a number of more powerful extensions of U-Net like UNet++ [15], Two-Stage U-Net [16], MultiResUNet [17], UNET 3+ [18] and TransUNet [19] at the moment, we selected the original U-Net model for our study because having a relatively simple architecture it still shows very good performance.

2 Materials and Methods

In this study we are performing the segmentation of fluorescence images of the breast tumor tissue slices. The images where obtained using Nikon TE200 epi-fluorescent inverted microscope equipped with the Photometrics 300 series CCD camera at 10x magnification and stored in RGB color system. The size of the images is 2048 × 2048 pixels in each of the three channels, the resolution is 0.2 μm/pixel, or 5 μm [14].

The protein estrogen receptor was used as a cancer indicator [1, 20]. In contrast to healthy cells, a protein cytokeratin appears in the cytoplasm of cancer cells. This protein is labeled with cyanine dye Cy3 and registered in the green color channel of the image. To label all nuclei, the 4,6-diamidino-2-phenylindole dihydrochloride (DAPI) dye was used. Its fluorescence was recorded in the blue channel. The cyanine dye Cy5 (recorded in the red channel of the image) was used to label the estrogen receptor, which is located primarily in the nuclei of cancer cells. Accordingly, two dyes, Cy5 and Cy3, are markers of cancer cells. A few patches of size 256 × 256 pixels of the experimental images are shown on Fig. 1.

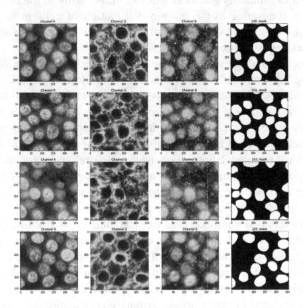

Fig. 1. Patches of immunohistology fluorescence images of a size 256 × 256 px. The red channel represents the cancer cell nucleus, the green channel represents the cytoplasm, and the blue channel show all nuclei, including healthy ones. Last column represents the ground truth.

For a better representation we separated the images into R, G, B color channels. The red channel represents the cancer cell nucleus, the green channel represents mostly the cytoplasm, and the blue channel show all nuclei, including healthy ones. Nine experimental images were labeled by experts initially semi automatically using CellProfiler (https://cellprofiler.org/) then manually. Labeled images (ground truth) are the binary images, where pixels of nucleus of cancer cells were set to 1, see the last column of images on Fig. 1.

The U-Net architecture, specially developed for a segmentation of biomedical images and showed good performance, was selected in our study. It is symmetrical neural net and has five sets of convolution/deconvolution layers, see Table 1 (in TensorFlow notation).

Table 1. Layer structure of U-Net

Encoder layers	Decoder layers
3 × 3 Conv + ELU, F = 16	2 × 2 ConvTranspose (S = 2), F = 128 (V)
Dropout = 0.1	3 × 3 Conv + ELU, F = 128
3 × 3 Conv + ELU, F = 16 (I)	Dropout = 0.2
MaxPool (S = 2)	3 × 3 Conv + ELU, F = 128
3 × 3 Conv + ELU, F = 32	2x2 ConvTranspose (S = 2), F = 64 (VI)
Dropout = 0.1	3 × 3 Conv + ELU, F = 64
3 × 3 Conv + ELU, F = 32 (II)	Dropout = 0.2
MaxPool (S = 2)	3 × 3 Conv + ELU, F = 64
3 × 3 Conv + ELU, F = 64	2 × 2 ConvTranspose (S = 2), F = 32 (VII)
Dropout = 0.2	3 × 3 Conv + ELU, F = 32
3 × 3 Conv + ELU, F = 64 (III)	Dropout = 0.2
MaxPool (S = 2)	3 × 3 Conv + ELU, F = 32
3 × 3 Conv + ELU, F = 128	2 × 2 ConvTranspose (S = 2), F = 16 (VIII)
Dropout = 0.2	3 × 3 Conv + ELU, F = 16
3 × 3 Conv + ELU, F = 128 (IV)	Dropout = 0.1
MaxPool (S = 2)	3 × 3 Conv + ELU, F = 16
Middle layers	1 × 1 Conv + Sigmoid, F = 1
3 × 3 Conv + ELU, F = 256	
Dropout = 0.3	
3 × 3 Conv + ELU, F = 256	

Abbreviations in the table: S – stride, F – number of filters. The following layers were concatenated (skip connections): (I)–(VIII), (II)–(VII), (III)–(VI), (IV)–(V).

Our realization of U-Net was based on the architecture that shown nice results in the 2018 Data Science Bowl Kaggle competition and available at GitHub (https://github.com/dubeyakshat07/Cell-Nuclei-Image-Segmentation-using-U-Net). The model has 1 941 105 learning parameters. We used binary cross entropy, see Eq. (1)

$$L = -\frac{1}{N}\sum\nolimits_{i=1}^{N} y_i \cdot \log(p(y_i)) + (1 - y_i) \cdot \log(1 - p(y_i)) \tag{1}$$

as the loss function, where y is the binary label 0 or 1, $p(y)$ is the probability that the output belongs to the y label y and N is a number of samples. Intersection over union (IOU, known also as Jaccard similarity coefficient, see Eq. (2))

$$IOU = \frac{|A \bigcap B|}{|A \bigcup B|} \tag{2}$$

calculated at the threshold 0.5, where A and B respectively correspond to the prediction result and to the ground truth, was used as the segmentation metric. The smaller the loss value, the better the learning effect. The larger the IOU metric – the better the segmentation (closer to the ground truth).

Taking into account the wide range and scalability of the application, we used a Python language environment to build the U-Net model, and selected the Jupyter Notebook to run and test the code. The main model components were implemented through the Keras library (TensorFlow kernel). Augmentation was performed using the Albumentations library (https://albumentations.ai/) and calculation of the loss function and the evaluation metric was done using the Segmentation models library (https://segmentation-models.readthedocs.io).

3   Results and Discussions

As we have only 9 labeled images (of size 2048 × 2048 px.) the main goal at deep learning is to increase a size of the training set. This can be done by splitting images into patches of smaller size. At the beginning we estimated the averaged nuclei size using a histogram of all masks found on the ground truth images. The average area of the cancer cell nuclei on our images is 1250 ± 800 pixels that corresponds approximately to the circle with radius of 20 px, see Fig. 2. In the Table 2 we summarized also the number of detected nuclei, the median and the first and third quartiles. It allows us to split the input images into a set of much smaller sizes – patches, thus defining a training set of optimal size.

The size of the patch is not trivial to guess because the segmentation results are obviously depended on how close to the ground truth is the predicted border of a nucleus. If we select small patch window the learning process will definitely suffer from the fact that probably most of nuclei will be located not in the center of the window, but over their borders. In opposite case we can get just rough estimation of the nuclei area. The answer to the question how many times an overlapped part of the image can be present in the training set is also not evident. The overfitting makes useless all our work otherwise.

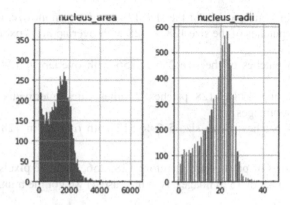

Fig. 2. Histogram of cancer cell nuclear area and radii in the annotated images. Left – histogram of cancer cell area, right – histogram of cancer cell radii.

Table 2. Descriptive statistics of cancer cell nuclear area and radii.

	Area of nucleus (px)	Radii of nucleus (px)
Count	7521	7521
Mean	1253.08	18.72
Std	740.10	6.97
25%	653.00	14.42
50%	1306.00	20.39
75%	1791.00	23.88

Therefore, to answer these questions we initially performed the segmentation of nuclei at different patch sizes and extraction strategies. At the second step we have studied several methods of preprocessing the patches such as image histogram equalization, standardization and normalization to the range [0, 1].

The U-Net model used in our study is described in details in the Materials and Methods section. We selected a simple augmentation including random 90-degree rotation, horizontal flipping and transposing. Although we utilized simple augmentation, it can effectively prevent overfitting. The intersection over union (at level 0.5) metric was set as a measure of accuracy of the segmentation. Seven images were used for training, one image for validation and one for testing. The same algorithm of preprocessing was applied to both training and validation images. The empty patches (the number of pixels less than 150) were removed from the training set. Number of epochs was set to 30. Earlier stopping callback with patience = 8 was used in the training process.

The first task is to obtain a sufficiently large training set and to avoid overfitting. We started with a patch size of 512 × 512 and decreased it to 64 × 64. The latter case gave much worse results, probably because the most nuclei crossed borders of patches, therefore we did not include it into the analysis. More specifically we studied the following cases:

1) simple splitting into patches of the size 128 × 128 without overlap;
2) splitting into patches of the size 128 × 128 with overlap in 64 px. (1/2 of the patch size);
3) splitting into patches of the size 256 × 256 with overlap in 128 px. (1/2 of the patch size);
4) random cropping 128 × 128 patches 8 times after intermediate splitting into 256 × 256 subimages;
5) splitting into patches of the size 512 × 512 with overlap in 128 px. (1/4 of the patch size).

The side lengths of patches are therefore 128, 256, and 512 pixels. At the case 1) we got the training set of 1576 images. A at the case 4) we got the training set of 12064 images.

The values of the loss function and the IOU metric on the test set are summarized in the Table 3. Other relevant information about the number of patches and the total number of pixels in the training set as well as the batch size, number of steps per epoch is also summarized there. The graphs of values of the loss function and IOU metric for 30 CNN epochs, obtained for both training and validation data, are shown in Fig. 3.

Table 3. Results of segmentation after different methods of patches creation

Parameters and metrics	Methods of patches creation				
	Case 1	Case 2	Case 3	Case 4	Case 5
Total number of patches	1576	5939	1508	12064	1177
Total number of pixels in all patches	25 821 184	97 304 576	98 828 288	197 656 576	308 543 488
Batch size	64	64	24	32	16
Steps per epoch	25	93	63	377	74
Loss function	0.222	0.188	0.156	0.156	0.157
IOU (th = 0.5)	0.786	0.830	0.837	0.837	0.839

In spite of the fact that in the case 5 we got the best metric value, we selected the case 4 with random extraction of patches of a size 128 × 128 to be the best. This conclusion came from the visual inspection of the segmentation results (data not shown). Here we use a simple but effective method to increase the size of the training set. In this case, patch overlap is useful, but when the number of overlapped regions reaches a certain level, then overfitting starts to occur. When the number of patches was the largest, we got the best results. In contrast, the maximum number of pixels was achieved in the case 5. One may come with a conclusion that if augmentation is performed then as larger the training set the better the result despite of the presence of overlapping areas of the images. To prove or reject this conclusion we did an experiment (data not shown) where we selected the case 2 but increased virtually twice (because of augmentation) the training set by selection of larger number of steps per epoch to get the same number of patches in the training process. We got slightly worse value of the IOU metric (= 0.834). Thus, the random extraction of patches is better.

We also tried the case with random extraction of four patches from 256 × 256 sub images. The result was worse than at the simplest case 1. Therefore, we proved that the random cropping is a powerful method but only when enough number of patches is extracted to obtain a complete coverage of the image. Also, we came to the conclusion that the patch of the size 128 × 128 px. is optimal for the segmentation of nuclei with the average radius of about 20 px.

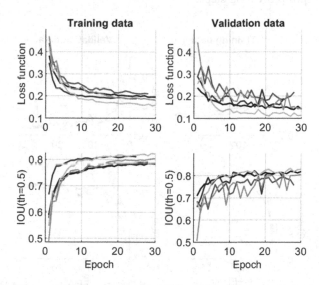

Fig. 3. Loss function and IOU metric for 30 CNN epochs, after cases 1–5 of patch extraction methods. Color coding: case 1 – red, case 2 – blue, case 3 – green, case 4 – black, case 5 – magenta. (Color figure online)

In the second step of our study, we picked out the case 4 of randomly selected patches with the side length of 128 pixels. The following methods of image normalization and standardization were studied: 1) raw data (without normalization); 2) normalization to the range [0, 1] where 1 corresponds to the maximum pixel intensity in the patch; 3) centering and scaling; 4) normalization to the range [0, 1] by initial patch histogram equalization followed by division to 255.

Surprisingly we obtained very similar results. The best method was the image histogram equalization (see Table 4 and Fig. 4).

The method of histogram equalization effectively increases the contrast of the cell nucleus, therefore supports its better segmentation. However, differences in the IOU metric are very small. Therefore, in our case, image normalization does not play a key role (see Table 4).

A few specific results of segmentation are shown in Fig. 5. From the images of the segmentation result, it can be seen that after using a variety of image sampling and normalization methods, the segmentation effect of the immunofluorescence image is also varying. The biggest problem in all cases is bad separation of touching or partially overlapped nuclei. The second problem is wrong prediction of nuclei on the patch boundary. All these suggest the necessity of the postprocessing step consisting in, for example, the watershed algorithm for separation of the overlapped masks and algorithm of correcting predictions on the borders. The result shown on top can be selected as the best one proving the accuracy of the chosen model and preprocessing algorithm. The result shown on bottom can be marked as the worst one indicating that the segmentation can be further improved by developing more sophisticated CNN models, preprocessing and postprocessing steps.

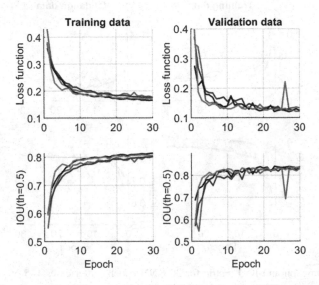

Fig. 4. Loss function and IOU metric for 30 CNN epochs after different methods of patch normalization. Color coding: case 1 – black, case 2 – red, case 3 – magenta, case 4 – blue. (Color figure online)

Table 4. Results of segmentation after different methods of patches normalization

Parameters and metrics	Methods of patches normalization			
	Case 1	Case 2	Case 3	Case 4
Batch size	32	32	32	32
Steps per epoch	377	377	377	377
Loss function	0.159	0.154	0.160	0.154
IOU (th = 0.5)	0.837	0.838	0.838	0.840

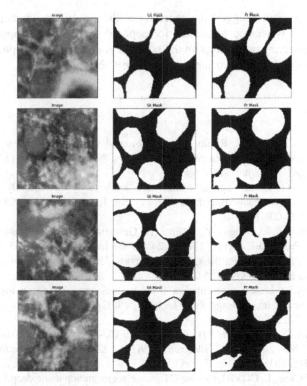

Fig. 5. Cancer cell nuclei segmentation results. Four sets of images are shown. Each set consist in the source image (patch) on the left, the ground truth in the middle and the predicted result (converted to the binary image at threshold 0.5) on the right.

4 Conclusion

The preprocessing of input images plays important role in the deep learning. Having only 9 whole slide labeled images of the size 2048 × 2048 pixels we were able to get satisfactory results in the segmentation of nuclei on the fluorescence images of the cancer cells of the breast tumor. We concluded that the random cropping is a powerful method for increasing the training set when the number of patches is high enough to obtain a complete coverage of the input image. The simple splitting of the image with overlap may be sufficient if the augmentation is used. Also, we came to the conclusion that the patch of the size 128 × 128 px. is optimal for the segmentation of nuclei with the average radius of about 20 px.

In our numerical tests the image normalization does not play a key role. Histogram equalization with subsequent normalization to the range [0, 1] demonstrated the best result. The method of histogram equalization effectively increases the contrast of the cell nucleus and thus supports the better segmentation.

Segmentation results suggest the necessity of the postprocessing step consisting in, for example, the watershed algorithm for separation of the overlapped masks and algorithm of correcting predictions on the borders. Another way to improve results is to select or develop more sophisticated model than U-Net.

References

1. Camp, R.L., Chung, G.G., Rimm, D.L.: Automated subcellular localization and quantification of protein expression in tissue microarrays. Nat. Med. **8**(11), 1323–1328 (2002). https://doi.org/10.1038/nm791
2. Ronneberger, O., et al.: Spatial quantitative analysis of fluorescently labeled nuclear structures: problems, methods, pitfalls. Chromosome Res. **16**(3), 523 (2008). https://doi.org/10.1007/s10577-008-1236-4
3. Lecun, Y., Bottou, L., Bengio, Y., Haffner, P.: Gradient-based learning applied to document recognition. Proc. IEEE **86**(11), 2278–2324 (1998). https://doi.org/10.1109/5.726791
4. Ronneberger, O., Fischer, P., Brox, T.: U-Net: convolutional networks for biomedical image segmentation (2015). arXiv:1505.04597
5. Todewale, N.S.: Lesion segmentation from mammogram images using a U-Net deep learning network. Int. J. Eng. Res. Technol. **V9**(02) (2020). http://dx.doi.org/10.17577/IJERTV9IS020213
6. Rehman, M.U., Cho, S., Kim, J.H., Chong, K.T.: BU-Net: brain tumor segmentation using modified U-Net architecture. Electronics **9**(12), 2203 (2020). https://doi.org/10.3390/electronics9122203
7. Saood, A., Hatem, I.: COVID-19 lung CT image segmentation using deep learning methods: U-Net versus SegNet. BMC Med. Imaging **21**(1), 19 (2021). https://doi.org/10.1186/s12880-020-00529-5
8. Simonyan, K., Zisserman, A.: Very deep convolutional networks for large-scale image recognition (2014). arXiv:1409.1556
9. He, K., Zhang, X., Ren, S., Sun, J.: Deep residual learning for image recognition (2015). arXiv:1512.03385
10. Long, J., Shelhamer, E., Darrell, T.: Fully convolutional networks for semantic segmentation (2014). arXiv:1411.4038
11. Szegedy, C., et al.: Going deeper with convolutions (2014). arXiv:1409.4842
12. Vu, Q.D., et al.: Methods for segmentation and classification of digital microscopy tissue images. Front. Bioeng. Biotechnol. **7** (2019). https://doi.org/10.3389/fbioe.2019.00053
13. Dakhare, S., Chowhan, H., Chandak, M.B.: Combined approach for image segmentation. Int. J. Comput. Trends Technol. **11**(3), 118–121 (2014). https://doi.org/10.14445/22312803/IJCTT-V11P125
14. Lisitsa, Y., et al.: Simulation model to study denoising methods. In: PRIP 2014, Collection, Minsk, pp. 157–160 (2014)
15. Zhou, Z., Siddiquee, M.M.R., Tajbakhsh, N., Liang, J.: UNet++: a nested U-Net architecture for medical image segmentation (2018). arXiv:1807.10165
16. Mahbod, A., Schaefer, G., Ellinger, I., Ecker, R., Smedby, Ö., Wang, C.: A two-stage U-net algorithm for segmentation of nuclei in H&E-stained tissues. In: ReyesAldasoro, C.C., Janowczyk, A., Veta, M., Bankhead, P., Sirinukunwattana, K. (eds.) ECDP 2019. LNCS, vol. 11435, pp. 75–82. Springer, Cham (2019). https://doi.org/10.1007/978-3-030-23937-4_9

17. Ibtehaz, N., Rahman, M.S.: MultiResUNet: rethinking the U-net architecture for multimodal biomedical image segmentation. Neural Netw. **121**, 74–87 (2020). https://doi.org/10.1016/j.neunet.2019.08.025
18. Huang, H., et al.: UNet 3+: a full-scale connected UNet for medical image segmentation (2020). arXiv:2004.08790
19. Chen, J., et al.: TransUNet: transformers make strong encoders for medical image segmentation (2021). arXiv:2102.04306
20. Chung, G.G., Zerkowski, M.P., Ghosh, S., Camp, R.L., Rimm, D.L.: Quantitative analysis of estrogen receptor heterogeneity in breast cancer. Lab. Invest. **87**(7), 662–669 (2007). https://doi.org/10.1038/labinvest.3700543

Simulation Modelling and Machine Learning Platform for Processing Fluorescence Spectroscopy Data

Mikalai M. Yatskou[✉] and Vladimir V. Apanasovich

Belarusian State University, 220030 Minsk, Belarus
yatskou@bsu.by

Abstract. A digital computational platform is proposed for processing fluorescence spectroscopy data, which implements complex analysis of experimental information based on the simulation modelling and machine learning algorithms. Data analysis includes partitioning biophysical data into clusters according to the degree of likeness in some measure of similarity, finding the median cluster members (medoids), applying a dimensionality reduction method and visualizing the experimental data in a two-dimensional space. Analysis of the medoids is carried out by analytical or simulation models of optical processes occurring in molecular systems. The visualization of data clusters in the original and transformed feature spaces is done with the aim of user interaction. As a demonstrative example, the platform FluorSimStudio is implemented for processing time-resolved fluorescence measurements (https://dsa-cm.shinyapps. io/FluorSimStudio). The digital platform is an open system and allows addition of complex analysis models, taking into account the development of new modelling and analysis algorithms.

Keywords: Fluorescence spectroscopy · Simulation modelling · Machine learning · Digital platform

1 Introduction

Experimental fluorescence spectroscopy methods are applied to study the optical properties of molecular compounds and are commonly used in the studies of artificial photonic materials, protein complexes, biopolymers, DNA sequencing, biological membranes, cell and tissues, medical diagnostics [1, 2]. The considerable development of methods is driven due to the improvements of effective molecular fluorophores, including genetically expressed proteins (for example, GFP), semiconductor nanoparticles and quantum dots, optical systems for laser excitation and registration of radiation, allowing high-precision measurements, computer technologies for data storage and processing [3, 4]. Novel experimental high-throughput techniques, integrating pulsed, phase and modulation methods for recording fluorescence decay times, form the basis of modern fluorescence microscopy and allow obtaining big data, characterized by high spectral, time and spatial resolution [4, 5]. The main fluorescence spectroscopy and microscopy techniques for studying complex molecular systems in "cuvettes" and living cells are fluorescence-lifetime imaging microscopy (FLIM),

© Springer Nature Switzerland AG 2022
A. V. Tuzikov et al. (Eds.): PRIP 2021, CCIS 1562, pp. 178–190, 2022.
https://doi.org/10.1007/978-3-030-98883-8_13

fluorescence recovery after photobleaching (FRAP) and its derivatives – fluorescence loss in photobleaching (FLIP) and fluorescence localization after photobleaching (FLAP), fluorescence fluctuation spectroscopy (FFS, combining fluorescence correlation spectroscopy (FCS), fluorescence cross-correlation spectroscopy (FCCS), photon counting histogram (PCH) and fluorescence intensity distribution analysis (FIDA)), fluorescence sensing (FS) [6, 7].

The existing data analysis approaches to processing fluorescence spectroscopy data can be divided into classical and modern, based on machine learning algorithms. Classical methods consider separate or joint analysis of datasets using deconvolution, least squares, maximum likelihood, Bayesian, target and global analysis to estimate the parameters of mathematical models of optical processes and systems [8]. New approaches are based on: i) projection transformations and following parameter estimation (for example – transformation of fluorescence intensities into the phasor space (phasor analysis), ii) using machine learning techniques, mainly artificial neural networks and ensemble algorithms, to estimate the model parameters, iii) segmentation of cell or tissue images and subsequent classification by a machine learning algorithm [8, 9]. The main disadvantages of existing data processing methods are limited or poor efficiency, that is due to the use of nonphysical analytical models (multi-exponential or polynomial decompositions), poor accuracy in parameter estimating when analyzing noisy data (phasor analysis, neural networks), slow computations (global and Bayesian analysis), the need for the large training datasets (neural networks), special requirements for computing resources (the usage of video cards or multiprocessor nodes to accelerate neural network computing), and finally the lack of specialized software for automated data processing. Therefore, the primary task is to develop an integrated data analysis approach and computational platform that eliminates the main drawbacks of existing methods, which would include physical models of the processes and systems under study, effective methods and software for processing a series of fluorescence spectroscopy data.

A computational approach for processing large sets of time-resolved fluorescence data using simulation modelling and data mining algorithms was developed [10, 11]. By this methodology it is possible to increase the accuracy of the estimated parameters of biophysical and optical processes occurring in the studied molecular systems. Specialized and general-purpose software tools and products, both commercial and freely available, have been developed for statistical processing, analysis and simulation of fluorescence spectroscopy data. However, there are no unified integrated software tools for processing large datasets using simulation modelling and machine learning methods. The development of a digital software platform for simulation and machine learning analysis of fluorescence data in various biophysical systems under experimental studies is a critically important and urgent task.

In this paper, we propose the conception of a digital software platform for the simulation modelling and machine learning analysis of optical processes in molecular systems studied by the fluorescence spectroscopy methods. As a demonstrative example, developed integrated methodology is implemented into the computational platform FluorSimStudio for processing fluorescence kinetic curves obtained through FLIM experiments.

2 Methodology

The section describes an integrated approach for processing large sets of fluorescence data using simulation modelling and machine learning algorithms, presents a review of the computational tools for constructing a digital platform, and introduces a conception of the simulation modelling and machine learning platform for processing fluorescence spectroscopy data.

2.1 Processing Fluorescence Data Using Simulation Modelling and Machine Learning Algorithms

The idea of an integrated approach is to study the object of research using simulation modelling of biophysical processes occurring in the object of investigation; comparison of simulated and the most informative experimental data, selected by the dimensionality reduction methods; determination of parameters of physical processes using optimization algorithms.

It is assumed that through a series of experiments generating big datasets some object, that is biophysical process or biomolecular compound, is investigated, whose essential properties or characteristics, for example, a set of biophysical parameters A, must be determined during data analysis. The registered object properties are known as features, attributes, or variables and can be of two types. The first ones, denoted X, are independent measurements, including external influences (this can also include time as a signal), set by the experiment designer or researcher. The second ones, denoted Y, are measurements depending on the selected values of the characteristics of the first group. Independent measurements X are usually called features (or inputs, predictors, independent variables), and dependent Y – target variables (or outputs, responses, dependent variables) that determine solutions to data analysis problems. As a result of measuring the properties of observations, a dataset (X, Y) is recorded that combines independent and dependent variables of observations. The data structure of an object is considered in terms of selected attributes X and dependent variables Y.

The scheme for studying a biophysical object using the integrated approach is shown in Fig. 1. The study of the object (block 1) is carried out by considering the physical model of the object (block 2) and a series of Q real and simulated experiments that form a global experiment (block 3). In block 5, the data of individual experiments are converted to a single format in order to reduce and eliminate inhomogeneities of various distortions associated with specific experiments. Filtering, normalization, vectorization, or special data transformations, such as logarithmic, are performed to reduce the effect of outliers. Sets of transformed data from various experiments are collected into a combined dataset (X, Y) for subsequent processing using machine learning and simulation modelling methods (block 9). The parameters of individual experiments $\alpha_1, \ldots, \alpha_Q$ and the model of object A are collected into a single set A and then refined during the analysis of the combined data. The analysis of individual experiments can be carried out independently or in a complex manner. The advantage of integrated analysis is the combination of data from various experiments into one large set, which provides a generalization and an increase in the statistical power of the results and, as a consequence, an increase in the accuracy of the analysis.

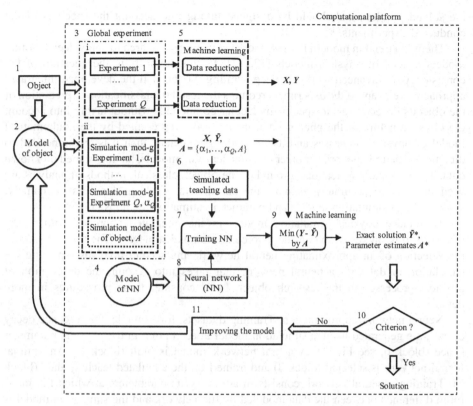

Fig. 1. Flow-chart of the fluorescence data analysis using simulation modelling and machine learning.

Some parameters A are fixed (they are global for the experiments), limited (in the case of dependent experiments), or remain free for accurate estimation using optimization methods. Data are compressed by the dimensionality reduction methods in order to exclude uninformative, redundant data or noise, and essential informative data are extracted. Optimization methods are used to evaluate free or adjustable parameters A^* of the global simulation model of the object, built on the basis of models of individual experiments (block 9). If the desired accuracy of the correspondence between the experimental and simulated data is achieved, which is determined by the given statistical criterion in block 10, then the analysis process is completed and a solution is provided (an estimated set of parameters and an accurate mathematical model of the object capable of predicting its behavior in the pre-cases of a desirable accuracy). Otherwise, in block 11, the description of the object is improved (including the deepening of the object formalization; collection of new data; changing models; conducting additional experiments; changing the parameters of the object or environment) and move to block 2 to perform the next iteration of data analysis. The presented scheme is a general approach, the specific implementation is determined by the type of the solved problem and should be designed taking into account the specifics of the conducted experiments.

There is a trend in modern fluorescence spectroscopy research to apply deep learning models instead of physical models [12, 13]. In this connection, the question of the consistency of advanced works on deep learning models and the developed integrated approach is relevant. If the experiment requires the result of classification or prediction of the object's observations to specific molecular compounds without taking into account the physical nature of the phenomenon under study, represented by the mathematical model of physical processes and its estimated parameters, then it is recommended to directly use neural networks or other machine learning models, having trained on known data. To study the physical background of the object, classical methods of analysis are used in order to accurately estimate the parameters of physical processes, namely, analytical and simulation models and parameter estimation methods [14].

To replace physical simulation models in the integrated approach with neural networks, it is suggested to consider two computational strategies. The first is based on the selection of an approximating neural network, the second involves replacing the simulation model with a neural network that takes into account the description of physical processes in the research object. Let's consider these procedures in more detail.

Neural network approximation. Training datasets, for example, fluorescence decay curves, are generated using a simulation model at each point in the physical parameter space (block 6, see Fig. 1). A neural network model is built (block 4). An optimal neural network is selected (block 8) and trained on the simulated teaching data (block 7). Training a neural network consists in adjusting its parameters at which the minimum difference between the data modeled by the network and the simulation model is achieved. The trained net at the input receives the fluorescence decay curve, and at the output gives out a set of estimated physical parameters and the corresponding fluorescence decay curve [15]. Here, the neural network is an analytical transformation that connects a point in the physical parameter space with the observed fluorescence decay curve. The computational convenience of this approach is that it is enough to apply a ready-made neural network from existing open libraries, such as Theano, TensorFlow, Keras, PyTorch, and to embed it into the platform of the integrated approach. The disadvantage is significant computational resources at the stages of generating simulated training datasets and training networks.

Physical model of a neural network. The idea is to develop a model of physical processes in the form of a neural network. A neural network can be considered as a solution of an equation or a system of equations on a computation graph, which is based on the decomposition of a complex function into a composition of simpler ones and more efficient computation of derivatives with respect to variables of those simple functions [16]. So the well-known libraries Theano and TensorFlow are designed for automatic differentiation on graphs, which is also known as training neural networks. Physical mathematical models are generally systems of equations or schemes for simulation modelling of physical processes. The simulation models of the integrated approach are based on the intuitive principles of drawing up a modelling scheme from the simplest blocks described by some probability distribution functions, the parameters of which are estimated during the analysis. Interactions of random variables with known distribution densities are simulated, which describe the component blocks of physical processes, constructed by the researcher in the modelling scheme. Analytical expressions of the distribution density functions implemented in the simulation model can be converted to a computation graph, to which a neural network is constructed. Thus the simulation scheme can be represented in the form of a graph and the optimal neural network can be designed. In this case, the integrated approach scheme includes a "physical" neural network (see Fig. 2, blocks 4, 6, 7).

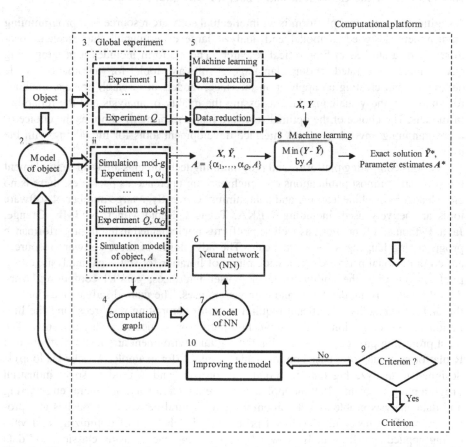

Fig. 2. Flow-chart of the fluorescence data analysis using the integrated approach with "physical" neural networks.

It should be noted that if the researcher deepens the consideration of physical processes and descends to the terminal level and the resulting element is replaced by a model of so-called black box, that is, its functioning is described by some mathematical relationship, then an alternative appears to using a "physical" neural network or a simulation model. If a neural network is more advantageous by some criteria, then it is used.

In the integrated approach, various methods and algorithms should be tried, moving from simple models to complex ones, performing a gradual complication of the models and increasing the circumstantiation of the process under consideration. When working with big data, it is necessary to choose an adequate level of refrainment of the mathematical model, corresponding to the desired depth of the object investigation, the volume of datasets and the power of the available computing resources.

2.2   Review of the Computational Tools for a Digital Platform

A digital computational platform is an intellectual software resource or a programming environment designed to model and analyze large experimental fluorescence spectroscopy data studied in biophysical research. The platform includes a programming environment, integrated coding languages, software tools for automation, code debugging and creating an application interface, models of research objects, methods for analyzing and visualizing data, assessing the quality of analysis and the reliability of models. The choice of the optimal software platform primarily implies the choice of a programming environment and interface development tools for interacting with the user.

Various computing platforms and programming technologies are used to implement the software. In most publications on benchmarking open access packages, there is no clear leader in machine learning and data mining. Currently, a large number of software tools are actively used, including WEKA, Tanagra, Rapid Miner, KNIME, Orange, Java, Python and R projects, as well as platforms implemented using high-performance programming languages C++ and Scala. The advantages of these software resources are computational performance, a wide range of libraries for statistical analysis, cross-platform integrity, the ability to develop user interfaces, parallel computing, work directly with existing databases and data warehouses. The main disadvantages include the lack of versatility, significant requirements for computing resources, and the limitation of the integration of the above fascinating properties in a single format. The most promising projects for organizing the digital environment are Scala-, Python- and R-platforms. A platform based on the Scala language (for example, Apache Hadoop) is designed to analyze big data in production projects and is used to solve industrial programming problems. Python applications are aimed at solving general engineering and data analysis problems with an emphasis on neural network approaches and programming. R-projects are developed primarily with the aim of optimizing and validating applied statistical analysis, which includes approaches using classical and data mining methods. Let take a closer look at the R environment.

The main advantages of the statistical programming environment R are the presence of optimized structures for representing data objects, which greatly simplifies data processing, optimization of programming tools and implementation of computation algorithms (in the sense of minimizing the introduction of errors into the program code), the ability to use a huge set of processing algorithms, statistical and data mining, various computing resources of the scientific community [17]. The main drawback is the low computational performance in the basic version of the environment layout, which is especially critical when working with large datasets and developing simulation models. This limitation can be partially or completely eliminated by connecting program codes of high-performance programming languages Scala, Java, C++ (packages rscala, rjava, Rcpp, inline), parallel computing procedures (managed by packages parallel, Rmpi, snow, snowfall), additional packages for efficient processing big data (readr, LaF, data.table, ff, bigmemory) and the use of third-party software resources (Microsoft R Open and Intel Math Kernel Library libraries, H2O big data analysis platforms, Apache Hadoop and Spark systems, with using h20, Rhadoop and SparkR packages).

An important issue is the development of the interface of a software application. The most popular R-code integrating user interface development packages are gWidgets, rpanel, svDialogs, RGtk2, qtbase, tcltk. A new direction in the development of R-applications for the analysis of biophysical systems [18] is associated with the creation of "reactive" web interfaces using the Shiny package and the subsequent placement of the software implementation on the shinyapps.io resource provided by the open source software developers RStudio. The advantage of this approach is the ability to remotely work with a web application for a wide scientific audience of users online via the global Internet. To implement the software application, the R computing environment and the Shiny package were chosen to create a web interface for the developed application.

The computing platform is organized according to the example of open projects of network resources CRAN (https://cran.r-project.org), R-Forge (https://r-forge.r-project.org), Bioconductor (https://www.bioconductor.org), Github (https://github.com). It is a programming and simulation environment that contains updated and supplemented libraries of analytical and simulation models of optical processes in molecular systems, built-in tools for machine learning methods and assessment of the quality of analysis and modelling, provides the scientific community with opportunities to develop new algorithms and simulation models.

2.3 Conception of the Digital Platform

The digital platform can integrate the research scheme for a certain biophysical process or molecular compound using a complex approach based on simulation modelling and machine learning methods. A schematic diagram of the methodology for spectral or/and time-resolved fluorescence spectroscopy data analysis of the platform is shown in Fig. 3. Consider the main stages of data analysis.

The platform is designed to analyze experimental or simulated data. Data loading and graphical presentation is carried out in block 1. Visual assessment of two-dimensional and three-dimensional fluorescence datasets allows predetermining the choice of a mathematical model for describing the physical processes, making a supposition regarding the number of data clusters, and limiting the choice of measures for calculating the similarity of samples based on the noise level of the data.

Modelling and visualization of fluorescence data are carried out in block 2. Integrated models of optical processes are considered. Simulation modelling is carried out using Monte Carlo algorithms [14]. The input characteristics of the simulation are the type and parameters of the model, the number of samples and the number of simulations. 2D or 3D visualization are intended for expert analysis of modeled data, study of the behavior of models when changing their parameters, manual selection of the most optimal modelling parameters, such as the number of simulations and data points, as well as initial approximations of parameters for subsequent precise determination during fitting using mathematical models. New and improved models of optical-physical processes in molecular systems can be developed and integrated into the software environment.

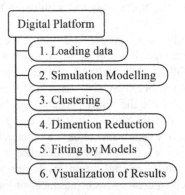

Fig. 3. Main stages of the fluorescence data analysis of a digital platform using simulation modelling and machine learning.

In block 3, cluster analysis of fluorescence data is performed in the space of experimentally detected features. Clusters of data are identified according to some degree of similarity (Euclidean, Minkowski, Manhattan, maximum or Canberra distance). The number of clusters is determined intuitively, automatically from the hierarchy dendrogram of data constructed on the basis of the cluster binding measure (Ward, single, complete, or average), or on the basis of a statistical criterion [19]. The median representatives of the clusters are calculated – medoids, samples or data objects having the smallest average distances to the rest of the objects of the corresponding clusters.

A data reduction is carried out in block 4. The consideration of a large group of uninformative experimentally detected features leads to difficulties in data analysis, namely, to their noise, an increase in the amount of data, and distortion of reliable information about clusters of similar samples. To improve the quality of data analysis, in particular, the visual assessment of data partitioning into clusters, it is expedient to carry out the stage of data analysis, which includes the transition to a low-dimensional space of new informative features, in which the fluorescence data form clusters. To perform this transformation, it is required to use data dimensionality reduction algorithms, among which the method of principal component analysis is the most widely known [20]. Conversion of fluorescence data using principal component analysis is performed. The proportion of relative variation attributed to principal components is set, limiting the number of components. Principal components are selected that correspond to a given variation in the data (for example, 0.95 out of 1). A diagram of the proportions of variation of the first ten principal components is constructed, according to which the contribution to the total variance in the data is estimated. Clusters and their medoids are displayed in the scatter diagram of the first two principal components.

Medoids are calculated in the space of initial features or in the space of the main components that explain a given value of variability. For example, if the data clusters are not separated, then it can be assumed that there is only one kind of fluorescent compounds. Otherwise, the presence of several forms of compounds (fluorophores) is allowed. For the convenience of visual control of cluster separability, histograms of frequencies are plotted on the axis of the first three principal components. Good separability of clusters is characterized by the presence of a multimodal form of histogram distributions.

In block 5, cluster medoids are analyzed to accurately determine the parameters of fluorescent compounds using an optimization algorithm and mathematical models. To approximate the fluorescence data, represented by the found medoids, analytical and simulation models for describing photophysical processes are used. Optimization methods are applied for the optimal selection of the parameters of mathematical models during the approximation of experimental data. In this work, the Nelder–Mead method [21] is chosen, which does not take into account the derivative of the objective function, which greatly simplifies the use of simulation models in the parameter estimation procedure. The best approximation is chosen according to a criterion (or a set of criteria) that determines the degree of deviation of the theoretical model from the experimental data. As a rule, such a criterion is presented analytically in the form of a function of experimental and theoretical data, the form of which is determined by the field of application, the direct modelling method and the conditions of the experiment. In our experiments, we consider the normalized chi-square criterion, diagrams of weighted residuals and their autocorrelation function [22, 23].

The visualization of the results and the analysis of graphical images of the estimated data clusters are carried out with the aim of interpreting, explaining, improving the understanding of the research object and its behavior (block 6). Reduced data are plotted in the three principal component space, the original feature space, and the principal component coordinates that explain the given fraction of the variation in the data. The presentation of a diagram of three main components, interactive for user, allows to visually assess the proximity of the found clusters and their shapes, the location of individual data points, the influence of experimental effects. Diagrams of a set of informative components enable to determine data clusters for a possible assessment of the parameters of models in the space of the main components. The latter helps to improve the accuracy of parameter estimation by reducing noise in the data due to the elimination of uninformative components describing the experimental noise. The procedure for estimating the parameters of models in the space of principal components can be additionally implemented in the platform. An interactive domain data cluster diagram lets to qualitatively explore groups of processed data.

3 Results

For the practical implementation of the digital platform conception integrating simulation modelling and machine learning algorithms the computational platform FluorSimStudio is developed for processing fluorescence kinetic curves in FLIM experiments. It is launched on an R server hosted on a network resource, such as shinyapps.io. To implement simulation models, it is proposed to use the C++ programming language. The choice and development of algorithms for data analysis is carried out by direct programming or by connecting ready-made machine learning packages provided by the scientific community of developers through open projects CRAN, Bioconductor, Github. The user's work is carried out through a web application. In the structure of the computational approach, the platform integrates the implementation of simulation models, analysis algorithms, provides computational tools for applying the developed simulation models and methods to the analysis of datasets, instruments for assessing its quality, visualizing and interpreting data.

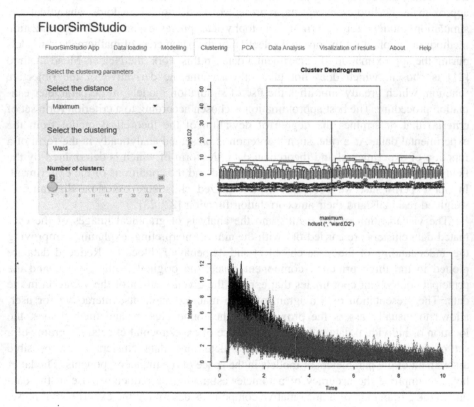

Fig. 4. FluorSimStudio web application interface window. Example of clustering fluorescence decay curves.

The programming implementation of the platform FluorSimStudio is organized using the Shiny R package and contains a set of functions that integrate the methodology for an integrated approach to data analysis. The web application is hosted at https://dsa-cm.shinyapps.io/FluorSimStudio. An example of the interface window is shown in Fig. 4. The main interface window consists of nine panels corresponding to six stages of analysis: loading, modelling and clustering data, reducing data dimensionality by the principal component analysis (PCA), fitting medoids (data analysis), visualizing and interpreting the results, information about the authors of the development, and instructions for using the computational resource.

The performance of the computational platform FluorSimStudio was tested by examples of the analysis of datasets representing systems of free fluorophores and in the presence of the Förster electronic excitation energy transfer process [1]. The obtained results are in good agreement with those previously published for analytical models of single- and stretch-exponential fluorescence decay laws [10]. Comprehensive analysis using simulation models and machine learning lets successfully to restore the parameters of optical processes from the experimental data.

4 Conclusions

The conception of a digital platform for processing fluorescence spectroscopy data has been developed, which is an implementation of an integrated approach for the complex machine learning analysis and modelling of optical processes in biophysical systems. Integrated data analysis pipeline comprises partitioning data into clusters, finding the cluster medoids, applying the dimensionality reduction method and visualizing the experimental data in a two-dimensional space, analyzing the medoids with analytical or simulation models. By this data analysis approach, it is possible to enhance the efficiency of the biophysical research. The digital platform is a programming environment designed to model and analyze large experimental fluorescence spectroscopy data. It includes a development framework, coding languages, tools for automation, code debugging and creating an application interface, models and methods for processing and visualizing data, assessing the quality of analysis. The R computing environment and the Shiny package are selected to create a web interface and online version for the developed software application. The C++ programming language is used for accelerating simulation modelling algorithms. The proposed methodology of the digital platform is realized in the computational platform FluorSimStudio, intended for processing fluorescence decay curves in molecular systems. FluorSimStudio provides high productivity of processing large fluorescence datasets, is hosted on the server and can be used in the educational process and for the study of experimental systems. Computational efficiency of the digital platform can be increased by connecting software tools for high performance big data computing (for example, H2O, Apache Hadoop, Spark resources).

References

1. Lakowicz, J.R.: Principles of Fluorescence Spectroscopy, 3rd edn. Springer, New York (2006). https://doi.org/10.1007/978-0-387-46312-4
2. Verveer, P.J. (ed.): Advanced Fluorescence Microscopy: Methods and Protocols. Springer, New York (2015)
3. Weinacht, T., Pearson, B.J.: Time-Resolved Spectroscopy: An Experimental Perspective. CRC Press, Boca Raton (2019)

4. Gryczynski, Z., Gryczynski, I.: Practical Fluorescence Spectroscopy. CRC Press, Boca Raton (2019)
5. Cox, G. (ed.): Fundamentals of Fluorescence Imaging. Jenny Stanford Publishing, Singapore (2019)
6. Jameson, D.M.: Introduction to Fluorescence. CRC Press, Boca Raton (2014)
7. Demchenko, A.P.: Introduction to Fluorescence Sensing: Volume 1: Materials and Devices, 3rd edn. Springer, Cham (2020). https://doi.org/10.1007/978-3-319-20780-3
8. Datta, R.T., Heaster, M., Sharick, J.T., Gillette, A.A., Skala, M.C.: Fluorescence lifetime imaging microscopy: fundamentals and advances in instrumentation, analysis, and applications. J. Biomed. Opt. 25(7), 1–43 (2020)
9. Datta, R., Gillette, A., Stefely, M., Skala, M.C.: Recent innovations in fluorescence lifetime imaging microscopy for biology and medicine. J. Biomed. Opt. 26(7), 1–11 (2021)
10. Yatskou, M.M., Skakun, V.V., Apanasovich, V.V.: Method for processing fluorescence decay kinetic curves using data mining algorithms. J. Appl. Spectr. 87(2), 333–344 (2020)
11. Yatskou, M.M., Skakun, V.V., Nederveen-Schippers, L., Kortholt, A., Apanasovich, V.V.: Complex analysis of fluorescence intensity fluctuations of molecular compounds. J. Appl. Spectr. 87(4), 685–692 (2020)
12. Smith, J.T., et al.: Fast fit-free analysis of fluorescence lifetime imaging via deep learning. Proc. Natl. Acad. Sci. USA 116(48), 24019–24030 (2019)
13. Ochoa, M., Rudkouskaya, A., Yao, R., Yan, P., Barroso, M., Intes, X.: High compression deep learning based single-pixel hyperspectral macroscopic fluorescence lifetime imaging in vivo. Biomed. Opt. Express. 11(10), 5401–5424 (2020)
14. Yatskou, M.M.: Computer simulation of energy relaxation and transport in organized porphyrin systems. Wageningen University, Wageningen, The Netherlands (2001)
15. Nazarov, P.V., Apanasovich, V.V., Lutkovski, V.M., Yatskou, M.M., Koehorst, R.B.M., Hemminga, M.A.: Artificial neural network modification of simulation-based fitting: application to a protein-lipid system. J. Chem. Inf. Comput. Sci. 44(2), 568–574 (2004)
16. Nikolenko, S., Kadurin, A., Arkhangelskaya, E.: Deep Learning: Immersion in the World of Neural Networks. Piter, Saint-Petersburg (2018)
17. Gentleman, R., et al.: Bioconductor: open software development for computational biology and bioinformatics. Genome Biol. 5(10), R80 (2004)
18. Yuan, V., Hui, D., Yin, Y., Peñaherrera, M.S., Beristain, A.G., Robinson, W.P.: Cell-specific characterization of the placental methylome. BMC Genomics 22(1), 6 (2021)
19. Shimodaira, H.: Approximately unbiased tests of regions using multistep-multiscale bootstrap resampling. Ann. Stat. 32(6), 2616–2641 (2004)
20. Jolliffe, T.: Principal Component Analysis. Springer, New York (2002). https://doi.org/10.1007/b98835
21. Nelder, J.A., Mead, R.: A simplex method for function minimization. Comput. J. 8(1), 308–313 (1965)
22. O'Connor, D.V., Phillips, D.: Time-Correlated Single Photon Counting. Academic Press, London (1984)
23. Demas, J.N.: Excited State Lifetime Measurements. Academic Press, London (2012)

A Bottom-Up Method for Pose Detection of Multiple People on Real-Time Video

Aliaksandr Leunikau[1], Alexander Nedzved[2]([✉]),
Alexei Belotserkovsky[3], and Stanislav Sholtanyuk[4]

[1] Minsk, Belarus
[2] Faculty of Applied Mathematics and Computer Science,
Belarusian State University, Minsk, Belarus
nedzveda@tut.by
[3] Department of Intelligent Information Systems, United Institute of Informatics
Problems of NAS Belarus, Minsk, Belarus
[4] Belarusian State University, Minsk, Republic of Belarus

Abstract. This article describes a realtime algorithm to determine a person's posture at a certain point in time.

Keywords: Human's pose recognition · Virtual human skeleton · Object movement analysis · Neural networks · Image recognition

1 Introduction

The pace of development of technology and robotics in the modern world is striding far into the future, but there are still many unsolved problems assigned exclusively to humans. Isolation of familiar faces from the environment, determination of the character and state of a person by non-verbal gestures and facial expressions, determination of emotions, type of activity, and occupation. All of these tasks are considered purely human. But thanks to the non-linear advances in technology, computer vision, machine learning, and artificial intelligence, robotics and almost any electronic device equipped with sufficient resources can learn how to solve these problems.

This research is aimed at solving creative, inherent only to humans, problems. Specifically, tasks related to pattern recognition and object positioning in space.

This topic is relevant for many areas of human life, from mass media systems to medicine and security. The algorithm can be used to analyze gestures in sign language translation, analyze people's behavior by security cameras, overlay animations in the film and game industries.

The purpose of this work is to create a new algorithm for analyzing people positioning in space and capable of increasing the efficiency of solving image recognition problems.

© Springer Nature Switzerland AG 2022
A. V. Tuzikov et al. (Eds.): PRIP 2021, CCIS 1562, pp. 191–204, 2022.
https://doi.org/10.1007/978-3-030-98883-8_14

2 Problem Review

Person's position recognition is a problem of localizing anatomical key points, later called body parts, which in physical terms are the joints points of the human body, with the exception of the face key points. This problem is mainly focused on finding body parts, combining them into a skeleton, and tracking it throughout the video sequence (see Fig. 1).

Recognizing the poses of several people in an image, especially socially active ones, presents a unique set of challenges:

- Each image can contain an unknown number of people appearing and disappearing at any position and scale.
- Interactions between people cause complex spatial interference, which is caused by occlusions, physical contacts between people, properties of joints, greatly complicate the unification of individual parts of the body in the limb, and later into the skeleton.

- The complexity increases with the number of people, which imposes significant restrictions in real-time.

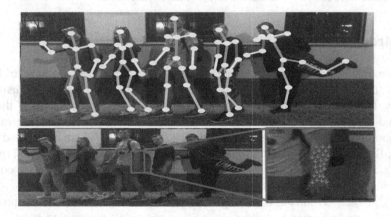

Fig. 1. The figure demonstrates how does the algorithm work, taking into account the above problems

There are two types of approaches: top-down and bottom-up. Top-down ones are characterized by the fact that they use body detectors and later apply positioning estimation to each person found. Such approaches significantly prevail over existing algorithms for recognizing postures for one person, but they also have several significant problems: if the body detector is interrupted, and this happens if several people are very close to each other, then subsequent iterations of detecting and evaluating poses are also interrupted. This problem is called the early confinement problem. In addition, the execution time of such algorithms proportionally depends on the number of people in the frame, for each person found, his pose is calculated, and the more people, the more expensive the computational cost of the algorithm.

In contrast, bottom-up approaches are attractive in that they provide robustness to the problem of early confinement and are able to abstract computational cost from the number of people in the frame. However, bottom-up approaches do not directly use global contextual cues from other parts of the body and other people. In practice, the bottom-up methods do not gain in efficiency, since the finalization of the analysis requires expensive computations. For example, Pishchulin proposed a bottom-up approach [5] that simultaneously marks candidates in body parts and associates them with specific people. However, solving an integer linear programming problem on a complete connected graph is NP-hard, and the average execution time is on the order of several hours. Insafutdinov [6] built on the Pishchulin algorithm [5] more powerful detectors based on ResNet and image-dependent pairwise estimates, which significantly improved the execution time of the algorithm, but the method still has several drawbacks:

- Execution time still takes several minutes for one frame
- The number of recognized body parts is limited in number.

Pairwise representations in Insafutdinov's method [6] are difficult to regress by themselves, so additional logistic regression must be used for this.

This work represents the most effective method for solving the problem of multiple assessment of people's postures, which shows better test results than all the above algorithms.

3   Solution Review

The algorithm is a bottom-up method for estimating associations through part affinity fields, a set of two-dimensional vector fields that encode the location and orientation of limbs in an image region.

The algorithm has three main steps:

1. Image preprocessing.
2. Simultaneous body parts detection and association.
3. Multiple people processing.

Step 1: Image Preprocessing. The method accepts a RGB image as an input image (see Fig. 2) and gives as an output 3D coordinates of anatomical key points for each person in the image.

Fig. 2. Input image

Step 2: Simultaneous body parts detection and association. The neural network simultaneously predicts a set of probability maps S of body parts positions and also a set of two-dimensional vector fields L of combining parts, which store the degree of compatibility between parts.

Step 2.1: Probability Mapping. The set $S = (S_1, S_2 ..., S_J)$ has J probability maps, one per a body part, where, $S_j \in R^{w \times h}$, $j \in \{1... J\}$ (as shown in Fig. 3).

Fig. 3. Probability mapping

Step 2.2: Body parts association. The set $L = (L_1, L_2 ..., L_C)$ has vector fields C, where, $L_c \in R^{w \times h \times 2}$, $c \in \{1... C\}$, each image position in is encoded by a 2D vector L_C (as shown in Fig. 4).

Fig. 4. Vector fields calculation

Step 3: Probability maps and body parts distribution. In the last step, the probability maps and the overlapping fields of the parts are analyzed by the final algorithm to output two-dimensional key points for all the people in the image (as shown in Fig. 5).

The result of the algorithm is a full-size virtual human skeleton, which displays the positioning of anatomical body parts, as well as the position of the whole body (as shown in Fig. 6).

3.1 Image Preprocessing

The first step of the algorithm is an image analysis by a convolutional network consisting of the first 10 layers of the VGG-19 network [1] and configured directly to generate characteristic maps, which, as a result of post-processing, send a set of these maps to the second step of the algorithm.

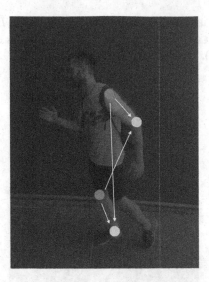

Fig. 5. Probability maps and body parts distribution

3.2   Simultaneous Body Parts Detection and Association

The neutral network simultaneously predicts probability maps and part compatibility fields that store the interconnection of the limbs. The network is divided into two branches: first branch predicts probability maps and the second one predicts the part compatibility fields. Each branch has an iterative-predictive architecture. Every iteration, according to the Wei's method [3], improves the network predictions with intermediate control after each stage.

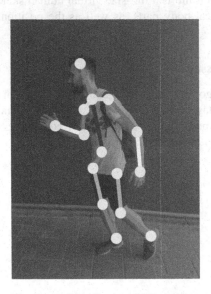

Fig. 6. Building a virtual 2D skeleton

At the first stage, the network creates a set of probability maps $S^1 = \rho^1(F)$ and a set of parts compatibility fields $L^1 = \phi^1(F)$, where ρ^1 and ϕ^1 are CNNs (convolutional neural networks) outputs for the first iteration. At each iteration, the predictions of both branches at the previous stage are combined with the initial characteristics F (1), (2) to obtain refinements of the network forecasts.

$$S^t = p^t\left(F, S^{t-1}, L^{t-1}\right), \forall t \geq 2 \tag{1}$$

$$L^t = \phi^t\left(F, S^{t-1}, L^{t-1}\right), \forall t \geq 2 \tag{2}$$

where p^t and ϕ^t - convolutional neural networks outputs at iteration t.

Figure 7 shows the adjustment of probability maps and compatibility fields of parts at different stages. Two loss functions are applied separately for each branch at the end of each stage to improve the output.

We use the margin of error L^2 between network predictions and known correct maps and fields. Here we spatially weight the error functions to get rid of the problem that some datasets do not completely label all people. The error functions (3) and (4) on both branches at stage t are:

$$f_S^t = \sum_{j=1}^{J} \sum_p W(p) * \left\| S_j^t(p) - S_j^*(p) \right\|_2^2 \tag{3}$$

$$f_L^t = \sum_{c=1}^{C} \sum_p W(p) * \left\| S_c^t(p) - S_c^*(p) \right\|_2^2 \tag{4}$$

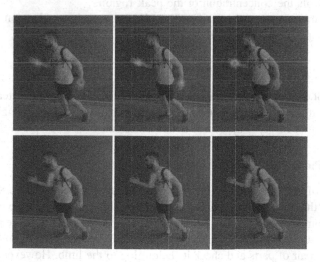

Fig. 7. Probability maps (top row) and compatibility fields of parts (bottom row) of the right forearm at different iterations of the network

where S_j is the probability map, L_c is the compatibility field, W is the binary mask, p is pixel of image. If $W(p) = 0$ there is no characteristic information in the pixel p.

The mask is used to avoid errors of positive predictions during training. Intermediate control (5) at each stage solves the vanishing gradient problem by periodically replenishing the gradient.

$$f = \sum_{t=1}^{T} (f_S^t + f_L^t) \qquad (5)$$

3.3   Probability Mapping

For f_S evaluation during training, we generate probability maps from two-dimensional key points. Each probability map is a two-dimensional representation of what happens to a specific body part for each pixel. Ideally, if there is one person in the image and corresponding body part is visible, only one peak should be present in each probability map. If there are more than one person occurs, there must be a peak corresponding to each visible part j for each person k.

First, we create individual probability maps, for each person k, $k \in R^2$. Let $x_j \in R^2$ be a position of body part j for person k. The value of the probability map at the point p $\in R^2$ is determined by the formula (6).

$$S_{j,k}^* = \exp(-\frac{\|p - x_{j,k}\|_2^2}{\sigma^2}) \qquad (6)$$

where σ controls the concentration of the peak region.

The probability map to be predicted by the network is a collection of individual probability maps (7) for all people.

$$S_j^*(p) = max_k(S_{j,k}^*(p)) \qquad (7)$$

We accept the maximum of all maps instead of the average to better demonstrate the accuracy of the peaks in occlusion. During testing, we predict probability maps (as shown in the first row in Fig. 7) and obtain candidates for body parts.

3.4   Body Parts Compatibility Fields Calculation

Having a set of detected body parts (shown as red and blue dots in Fig. 8), we process them to form the poses of an unknown number of people. To do this, we need a reliable measure of compatibility for each pair of detected body parts. One of the possible ways to measure association (compatibility) is to introduce an additional point - the middle between each pair of parts and check its belonging to the limb. However, when people come together, these midpoints are likely to give false associations (shown by the green lines in Fig. 8). These false associations arise from two limitations.

- This method encodes only the position, not the orientation of each limb.
- It reduces the support area of the limb to one point.

To address these limitations, a new representation, called part compatibility fields, is created that retains both location information and orientation across the entire support area of the limb (shown by yellow arrows in Fig. 8). The compatibility (affinity) of the parts is a two-dimensional vector field for each limb. For each pixel in an area belonging to a specific limb, the 2D vector encodes a direction from one part of the limb to another. Each type of limb has a corresponding field of compatibility connecting its two connected body parts into a limb.

Consider the limb shown in Fig. 9.

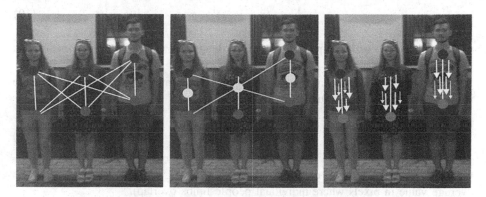

Fig. 8. Distribution body parts between people (Color figure online)

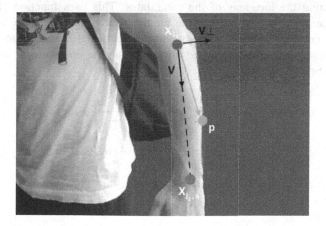

Fig. 9. An example of the distribution of vectors in a limb

Let $x_{j_1,k}$ and $x_{j_2,k}$ be the positions of the joints of body parts j_1 and j_2 for a k-person. If point p lies on a limb, the value of $L_{c,k}^*(p)$ is a unit vector that points from j_1 to j_2, for all other points, the vector is zero.

We determine the vector compatibility field at the point p by formula (8).

$$L_{c,k}^*(p) = \begin{cases} v \, if \, p \, belongs \, to \, limb \, c, k \\ 0 \, otherwise \end{cases} \tag{8}$$

here $v = (x_{j_1,k} - x_{j_2,k})/\|x_{j_1,k} - x_{j_2,k}\|_2$ is the unit vector in the direction of the limb.

The set of points on the limb is defined as the number within the segment, that is, those points p for which inequalities (9) and (10) hold.

$$0 \leq v * (p - x_{j_1,k}) \leq l_{c,k} \tag{9}$$

$$|v_\perp * (p - x_{j_1,k})| \leq \sigma_l \tag{10}$$

where σ_l is a limb width in pixels, $l_{c,k}$ is limb length, $k = \|x_{j_1,k} - x_{j_2,k}\|_2$, and $v_\perp$ is a vector perpendicular to v.

The general vector proximity field averages the proximity fields of all people in the image and is given by formula (11).

$$L_c^*(p) = \frac{1}{n_c(p)} \sum_k L_{c,k}^*(p) \tag{11}$$

where $n_c(p)$ is the number of nonzero vectors at point p for all k people (i.e., the average value in pixels where individual people limbs overlap).

During testing, we measure the relationship between the identified candidates by calculating the linear integral (12) over the corresponding vector field along the segment connecting the locations of the candidates. This uses function (13). In other words, we measure the alignment of the predicted field with the limb, which will be formed by connecting the detected body parts. In particular, for candidates, we project the compatibility field of the predicted portion along the line segment to measure the accuracy of their relationship.

$$E = \int_{u=0}^{u=1} L_c(p(u)) * \frac{d_{j_1} - d_{j_2}}{\|d_{j_2} - d_{j_1}\|_2} du \tag{12}$$

$$p(u) = (1 - u)d_{j_1} + u d_{j_2} \tag{13}$$

In practice, we approximate the integral by sampling and summing uniformly distributed values u.

3.5   Multiple People Affine Fields Processing

The algorithm does not perform the maximum suppression on the probability maps to obtain a discrete set of candidates for the next processing steps. Due to the analysis of all people at once or errors in image processing, several candidates may arise at once for each part of the body (as shown in Fig. 10). These candidates create a large set of possible limbs. We evaluate each limb using the linear integral (12) above.

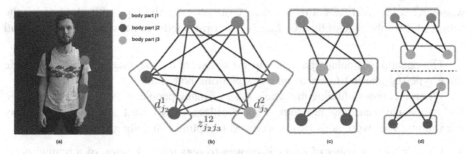

Fig. 10. Algorithm for testing compatibility fields

The optimal selection problem corresponds to the K-dimensional match problem, which is known to be NP-hard (as shown in Fig. 10). This seems to be a rather expensive relaxation that consistently determines high-quality matching of parts in the limb. This is because the pairwise associative evaluation implicitly encodes the global context due to the high sensitivity of the compatibility fields.

First, we get a set of candidates D_J for several people, where $D_J = \{d_j^m, \text{for} j \in \{1...J\}, m \in \{1...N_j\}\}$, N_j is the number of candidates for part j, and $d_j^m \in R^2$ is the location of the mth candidate for body part j. These candidates still need to be associated with other body parts from the same person. In other words, we need to find candidate pairs that are actually a connected limb. For this, a variable $z_{j_1,j_2}^{m,n} \in \{0,1\}$ is introduced, which is a flag indicating whether the two candidates are connected to each other. The goal is to find the optimal assignment for the set of all possible connections (14).

$$Z = \{z_{j_1,j_2}^{m,n} : \text{for} j_1, j_2 \in \{1...J\}, m \in \{1...N_{j_1}\}, n \in \{1...N_{j_2}\}\} \qquad (14)$$

If we consider one pair of parts j_1, j_2 (for example, the neck and the right thigh) for the c-th limb, then the search for the optimal match is reduced to the problem of matching bipartite graphs with maximum weight. In this problem, the nodes of the graph are the candidates for detecting a body part, and the edges are all possible connections between pairs of candidates. In addition, each edge has its own weight. A concordance in a bipartite graph is a subset of edges selected such that no two edges separate a node. Our goal is to find a match with the maximum weight for the selected edges (15), (16), (17).

$$max_{Z_c} E_c = max_{Z_c} \sum_{m \subset D_{j_1}} \sum_{n \subset D_{j_2}} E_{m,n} * z_{j_1,j_2}^{m,n} \qquad (15)$$

$$\forall m \in D_{j_1}, \sum_{n \subset D_{j_2}} z_{j_1,j_2}^{m,n} \leq 1 \qquad (16)$$

$$\forall n \in D_{j_2}, \sum_{m \subset D_{j_1}} z_{j_1,j_2}^{m,n} \leq 1 \qquad (17)$$

where E_c is the total weight of the correspondence for the type of limb C, Z_c is the subset of Z for the type of limb C, $E_{m,n}$ is the correspondence between the parts $d_{j_1}^m$ and $d_{j_2}^m$.

The equations stipulate that two ribs do not share a node, that is, two limbs of the same type (eg, the left forearm) do not share one body part.

When it comes to finding the whole pose of many people, the Z definition task is a K-dimensional matching problem. This problem is NP hard and there are many relaxations. This work adds two relaxations to optimize the algorithm:

- The minimum number of edges is chosen to obtain the skeleton of a human pose, rather than using the full graph (as shown in Fig. 10).
- The matching task is decomposed into a set of bidirectional matching subtasks and independently determines the matching in adjacent tree nodes.

With these two relaxations, the optimization is presented in formula (18).

$$max_Z E = \sum_{c=1}^{C} max_{Z_c} E_c \qquad (18)$$

Therefore, candidates for limb connection are obtained independently of each other. These candidates are then assembled into limbs and combined into full body poses for multiple people (As shown in Fig. 11).

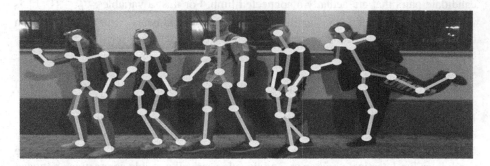

Fig. 11. The result of assembling and combined limbs into a full body pose

4   Solution Testing and Results

The algorithm is evaluated according to two criteria:

- MPII multiuser dataset
- COCO milestone dataset

These two datasets contain images with different scenarios that contain many real-world problems such as large numbers of people, zooming, occlusion, and contact.

4.1 Test Results on MPII Multi-person Dataset

For comparison on the MPII dataset, we measure the mean accuracy (mAP) of all body parts based on the PCKh threshold. Table 1 shows mAP and the average processing and optimization times comparison between our method and other approaches.

For a subset of 288 images, our method outperforms previous modern bottom-up methods by 8.5% mAP. It is noteworthy that our inference time is 6 orders of magnitude less than competing algorithms. Comparing mAP with previous bottom-up approaches shows that the compatibility fields approach is very effective for linking body parts. Based on a tree structure, our expensive processing method provides better accuracy than a graph optimization formula based on a fully coupled graph structure.

Table 1. MPII test results (288 images subset)

Algorithm	HEA	SHO	ELB	WRI	HIP	KNE	ANK	mAP	Seconds/image
Deepcut	72,6	71,3	57,3	40,1	72,6	45,1	32,3	54,2	57604
Iqbal	69,7	64,9	54,4	45,9	69,7	47,5	44,1	54,8	15
Current	94,0	91,7	80,3	94,0	77,1	72,7	68,3	78,9	0,008

4.2 Test Results on COCO Keypoints Challenge Dataset

The COCO training set consists of over 100,000 people with over 1 million major key points (body parts) and more then 20K images.

The COCO score determines the comparability of the recognized points (OKS) and uses the average accuracy (AP) at more than 10 OKS thresholds as the main scoring criterion. OKS is calculated based on the size of the person and the distance between the predicted points. Table 2 shows the results from the best teams for a task. It should be noted that our method has lower accuracy than top-down methods for people with smaller scales. The reason is that our method has to deal with a much wider range of scales covered by all the people in the image in one frame. Top-down methods, on the other hand, can scale each deterministic region to a larger size and thus reduce the error at smaller scales.

Table 2. COCO test results

Algorithm	AP	AP-50	AP-75	*AP-L*	*AP-L*
G-RMI	59.8	81.0	65.1	**56.7**	66.7
R4D	49,7	74,9	54,4	54,9	55,9
Current	**60.5**	**83.4**	**66.4**	55.1	**68.1**

References

1. Sun, M., Savarese, S.: Articulated part-based model for joint object detection and pose estimation. In: ICCV (2011)
2. West, D.B.: Introduction to Graph Theory, vol. 2. Prentice Hall, Upper Saddle River (2001)
3. Weil, S.E., Ramakrishna, V., Kanade, T., Sheikh, Y.: Convolutional pose machines. In: CVPR (2016)
4. Yang, Y., Ramanan, D.: Articulated human detection with flexible mixtures of parts. In: TPAMI (2013)
5. Newell, A., Yang, K., Deng, J.: Stacked hourglass networks for human pose estimation. In: Leibe, B., Matas, J., Sebe, N., Welling, M. (eds.) ECCV 2016. LNCS, vol. 9912, pp. 483–499. Springer, Cham (2016). https://doi.org/10.1007/978-3-319-46484-8_29
6. Pishchulin, L., et al.: DeepCut: joint subset partition and labeling for multi person pose estimation. In: CVPR (2016)
7. Insafutdinov, E., Pishchulin, L., Andres, B., Andriluka, M., Schiele, B.: DeeperCut: a deeper, stronger, and faster multi-person pose estimation model. In: Leibe, B., Matas, J., Sebe, N., Welling, M. (eds.) ECCV 2016. LNCS, vol. 9910, pp. 34–50. Springer, Cham (2016). https://doi.org/10.1007/978-3-319-46466-4_3
8. Lin, T.-Y., et al.: Microsoft COCO: common objects in context. In: Fleet, D., Pajdla, T., Schiele, B., Tuytelaars, T. (eds.) ECCV 2014. LNCS, vol. 8693, pp. 740–755. Springer, Cham (2014). https://doi.org/10.1007/978-3-319-10602-1_48
9. Chen, X., Yuille, A.: Articulated pose estimation by a graphical model with image dependent pairwise relations. In: NIPS (2014)

Authentication System Based on Biometric Data of Smiling Face from Stacked Autoencoder and Concatenated Reed-Solomon Codes

Boris Assanovich$^{(\boxtimes)}$ ⓘ and Katsiaryna Kosarava ⓘ

Yanka Kupala State University of Grodno, 230023 Grodno, Belarus
bas@grsu.by

Abstract. A new authentication system based on video frames sampled from three main phases of a user smile has been proposed. This biometric system is implemented by exploiting the neural network model of stack autoencoder and fuzzy commitment scheme applying the concatenated RS and linear error-correcting codes. The performance of system verified with smiles from UvA-NEMO database has shown the achievement of FRR <1% for secret key lengths 90–180 bits with the use of non-binary codes of size 31 and 63 elements.

Keywords: Autoencoder · Biometric features · Smile imprint · Fuzzy commitment · Concatenated Reed-Solomon codes

1 Introduction

A human smile that is a key factor in determining person's psychological state, can also be used as a behavioral biometric identification element. Recently, several applications have appeared that implement the concept of SmileID [1] related to the face biometrics where identity is verified remotely. Previously, facial biometry has become one of the most preferred biometric methods both in video surveillance and in banking [2] due to the fact that it does not require precision equipment and uses a non-contact data processing method. A few years ago Murat Taskiran et al. [3] have applied dynamic face features extraction from videos and used them for face recognition. The authors performed the analysis of face videos and extracted the statistical properties of facial distances during several phases of spontaneous and posed smiles on the UvA-NEMO smile database that have been created before for biometric applications by Dibeklioglu et al. [4]. Despite the fact that there are a number of techniques that use facial dynamics to identify a person with various spatiotemporal parameters extracted from face, the deep learning methods are increasingly being exploited for recognition tasks.

Modern face recognition systems are commonly based on deep learning architectures, which train a multi-layer neural network (NN) to learn a set of representative face features from images of a person's face. Recently, it has been

© Springer Nature Switzerland AG 2022
A. V. Tuzikov et al. (Eds.): PRIP 2021, CCIS 1562, pp. 205–219, 2022.
https://doi.org/10.1007/978-3-030-98883-8_15

shown that face features can be "inverted" to recover an approximation of the original face image and that they can reveal additional information about the underlying person (e.g., gender, race, age) [5,6]. These findings indicate that the face features are rich with personally identifiable information, which may represent a threat to the privacy of the system's users if their face features are leaked to an adversary.

So for the past decade the Biometric Template Protection (BTP) research field, which strives to develop effective ways of protecting our biometric "templates" (images or features) is quickly developing. Biometric template is a digital representation of the unique features that have been extracted from a biometric sample (facial image, voice recording or a fingerprint) and is stored in a biometric database. These templates are then used in the biometric authentication and identification process.

One of the most commonly studied algorithms for the protection of face features (using pre-trained NN models) is homomorphic encryption (HE) [7–10]. HE allows to perform operations on encrypted data without having to first decrypt it, i.e. HE allows to compare reference and probe encrypted templates (generated during the enrollment and authentication stages, respectively) directly in the protected domain. Besides, using HE for BTP, theoretically doesn't lead to loss in the resulting recognition accuracy, since the comparison score obtained in the encrypted domain should be the same as that obtained in the original (unprotected) domain. The two main disadvantages of HE are computational complexity which has rendered it impractical for the application in face BTP until fairly recently, and that the encrypted templates remain secure only insofar as the corresponding decryption key remains secret.

Another approach to encoding face templates is using cryptographic hash functions. This function creates a fixed-size, predictable output called a "hash" from each instance of the same input data (e.g., a password), so that it is mathematically impossible to recover the original input from its computed hash. Considering the sensitivity of these functions to small changes in the input, face BTP methods that employ cryptographic hashing often apply the hashing algorithm not to the face templates themselves but to randomly generated, external codewords, which are related to the face templates by some sort of mathematical function. A well-known example of such a method is the Fuzzy Commitment scheme [11]. Its variants were investigated for the protection of NN-extracted face features in [12,13].

In [14] the application of the unlinkable fuzzy vault scheme to facial feature vectors extracted through deep convolutional neural networks (DCNN) is investigated. Firstly, a real-valued feature vector is extracted from a face image using a DCNN. Then, based on a training step, the feature vector is quantized to an integer vector which is then binarized. And lastly, an integer set is obtained from the binary vector through the feature set mapping. At key binding a public bijection is firstly applied to the integer set, then the resulting integer is projected onto a secret polynomial defined by a key, and is stored in addition with a hash of the key. At key retrieval the polynomial reconstruction is performed.

Finally the correctness of the retrieved key is validated by comparing its hash value to the stored one. The proposed template protection scheme is agnostic of the biometric characteristic and, thus, can be applied to any biometric features computed by a deep neural network.

In [15] a cryptographic hash function is directly applied to the face template. First a stacked denoising autoencoder is trained to extract face features from different local regions of the face image. Then each local feature vector is quantized and cryptographically hashed. In [16,17] the study of deep autoencoders to reduce the dimension of feature representation has shown that this nonlinear technique is more effective than known the PCA method.

Further, to create the BTP with processing a series of different video frames of faces with reduced sensitivity to intraclass variations, and then apply error correction codes with hashing, we can achieve a good performance using the known Fuzzy Commitment (FC) scheme [11] that can be revoked if compromised.

In this paper, we consider the use of a stacked autoencoder (SAE) to extract features from a sequence of video frames from user smiling face in order to authenticate him and provide the access to digital services. Our contribution is threefold. First, we describe the method of creating biometric templates with the use of Juels and Wattenberg (JW) FC scheme based on the equidistant quantization of real data at the output of SAE for further quantization and encoding by concatenated Reed-Solomon (RS) codes. Second, we propose an approach to assessing the reliability of biometric data and an algorithm for its use to perform soft decoding of RS codes with error and erasure correction. Third, we develop the biometric cryptosystem based on the JW FC scheme using the additional Helper Data (HD) to implement the error correction with RS codes, improving the overall system performance. The first section presents an introduction. It continues in Sect. 2 by reviewing the related structure of an autoencoder and the error correcting code parameters. In Sect. 3 we describe the BS structure and the errors-and-erasures decoding algorithm for the applied RS codes. Section 4 demonstrates the experimental results of this study. The paper concludes in Sect. 5 and also provides some direction for future work.

2   Autoencoders and Error Correcting Codes

2.1   Autoencoders

There are several types of autoencoders. Sparse Autoencoder has a dimension of the hidden layer that is greater than the input. It consists of two parts: coder (encoder) G and decoder F as depicted in Fig. 1 [18]. The encoder translates the input signal into its representation (code): $y = G(x)$, and the decoder restores the signal by its code: $x' = F(y)$. Moreover, the transformation functions F and G contain activation function, weights and biases of trained artificial NNs. By changing the mappings G, autoencoder tends to learn the identity function $x' = F(G(x))$, minimizing the kind of error based on some functional $L = (x, F(G(x))$. Let us consider that a vector $x \in R$ connected to the input of an autoencoder. Then the encoder maps the vector x to another vector $y \in R$ as follows

$y = h^i \left(W^i x + b^i \right)$, where the superscript i indicates the i-th layer. Then h^i is a transfer function for the encoder, $W^i \in R$ is a weight matrix, and $b^i \in R$ is a bias vector. Hence, the decoder maps the encoded representation y back into an estimate of the original input vector x, as follows: $x' = h^{i+1} \left(W^{i+1} x + b^{i+1} \right)$, where the superscript $i+1$ represents the $i+1$ layer. Then a transfer function h^{i+1} for the decoder has a factor $W^{i+1} \in R$ that is a weight matrix, and $b^{i+1} \in R$ is a bias vector correspondingly. If the encoder has only two layers then the expression for the transfer function can be represented as $x' = h^2 \left(W^2 x + b^2 \right)$. In our setup we applied so-called stacked autoencoder (SAE) that is a NN including only 2 layers where output of each hidden layer is connected to the input of the successive hidden layer. The effectiveness of user comparisons depends on similarity rates, which are often determined by the distribution of root mean square (RMS) distances of their characteristics.

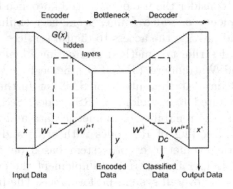

Fig. 1. Autoencoder structure.

The more the two distributions are separated and the smaller the standard deviation for each distribution, the better is the separation of the classified classes. This property of distributions is estimated by such a parameter as decidability index

$$DI = \frac{|\mu_g - \mu_i|}{\sqrt{(\sigma_g^2 + \sigma_i^2)/2}}, \tag{1}$$

where μ_g, μ_i and σ_g^2, σ_i^2 are the means and standard deviations of genuine and imposter distributions.

In addition to the decidability index, an equal error rate (ERR), which is the error rate at which a false accept rate (FAR) is equal to a false rejection rate (FRR), is normally used as a measure of biometric system verification accuracy. In biometrics FAR is the rate at which an imposter print is incorrectly accepted as genuine and FRR is the rate at which a genuine print is incorrectly rejected as imposter.

The use of autoencoders will make it possible to compactly present biometric features and then apply the scheme to organize Human Computer Interface (HCI), where instead of tokens and passwords, a biometric key can be exploited for authentication To handle the variability inherent in biometric authentication, it is necessary to create and store a template for each user. To create it, we will use the fuzzy commitment scheme with application of error correcting codes (ECC).

2.2   Error Correcting Codes

In this paper, in contrast to the generally accepted application of binary ECC in Biometric Cryptosystem (BC), we consider the use of non-binary RS codes. However, the parameters we enter for evaluating the effectiveness of biometric systems can easily be used for the binary error correcting codes.

More formally, a non-binary ECC consists of a set $C^* \in 0, q-1$, where q is some integer, and is often chosen to be a multiple of some power 2^n to form the finite field GF(2) expansion. The use of the code is aimed at encoding a message of length k with the addition of redundancy $r = n - k$, so that if a certain number of characters is corrupted, it is still possible to get the correct codeword C and message R. The robustness of an ECC depends upon some distance between codewords. Let the RS code be defined over the $GF(2^m)$ field with a redundancy of $n - k$ symbols and let the Symbol Error Rate (SER) caused by the fuzziness of biometric data or so called "biometric noise" be p. The important performance parameters to consider when using EEC in BC are still FAR and FRR. The FRR, which depends on SER of RS code, can actually be upper bounded by the probability that more than $t = (n-k)/2$ errors occur, i.e. [19]:

$$FRR \leq \sum_{i=\lfloor(n-k)/2\rfloor+1}^{n} \binom{n}{i} p^i(1-p)^{n-i} \approx (np)^{\lfloor(n-k)/2\rfloor+1}, \qquad (2)$$

where n, k are the ECC parameters defined above, and t is its error correction capacity, i.e. the ability to correct any set of up to t symbol errors.

Considering that an imposter produces a random syndrome during decoding for uncorrectable error patterns, made up of q-ary symbols, and it is accepted by BC, FAR will be the probability that it is valid, i.e.

$$FAR = \sum_{i=0}^{\lfloor(n-k)/2\rfloor} \binom{n}{i} (n+1)^{-(n-k)} \approx (q)^{-(n-k)/2}, \qquad (3)$$

From (1) and (2), we see that FRR, FAR can be reduced by increasing $(n-k)$ and t.

The dimension of the $GF(2^m)$ field and the redundancy of the RS code significantly affect the length of the cryptographic key R in the biometric JW scheme. The use of non-binary RS codes has the advantage which lies in the fact that an increase in the symbol dimension leads to an increase in the length of their bit representation. On the other hand, in order to obtain high error correction capacity t of ECC, it is necessary to increase the redundancy, which reduces the code rate k/n and leads to the need to use several ECC codewords. For example, to obtain a user's secret key R with a length of more than 128 bits, when using RS(31,9) code with $k = 9$ over $GF(2^5)$ with a code rate k/n of about 0.3, only 45 bits can be placed in one codeword. Hence for the key length of more than 128 bits, 3 such codewords are required. Whereas when using the RS(63,15) code with the rate 0.24 over $GF(2^6)$, the key length 180 bits can be distributed between two codewords of this ECC.

To evaluate the effectiveness of these codes, the corresponding FRR values have been calculated using (2) at different symbol error probabilities and placed in Table 1.

Table 1. Evaluation of FRR for RS codes (63,15), (31,9).

HSER	FRR: RS(63,15)	FRR: RS(31,9)
0.0050	$2.8692 \cdot 10^{-13}$	$1.9230 \cdot 10^{-10}$
0.0100	$9.6275 \cdot 10^{-6}$	$7.8766 \cdot 10^{-7}$
0.0150	0.2431	$1.0220 \cdot 10^{-4}$

It follows from Table 1 that with the increase of p, FRR grows exponentially and, taking into account (2), to reach FRR = 1.0e−04 for RS code (63,15), it is necessary to reduce SER by 1.36 times. Thus, in order to achieve the required performance of the biometric system, it is necessary to introduce a significant redundancy by ECC applied. In this case one of the efficient ways to increase the efficiency of error-correcting coding is the transition to concatenated ECC. It is a class of error-correcting codes derived by combining an inner code and an outer code that can be tuned in a given way and show better performance than ECC of a certain type. According to our estimates, to reduce SER by several times, it is sufficient to use a class of linear codes with a suitable length.

One of the efficient high-redundancy code, also referred to as a linear one, is the repetition (REP) code. The use of a binary REP code makes it possible to reduce the probability of erroneous decoding of an m-bit code block P_m by an order of magnitude. To find the required m value when using REP codes, one can use a calculated approximation of the binomial distribution based on the Stirling formula [20]:

$$m \approx 2 \frac{\log_2 P_m}{\log_2(4p_e(1 - p_e))}, \tag{4}$$

where p_e is Bit Error Rate (BER) of a Binary Symmetric Channel (BSC) model, which is often used to analyze ECC performance at the bit level. For example, if a BSC with $p_e = 0.1$ is used, then to obtain $P_m = 0.01$, a REP code with a block length of approximately $m = 9$ bits is required. However, it should be taken into account that formula (4) is an estimate, since this approximation is used for large m and small P_m.

Moreover, in practice, to correct single and multiple bit errors, more efficient linear codes, with a higher code rate k/n are used. The mathematical representation developed for them makes it possible to use the fast (syndrome) decoding algorithms. A detailed description of their properties, as well as the principles of encoding and decoding, can be found in a number of textbooks, for example [20,21]. In this case, an estimate of their efficiency for the bounded distance decoding can be determined by formula (2), using the parameter p_e for BSC instead of p.

3   Proposed System

3.1   System Structure

In this paper, we have used an autoencoder to obtain the biometric data on a person's smile and bind it to a secure user key. Due to the fact that biometric data has instability, error correction codes should be adopted to ensure that the fuzziness of biometric data can be alleviated.

In this study we propose to apply the concatenated ECC using the Hard Decision Decoding (HDD) and Soft Decision Decoding (SDD) techniques for RS codes based on their symbol reliability. Further, in this paper we consider the classical structure of encoding-decoding for the concatenation of codes.

Initially, the user key will be encoded with a non-binary RS code, and then the bit representations of the symbols will be additionally encoded with a linear binary code. After imposing "biometric noise" on the received code vectors, the key is extracted by decoding the code constructions in reverse order.

We denote by $\mathbf{y} = (y_1, \ldots, y_n)$ an n-dimensional feature vector from set of real numbers Y, by $\mathbf{z} = (z_1, \ldots, z_n)$ - its quantized version and by $\mathbf{C} = (c_1, \ldots, c_n)$ - the corresponding codeword of RS code from the space C of integers.

The model of the proposed system is depicted in Fig. 2. We will introduce the term *Smile Imprint* of biometric data obtained from SAE output layer to form a concatenated supervector $\overline{Y} = \mathbf{y}^1 \cup \mathbf{y}^2 \ldots \cup \mathbf{y}^M$ from several vectors $\mathbf{y}^i$, where M is a number of processed frames. It should be noted that the *Preprocessor* block also performs such operations as smile detection and smile frames selection related to its main three phases (onset, apex, offset) as it is also described in [22].

At the stage of *Qantization*, the real values Y are converted into their quantized versions $\mathbf{Z}$ producing also deviations W^* of encoded by SAE data values Y relative to mean values or centers of quantization intervals used as HD1. The set Z^* contains not absolute values, but data deviations and can serve as open information in HD1. In the *Encoder* block, the user's password or Key R is encoded with one or more ECC codes, depending on the required password strength and FRR, which will be discussed below. Further, for a biometric authentication purposes the bit representation of the resulting codeword is added modulo 2 to the encoded version $\mathbf{C}$ of quantized data $\mathbf{Z}$, which results in W that serves as HD2. In this study, we will consider the authentication scenario, although this BS can also implement the identification process.

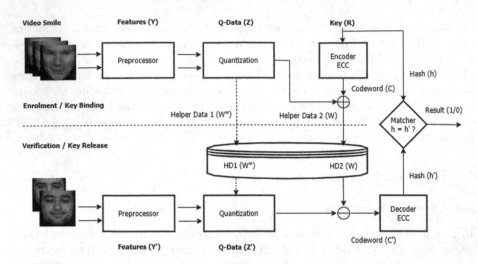

Fig. 2. A system model.

The proposed system works in two operating modes (see Fig. 2). In the first mode, the user is registered and his smile imprint is obtained from SAE, and with the use of HD1 and HD2 linked to the secret Key R, the h-hash of which is calculated and stored in the Biometric Database (BD). During verification, the reverse process of decoupling the "auxiliary" data HD1, HD2, decoding $\mathbf{C}$' and comparing two hashes h and h' are performed.

Thus, the user smile imprint captured from his video can serve as the biometric key to organize the access to different external digital services. At the same time, the proposed system implements the JW scheme using both helper data samples of HD1 and HD2 or only one sample of HD1 that can be stored in the public domain data base. To represent information in HD1 and HD2, various methods can be used up to encryption, which is determined by the complexity and the required speed of the implemented biometric system. System parameters such as the length of the cryptographic key, the type and characteristics of ECC must be determined by the quality of biometric data, the number of users, resistance to external attacks, etc.

3.2   Algorithms for RS Codes Decoding

To decode the Reed Solomon codes, we can use an algebraic HDD method based on a number of steps, which makes it possible to implement it both by means of software and hardware elements. As a rule, after finding the syndrome, it includes the following actions [21, 23]: finding the error locator and evaluator polynomials with Berlekamp-Massey (BM) Algorithm; Chen's search procedure; error magnitudes determination based on Forney's formula; error correction. Assuming that the result of decoding is either a decoded message or a decoding error, we will actually have a hard-decision RS decoder.

However, RS code can correct not only errors, but also the erasures, i.e. so-called "lost" symbols that are not included in the set of q elements. If N_{er} symbols of RS code are erased and the remaining $n - N_{er}$ symbols contain N_e errors, the BM algorithm can find the correct codeword as long as [23].

$$N_{er} + 2N_e \leq 2t < d. \tag{5}$$

If $N_{er} = 0$, the decoder is used as an errors-only decoder, and if $0 < N_{er} \leq d - 1$, the decoder is called an errors-and-erasures decoder (EED). However, to apply the EED principle we must determine which symbols are incorrect or erased, and find the correct value of the incorrect symbols.

There are several approaches to solving this problem [23] by the use of side information to search for "unreliable" symbols based on certain criterion. In this work, we use the LLR estimate of the code symbol reliability, which is based on the absolute value of the deviation in magnitude relative to its mean for the i-th element $D_i = |y_i^j - \mu_i|$ in j biometric measurement that is expressed as

$$LLR_i = \ln \frac{D_i'}{D_i}. \tag{6}$$

Thus, the real-valued deviations found by (6) at the stage of verification in biometric system can serve as the additional information for EED implementation. To do this, in the processed codeword, we must mark N_{er} symbols from n as erasures and form the erasure vector $\mathbf{E} = (e_1, .., e_n)$, consisting of the position numbers (flags) marking the erasures. This vector of length n will be formed with the use of experimentally found threshold T as follows. First of all, a vector $\mathbf{L} = (l_1, ..., l_n)$ is created from $l_i = |LLR_i|$ values, then sorting is performed in descending order of n its values, and the vector of indices $\mathbf{K} = (k_1, ..., k_n)$ corresponding to the ranking of symbols in this order of unreliability is formed, from which then vector $\mathbf{E}$ is constructed.

We form a vector containing the erasure flags in N_{er} positions. It contains binary elements with the assignment $e_i = 1$, if the selected position is assumed to be erased and $e_i = 0$ – otherwise. This vector is called the erasure vector and, together with the codeword found after subtraction (see Fig. 2), is used for EED.

The EED procedure is performed by updating vector $\mathbf{E}$, in which the elements are cyclically shifted in case of HDD failure based on the HDD algebraic method described above. The decoding procedure ends when decoding is successful and the message (key R) is found, or after all cyclic shifts of the initial erasure vector are completed. Since the positions of the most unreliable symbols will be at the beginning of $\mathbf{K}$, the correct decoding is achieved after a few shifts.

However, in contrast to work [23], in our case the threshold T is defined with the use of LLR-values (6) and is applied to create a one-component EED, although it can be easily extended to the multi-component case. In the proposed biometric system, the SDD based on EED algorithm for the applied RS codes consists of the following steps.

1. Read vector $\mathbf{D} = (D_1, ..., D_n)$ from W^* belonging to HD1.
2. For a set M of vectors $\mathbf{y}' = (y_1', ..., y_n')$, calculate $\mathbf{D}' = (D_1', ..., D_n')$ and LLR_i based on (6).
3. Get vector $\mathbf{C}' = (c_1', ..., c_n')$ for a new biometric sample after the operations of quantization and subtraction from W (HD2) are completed.
4. Find vectors $\mathbf{L}$, $\mathbf{K}$.
5. Perform the EED for every pair of $\mathbf{E}$ and $\mathbf{C}'$.
6. In case of failure decoding shift $\mathbf{E}$ by one position and go to 5.
7. If decoding with $\mathbf{C}'$ is successful, then output a key R (or part of it), otherwise declare an authentication error.

Note that algorithm does not describe the bit-level data processing procedures. The size of the R part, resulting from the above-described decoding, is determined by the number of codewords M to form the dimension of R.

Thus, the basic procedure in the proposed EED algorithm for the SDD of RS codes is the application of HDD and the use of HD1 and HD2. In the case of using only HD2, HDD is performed and steps 1, 2, 4, 5, 6 are excluded.

4 Experiments Performed

4.1 SAE and RS Simulation

A series of experiments were performed with SAE to get good compact biometric features. To reduce time spent, in these experiments the subsets of 40 subjects randomly selected from the entire UvA-NEMO Database were used, reproducing a posed smile. Then normalized grayscale images from corresponding video of 112×112 pixels in size, scaled to 50%, creating a vector length of the input layer of 6272 elements have been used for unsupervised learning of SAE. Combinations of the second and third SAE layer dimensions had values 255/63, 127/63, 127/31, and 63/31. The selected values were determined by the length of the applied RS-codes, as well as the chosen dimension of equidistant quantization.

To perform quantization and encoding, the following structures were chosen 127/63 and 63/31.

To evaluate the quality of training, on the basis of latent layer data Y, such values as FRR, FAR, GAR, ERR and DI were calculated and the ROC-characteristic was monitored, as well as the values of MSE for controlling the intra-class and inter-class distance distribution. Unsupervised learning results and then supervised tuning of SAE with parameters 127/63 for 40 users in the form of histograms are shown in Fig. 3. It can be seen from the figure that due to the fine-tuning procedure, the interclass distributions expanded significantly relative to each other when applying NN model compared with the processing of HOG features in [24].

Then several experiments have been carried out to train SAE for 10 different groups of 40 users each, randomly selected from the UvA-NEMO database. For this compiled dataset the encoding-decoding procedures were modeled using the above-mentioned ECC. For processed 400 subjects from the dataset, the

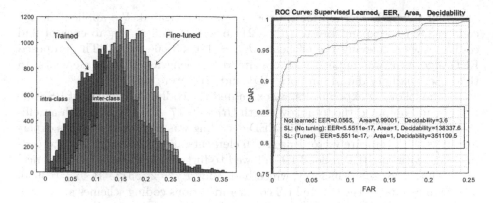

Fig. 3. Learning results of the SAE with parameters 127/63

real-valued data with lengths of 63 and 31 elements obtained from SAE and equidistantly quantized have been encoded with non-binary RS codes.

The schemes of ECC used in modeling included: 1). RS code (63,15) concatenated with linear code (6,3,1) and separately with repetition (REP) codes (3,1,1); 2). RS code (31,9) concatenated with REP codes (3,1,1), as well as the same code constructions without concatenation. The conversion of symbols to bits was done based on Gray's code representation [21].

A number of experiments on the design of RS codes and the use of concatenated structures were carried out.

Initially, the code RS (63,15) was used with elements from $GF(2^6)$ that were represented by 6 bits, which made it possible to obtain a block with a length of $n = 6 \cdot 63 = 378$ bits. After grouping bits by 3 elements and representing them with Gray code in this block, they were further encoded with a linear code (6,3,1). As a result, 126 groups of 6 bits were formed with a resulting length of 756 bits. When using one code block of this construction, we have the key length $|R| = 6 \cdot 15 = 90$ bits. The efficiency E_f or the resulting code rate of ECC construction is $E_f = 90/756 = 0.119$. To implement the FC scheme, 2 biometric samples with a length of 63 elements and 2 samples from HD2 are required for HDD of RS codes. To increase a key length by 2 times, 2 codewords of the RS code (63,15) and 4 biometric samples are needed.

We have also considered an alternative scheme of the RS code (63,15) together with REP (3,1,1) code use at the 2nd stage. For the password length $|R| = 90$ bits, the efficiency dropped to the value $E_f = 90/378 \cdot 3 = 0.0794$. Next, we examined RS codes (31,9), which in bit representation made it possible to obtain blocks with a length of $31 \cdot 5 = 115$ bits with the ability to use only $9 \cdot 5 = 45$ bits for a key, that is not enough for a BS. To expand $|R|$ and improve the noise immunity, the 2nd stage of coding with the REP code (3,1,1) was used, which ultimately determined the $E_f = 90/115 \cdot 3 \cdot 2 = 0.0968$. In this case, we have to use 6 biometric samples with a length of 31 elements.

Then the SDD method for RS codes was investigated. We applied the RS code (63,31) to expand key to $|R| = 21 \cdot 6 = 126$ bits in the absence of 2nd coding stage, achieving the efficiency $E_f = 126/63 \cdot 6 = 0.33$. The proposed EED algorithm was applied with erasure vector lengths of 21–19 elements. In this case, auxiliary data from both HD1 and HD2 were used.

In the following experiments, we examined the coding of 2 blocks of RS code (31,17) and obtained the total key length $|R| = 2 \cdot 17 \cdot 5 = 170$ bits with an efficiency of $E_f = 85/115 = 0.36$. The EED decoding was used as in previous experiments with the erasure vector length of 6 elements. The addition of the 2nd coding stage with the REP code (3,1,1) allowed to further improve the performance, but with a decrease in efficiency, which had value $E_f = 2 \cdot 85/3 \cdot 31 \cdot 5 = 0.3656$. The final results for the selected RS codes and various coding schemes are shown in Table 2. The FRR value in the last row of the table corresponds to error-free decoding in 5 cases with integrated processing of 2400 blocks of concatenated encoding.

From Table 2 follows that by reducing the RS code length and complicating coding scheme, it is possible to improve the performance of BS in terms of the FRR parameter by increasing the processing time. Thus, there is a trade-off between a decrease in FRR and an increase in the number of processed video frames.

Table 2. Evaluation of FRR and Key size for concatenated ECC

Inner code	Outer code	FRR, %	Key, $|R|$ (bit)/Frames × Dimension	Efficiency, E_f
$RS(63, 15)$	Linear(6,3,1)	1.0	90/2 × 63(180/4 × 63)	0.119
$RS(63, 15)$	REP(3,1,1)	0.5	90/3 × 63(180/3 × 63)	0.0079
$RS(31, 9)$	REP(3,1,1)	0.5	90/6 × 31	0.0968
$RS(63, 21)$	–	0.7	126/1 × 63	0.33
$RS(31, 17)$	–	0.3	170/2 × 31	0.5
$RS(31, 17)$	REP(3,1,1)	<0.1	170/6 × 31	0.1828

4.2   Security Issues

In biometric authentication systems a secret key R is bound to biometric data and is used to regulate access to services, and different environments. The secret keys are chosen during an enrollment when the biometric samples are captured for the first time and are reconstructed after new biometric data are observed again to realize the authentication. To combat with biometric noise, a reliable BS also uses helper data (HD1 and HD2 in our case) obtained from the biometric measurements at the enrollment stage. The helper data are assumed to be public, do not contain information on R, and facilitate reliable reconstruction of it in the authentication process. One of the important parameter of BS is the information that HD1 and HD2 contain (leak) about the biometric measurement. This parameter is called privacy leakage, and should be small, to avoid biometric data of a user to become compromised.

Moreover, the secret-key is also characterized by the secret-key length $|R|$ and rate (Efficiency E_f in our case) that should be large to minimize the probability of a successful secret guess by an unauthorized user. Despite the fact that the fundamental trade-offs between the rate of secret key leakage in biometric systems have been well studied from an information-theoretical point of view [25], in specific practical implementations, their assessment is required.

For these purposes, for a random user, in the proposed BS we calculated the entropy values of the biometric sample $H(Y)$ and random key encoded by RS code (63,21) $H(C)$, and compared them with the values of mutual information $I(Y, W)$ and $I(Y, W^*)$ based on the method from [26]. Calculations have shown that $H(C) \approx H(W) \gg I(Y, W) > I(Y, W^*)$, and are almost two orders of magnitude less than $H(Y)$. For example, for the selected first frame of the 1-st user from UvA-NEMO Database when applying the above RS code, we have $H(Y) = 4.6793$, $H(C) = 5.3819$, $I(Y, W) = 0.0429$, $I(Y, W^*) = 0.0769$.

With regard to the secret key leakage, it should be noted that by using the shorter RS codes and increasing their efficiency, the leakage rate will decrease, as can be seen from Table 2.

5   Conclusions

In this article, we examined the principles of implementing a cryptographic system based on the use of facial smile imprints. Video frames of the main smile phases (onset, apex and offset) were used to obtain biometric data, on the basis of SAE consisting of two inner layers and trained with the use of smile videos of 400 subjects taken randomly from UvA-NEMO database. The real data of the output layer was quantized and encoded by the RS codes (63,15) and (31,9) with a redundancy of more than 70%, which affects the entropy loss or leakage rate [27].

Simulation experiments have shown the ability to achieve the FRR parameter of less than 1% for key lengths of 90–170 bits and have demonstrated more efficient use of RS codes compared to their application for iris biometrics [28] and better performance in relation to the results from [29] for face template protection.

In our setup, we have used rather simple NN structures and concatenated ECC based on non-binary RS codes which made it possible to obtain small values of FRR for the proposed BS. Moreover, it can be seen, that a decrease in the FRR parameter is possible, firstly, by increasing the redundancy of the concatenated ECC, and secondly, by using the additional information from HD samples when exploiting the EED for RS codes, which, in fact, is an extension of the results in [30].

The direction of further work can be both the study of other NN structures to obtain deep features of a smile facial imprint, and the implementation of proposed algorithms and data structures for HD1 and HD2 storage.

Acknowledgments. This material is based upon work partially supported by the COST Action CA16101. The authors would like to thank Dr. Hamdi Dibeklioğlu for providing access to the data base UvA-NEMO.

References

1. Smileid. New Standard for Face Biometrics. http://www.electronicid.eu/en/solutions/smileid. Accessed 05 May 2021. Accessed 4 Nov 2021
2. Cook, S.: Selfie banking: is it a reality? Biom. Technol. Today **3**(2017), 9–11 (2017)
3. Taskiran, M., et al.: Face recognition using dynamic features extracted from smile videos. In: IEEE International Symposium on INnovations in Intelligent Systems and Applications (INISTA), Sofia, pp. 1–6 (2019)
4. Dibeklioğlu, H., Salah, A.A., Gevers, T.: Are you really smiling at me? Spontaneous versus posed enjoyment smiles. In: Fitzgibbon, A., Lazebnik, S., Perona, P., Sato, Y., Schmid, C. (eds.) ECCV 2012. LNCS, vol. 7574, pp. 525–538. Springer, Heidelberg (2012). https://doi.org/10.1007/978-3-642-33712-3_38
5. Fabian, I., Gulyas, G.: De-anonymizing facial recognition embeddings. Infocommun. J. **2**(12), 50–56 (2020)
6. Terhorst, P., Fahrmann, D., et al.: Beyond identity: what information is stored in biometric face templates? In: IEEE International Joint Conference on Biometrics (IJCB), Houston, pp. 1–10 (2020)
7. Boddeti, V.N.: Secure face matching using fully homomorphic encryption. In: 2018 IEEE 9th International Conference on Biometrics Theory, Applications and Systems (BTAS), Redondo Beach, pp. 1–10 (2018)
8. Jindal, A.K., et al.: Secure and privacy preserving method for biometric template protection using fully homomorphic encryption. In: 2020 IEEE 19th International Conference on Trust, Security and Privacy in Computing and Communications (TrustCom), Guangzhou, pp. 1127–1134 (2020)
9. Drozdowski, P., et al.: Feature fusion methods for indexing and retrieval of biometric data: application to face recognition with privacy protection. IEEE Access **9**, 139361–139378 (2021)
10. Osorio-Roig, D., et al.: Stable hash generation for efficient privacy-preserving face identification. IEEE Trans. Biom. Behav. Identity Sci. **99**, 1–1 (2021)
11. Juels, A., Wattenberg, M.: A fuzzy commitment scheme. In: ACM Conference on Computer and Communications Security, Singapore, pp. 28–36 (1999)
12. Mohan, D.D., et al.: Significant feature based representation for template protection. In: 2019 IEEE/CVF Conference on Computer Vision and Pattern Recognition Workshops (CVPRW), Long Beach, pp. 2389–2396 (2019)
13. Gilkalaye, B.P., Rattani, A., Derakhshani, R.: Euclidean-distance based fuzzy commitment scheme for biometric template security. In: 2019 7th International Workshop on Biometrics and Forensics (IWBF), Cancun, pp. 1–6 (2019)
14. Rathgeb, C., Merkle, J., et al.: Deep face fuzzy vault: implementation and performance. Comput. Secur. **113**, 102539 (2022)
15. Pandey, R.K., Zhou, Y., Kota, B.U., Govindaraju, V.: Learning representations for cryptographic hash based face template protection. In: Bhanu, B., Kumar, A. (eds.) Deep Learning for Biometrics. ACVPR, pp. 259–285. Springer, Cham (2017). https://doi.org/10.1007/978-3-319-61657-5_11
16. Siwek, K., Osowski, S.: Autoencoder versus PCA in face recognition. In: 18th International Conference on Computational Problems of Electrical Engineering (CPEE), Kutna Hora, pp. 1–4 (2017)

17. Usman, M., Latif, S., Qadir, J.: Using deep autoencoders for facial expression recognition. In: 13th International Conference on Emerging Technologies (ICET), Islamabad, pp. 1–6 (2017). https://doi.org/10.1109/ICET.2017.8281753
18. Assanovich, B.: Autoencoders for denoising and classification applications. In: Open Semantic Technologies for Intelligent Systems (OSTIS), Minsk, pp. 309–312 (2020)
19. Vinck, A.J.H.: Coding Concepts and Reed-Solomon Codes. Institute for Experimental Mathematics, Essen (2013)
20. MacKay, D.J.C.: Information Theory, Inference and Learning Algorithms. Cambridge University Press, Cambridge (2003)
21. Rao, K.D.: Channel Coding Techniques for Wireless Communications. Springer, New Delhi (2015). https://doi.org/10.1007/978-81-322-2292-7
22. Assanovich, B., et al.: Recognition of genuine smile as a factor of happiness and its application to measure the quality of customer retail services. In: Proceedings of the 14th International Conference on Pattern Recognition and Information Processing (PRIP 2019), Minsk, pp. 84–89 (2019)
23. Atieno, L., Allen, J., et al.: An adaptive Reed-Solomon errors-and-erasures decoder. In: Proceedings of the 2006 ACM/SIGDA 14th International Symposium on Field Programmable Gate Arrays (FPGA 2006), Monterey, California, pp. 150–158 (2006)
24. Assanovich, B., Veretilo, Yu.: Biometric database based on HOG structures and BCH codes. In: Proceedings of Information Technologies and System 2017 (ITS 2017), Minsk, pp. 286–287 (2017)
25. Ignatenko, T., Willems, F.M.J.: Information leakage in fuzzy commitment schemes. IEEE Trans. Inf. Forensics Secur. 2(5), 337–348 (2010)
26. Moon, Y.I., Rajagopalan, B., Lall, U.: Estimation of mutual information using kernel density estimators. Phys. Rev. E Stat. Phys. Plasmas Fluids Relat. Interdiscip. Top. 3(52), 2318–2321 (1995)
27. Immler, V., Uppund, K.: New insights to key derivation for tamper-evident physical unclonable functions. IACR Trans. Cryptogr. Hardw. Embed. Syst. 3(2019), 30–65 (2019)
28. Adamovic, S., et al.: Fuzzy commitment scheme for generation of cryptographic keys based on iris biometrics. IET Biom. 6(2), 89–96 (2017)
29. Chen, L., et al.: Face template protection using deep LDPC codes learning. IET Biom. 3(8), 190–197 (2019)
30. Assanovich, B.: Towards creation of SmileID obtained from face biometrics binded to concantenated error-correcting codes. In: Proceedings 15th International Conference on Pattern Recognition and Information Processing (PRIP 2019), Minsk, pp. 65–69 (2021)

Detection of Features Regions of Syndrome in Multiple Sclerosis on MRI

Ivan Kosik[1,2], Alexander Nedzved[1,3(✉)], Ryhor Karapetsian[2],
Vera Yashina[4], and Igor Gurevich[4]

[1] Belarusian State University, 4 Nezavisimosti Avenue, 220030 Minsk, Belarus
nedzveda@tut.by
[2] Belarusian Medical State University, 83 Dzerjinskogo Avenue, Minsk, Belarus
[3] UIIP of NAS Belarus, 6 Surganova Street, Minsk, Belarus
[4] Federal Research Center "Computer Science and Control" of the Russian
Academy of Sciences, Moscow, Russia

Abstract. In this paper regions of multiple sclerosis on radiological images are detected by model of convolutional neural network. The specific image preprocessing allows to improves quality of dataset. In result the model UNet 3+ detect regions with pathology with high probability. The proposed solution significantly increases the speed of analyzing the state of the pathological pattern.

Keywords: Multiple sclerosis · Medical image analysis · UNet 3+ · Regions detection · Segmentation · Dataset preprocessing

1 Introduction

Multiple sclerosis is a serious disease of the central nervous system that leads to disability among people, including young people of working age. Insufficient knowledge of the pathogenesis of this disease and an increase in the frequency of its occurrence require the intensification of studies of this pathology [1].

The most important symptom of multiple sclerosis is a focal lesion of the central nervous system caused by auto aggression against myelin proteins in the brain and spinal cord. In this case sites of demyelination occur and sclerotic plaques appear in the small veins of the brain, in the cerebellum, in the spinal cord, in the optic and other cranial nerves. They are an important diagnostic feature of multiple sclerosis.

Magnetic resonance imaging (MRI) is the most effective tool for visualization of demyelination sites nowadays. However, for an objective description of the state and dynamics of the pathological process, visualization of foci on MRI sections should be supplemented with data on the size, intensity and localization [2].

Detection of lesions is the first step towards obtaining additional quantitative information from MRI images. In most cases, their boundaries are blurred and have poor contrast against the background of the brain tissue. Therefore, the detection of pathological sites is the most time consuming and at the same time the most important stage. The accuracy of the diagnostics largely depends on the accuracy of the detection. Meanwhile, in medical practice, segmentation of foci is carried out either by manual

© Springer Nature Switzerland AG 2022
A. V. Tuzikov et al. (Eds.): PRIP 2021, CCIS 1562, pp. 220–233, 2022.
https://doi.org/10.1007/978-3-030-98883-8_16

methods (contouring), or by semi-automatic methods (for example, by algorithms of area growth or "smart brush"). The diagnostician must first visually assess the information content of the image area in terms of the level of brightness and localization, and then carry out the recognition procedure. Considering that the radiologist has to analyze at least 120 slices (50 + 40 + 30 in three orthogonal projections), it is easy to understand how difficult this work is. This affects the accuracy of the results, especially when examining multifocal patterns [3].

The use of advanced methods of volumetric reconstruction of MRI images, based on fully automatic segmentation of informative objects by neural networks, contributes to an increase in the productivity and accuracy of the study.

2 Dataset Preparing

2.1 Properties of Multiple Sclerosis Images

In patients who are suspected of having multiple sclerosis, conventional Magnetic Resonance imaging (MRI) has been formally included in the diagnostic work-up through the definition of ad hoc sets of criteria to show disease dissemination in space and time. the strength of the association of conventional MRI findings with the subsequent clinical manifestations of the disease remains modest, at best, in patients with definite multiple sclerosis. This is likely due to the relative lack of specificity of conventional MRI in evaluation of the heterogeneous pathologic substrates of the disease, the inability of MRI to provide accurate estimates of such damage outside focal lesions, and the fact that MRI cannot be used to identify the mechanisms through which the central nervous system recovers after tissue injury has occurred. Structural, metabolic, and functional Magnetic Resonance techniques have provided new markers that are more closely linked to the pathologic features of the disease, which may in part overcome the limitations of conventional MRI.

For images dataset, we used the data of patients with multiple sclerosis. They were diagnosed at the 9th City Clinical Hospital of Minsk. The data included MRI series of images. They were saved as Dicom files and compiled by the standard method of the conclusion of a specialist neuroradiologist. We used MRI-series of 50 patients obtained in different modes (T1, T2, Flair, etc.) for training the neural network.

The definition of MRI criteria for a diagnosis of multiple sclerosis is based on the demonstration of lesion dissemination in space and time on dual-echo and postcontrast T1-weighted magnetic resonance studies of the brain and on the exclusion of alternative neurologic conditions. A series of MRI markers, derived from evidence-based findings and educated guesses, have also been identified in the setting of clinically suspected multiple sclerosis. The detection of a new high-signal-intensity lesion on T2-weighted MRI can identified at any time since the performance of a reference magnetic resonance study. The revised criteria can be clarified the use of spinal cord MRI to demonstrate disease dissemination in space.

2.2   Annotation Software

To prepare a dataset and annotation of images, the special software was developed. It includes a function of semi-automatic segmentation with the graphic primitive "Smart Brush".

This function allows you to quickly select regions of lesions by breaking all pixels under the brush into background and tumor. The user sets brush radius for definition size of extracted regions. The spot with this radius includes all pixels around the current cursor position. Then, pixels are divided into 2 clusters in terms of brightness by k-means clustering algorithm. After that, one of the clusters is selected as a tumor interactively:

a) lighter region: with a higher average brightness of all pixels in the cluster;
b) darker region;
c) the cluster into which the current pixel under the cursor.

If first item is selected, then only the lighter areas of the image the spot regions are highlighted (see Fig. 1).

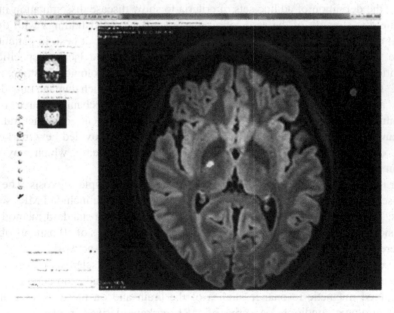

Fig. 1. The result of selection with a brush in the light mode.

If second item is selected, then the brush spot extracts the darker regions of the image in the spot. This tool is leaving the bright, light regions as not painted over (see Fig. 2). This mode is more convenient to use in the T1-weighted mode for image. The spot size can be changed interactively.

If the last item is selected, then the user can additionally use the selection of connected regions only. In this way, only that part of the cluster is extracted that is one connected area together with the pixel under the cursor (see Fig. 3).

The k-means algorithm initially selects random cluster centers and assigns each pixel to the closest cluster in brightness. After that, at each iteration, the center of each cluster from previous step is recalculated, and the pixels are divided into clusters again.

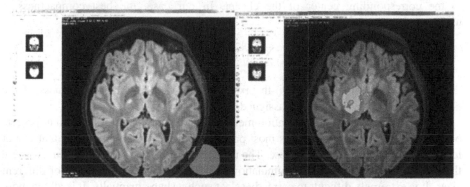

Fig. 2. The result of selection with a brush of darker regions.

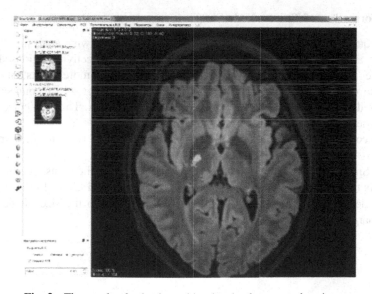

Fig. 3. The result of selection with a brush of connected regions.

The algorithm is finished when the cluster centers change by less than a specified value epsilon or after a specified number of iterations. In our case, we used epsilon = 1, the number of iterations = 10.

In addition, the algorithm processes several randomly selected cluster centers. From the data of processing result, the clustering option is selected, where the clusters had the best compactness.

Compactness is estimated as the sum of the squares of the distances from each point to the corresponding center of the cluster. In our case, the best compactness is understood as the minimum:

$$C = \sum_i \left(p_i - center_{p_i}\right)^2, \tag{1}$$

where p_i is brightness of the i-th pixel, $center_{pi}$ is the average brightness of the cluster to which the i-th pixel is assigned.

The first and third of segmentation methods can be conveniently applied to objects of complex shapes. The second is most productive for objects with shape, that can at least approximate by circle or ellipse. The third method is most effective in cases where the demyelination node is an accumulation of closely spaced, ragged foci of different sizes. It is extremely difficult to correctly select such a shape manually. It is all the more difficult to maintain a high repeatability, which means the reliability of the result.

2.3   Correction of Tumor Node Shape

After sequential cross-cut segmentation of every layer, pairwise analysis of adjacent slices is carried out. It is necessary for determination of connectivity regions. There are binary regions on neighboring slices, which include one or more points (pixels) with the same coordinates along the horizontal axis. These regions of connectivity are interpreted as lying in different horizontal slices of one focus. They are corrected by a volumetric model of the focus of demyelination.

The construction of volumetric models is carried out in two versions: spline and voxel.

The Smart Brush tool does not select only the borders of the focus, but immediately segments the area that falls within the brush (see Fig. 4 and Fig. 5). In Fig. 4, the size of the selected lesion is larger than the lesion in Fig. 5, so the size of the brush is chosen large.

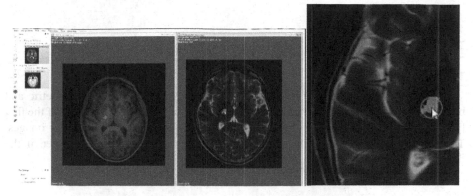

Fig. 4. Demonstration of selection with the "brush" tool of a medium tumor node, T1 mode processing is represented on the left picture, T2 mode processing is represented in the center, and detailing of representation of selection process on scaling the picture.

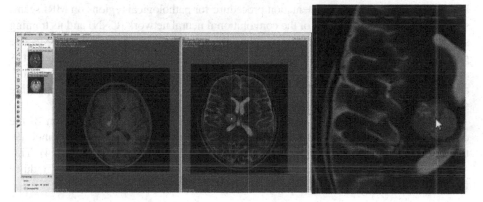

Fig. 5. Demonstration of selection with the "brush" tool of a big tumor node, T1 mode processing is represented on the left picture, T2 mode processing is represented in the center, and detailing of selection process on scaling the picture.

This method is distinguished by its performance and low investment in time required to complete the task. Moreover, the quality of the result is the highest.

2.4   Preparation of Training Images

In addition, data augmentation was used. It is the technique for generation additional training data from the initially available initial set of images [4, 5]. In our case, the initial training set consisted of 455 3D-series. It corresponds to different modes and different studies of 50 patients.

For the augmentation the Albumentations library (https://albumentations.ai/) was used. We chose the following parameters for augmentation:

– rotations up to 20°;
– shift;
– scaling;

- horizontal reflection;
- vertical reflection;
- sharpening;
- spectrum change;
- optical distortion.

To increase the volume of initial data, we used methods based on geometric and brightness variability for informative objects in the original images. Methods of the first type increase the data volume by reorienting and scaling the available input images. This allowed the network to learn invariance to this kind of distortion, even if the distortion was absent in the original images.

3   Definition of CNN Model

3.1   Model on Base DenseNet

For full automation of the segmentation procedure for pathological regions on MRI scans, such algorithms include model of the convolutional neural network (CNN) and its training strategy [6]. The learning strategy is based on the most complete extraction and effective generalization of meaningful information concentrated in the initial data. The effect is achieved due to the automatic generation of additional data from them. The network architecture consists of a tapered section for capturing context, and a symmetrical expanding section for more accurate localization and contouring of objects like as U-Net [7].

To solve the problem of segmentation of the tumor area, a modernization of the classical U-Net [8] was proposed by integration DenseNet model into the branch [9] that converts the image into a set of features as a subnet (backbone) (see Fig. 4). This solution was developed by the Python programming language with separate modules for the popular Keras library focused on working with neural networks.

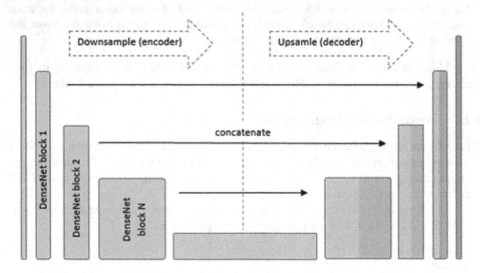

Fig. 6. Graphical representation of U-Net architecture with DenseNet backbone.

DenseNet [10] is an evolution of the ResNet model, which is highly efficient in MRI image segmentation. A number of disadvantages of the previous generation networks were taken into account in these models of CNN. First of all, a method of reducing of number of layers was used in it. The excess of layers number influence to the quality of recognition by the neural network of informative regions on validation and training images.

3.2 Model on Base U-Net 3+

For the most complete automation of the procedure for segmentation of pathological areas on MRI scans, a selection of the architecture of a convolutional neural network (CNN) and a strategy for its training was performed, which would allow obtaining a high return with a limited initial sample. The learning strategy is based on the most complete extraction and effective generalization of meaningful information concentrated in the initial data. The effect is achieved due to the automatic generation of additional data from this data. The network architecture consists of a tapered section for capturing context, and a symmetrical expanding section for more accurate localization and con-touring of objects. This network organization is called U-Net 3+ [11] like as Fig. 5.

The UNet 3+ gives simplified overviews of UNet, UNet++. Compared with UNet and UNet++, UNet 3+ combines the multi-scale features by re-designing skip con-nections as well as utilizing a full-scale deep supervision, which provides fewer parameters but yields a more accurate position-aware and boundary-enhanced seg-mentation map [12, 13].

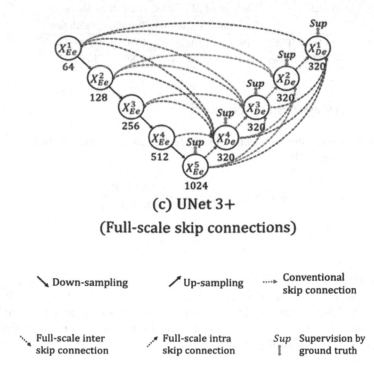

(c) UNet 3+

(Full-scale skip connections)

Fig. 7. The model of UNet 3+ [6]. The depth of each node is presented below the circle. (Color figure online)

4 Neural Network Training

The series were divided into training set and validation one in a ratio of 75% to 25%, respectively. The formation of sets of training and validation images by series allows you to include all MRI slices of the series in only one sample (training or validation). This is justified by the fact that similar regions belonging to neighboring slices will lead to overfitting if they get in different samples. An additional set of test images for a separate small group of patients is formed during the testing phase of the final version of the neural network.

The next step in the training procedure is to obtain training images (MRI slices) from the 3D series, divided into training set and validation one. Sections without pathological regions are not used in training, since preliminary tests showed that training on all sections gives worse results. Examples of the formation of training sets are given below. It is clear that the number of series selected for the same MRI scan mode exceeds the number of unique patients, since several series (taken at different times) can belong to the same patient.

Two neural networks were trained: one on MRI series obtained in the T2 TSE scan mode; the second on all images (all modes were used). The amount of training data is shown in Table 1.

Table 1. Amount of training data for each model

Model	Number of 3D-series		Number of slices	
	Training	Validation	Training	Validation
Mode T2 TSE	119	40	1500	506
All MRI-modes	341	114	4789	1452

5 Quality Assessment of Network

To assess the quality, the Intersection Over Union metric (or Jaccard index) was used, given by the formula (2):

$$IoU = \frac{TP}{TP + FP + FN} = \frac{Im_1 \cap Im_2}{Im_1 \cup Im_2}$$

$$= \frac{Im_1 \cap Im_2}{Im_1 + Im_2 - Im_1 \cap Im_2} \quad (2)$$

where TP (true positive) is selection of a pixel that actually belongs to the focus of demyelination; FP (false positive) is false selection of a pixel that does not belong to the focus; FN (false negative) is false marked pixel as not belonging to the focus; Im_1 is an area identified by an expert as a focus of demyelination; Im_2 is area identified by the neural network as a focus of demyelination.

The metric can take values from 0 to 1. It assesses how closely the area of the real focus Im_1 (selected interactively by the expert) matches the area Im_2, segmented automatically by the neural network. The higher the metric value, the greater the coincidence, and, therefore, the more reliable the neural network model works. In Fig. 6, the same focus is highlighted by an expert (green) and a neural network (brown).

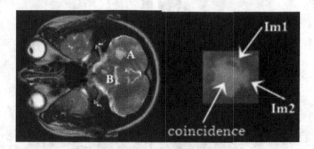

Fig. 8. The *IoU* metric demonstration: total image of MRI-section, with highlighted foci A and B (a); fragment of the MRI image with focus A (b)

There is an overlap of areas of green and brown in Fig. 6b. In Fig. 6b, the overlapping areas of green and brown correspond to the area selected by both the expert and the neural network.

6   Discussion and Conclusion

The best accuracy was obtained for the trained model with the input image size 352 × 352 and the batch-size 9. It is equal to 0.62 (IoU, Jaccard index). combination of the binary cross-entropy and the Sørensen loss function (Dice loss). This model was trained for 100 epochs using a GeForce GTX 1080 Ti graphics card. The training lasted 4 h.

Examples of the results of segmentation of areas of destruction of the myelin sheath are shown in Fig. 7 and 8. The color of individual areas corresponds to the color (see Fig. 6): green corresponds to the selection of the focus by the expert, brown to the selection of the focus by the neural network. The overlapping areas of green and brown correspond to the area selected by both the expert and the neural network.

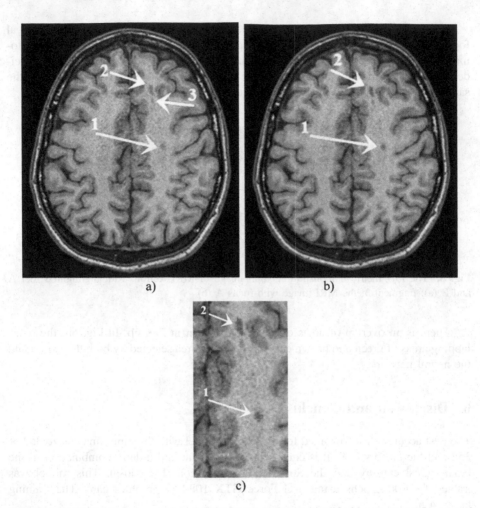

Fig. 9. Myelin sheath lesions: original T1W image (a); areas identified by an expert (b); part of an enlarged image (c)

The Fig. 8 shows that, the network found all the affected areas. For two of them, the highlighting coincided with the expert's opinion, one is highlighted contrary to the expert's opinion. In such cases, additional validation is required.

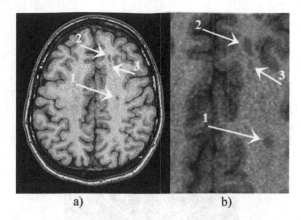

a)   b)

Fig. 10. Myelin sheath lesions: areas identified by neural network (a); a enlarged part of the image with the result of comparing the lesions identified by the expert and the network (b)

In Fig. 9, the network also highlighted all the foci (the areas highlighted by the expert and the network changed color when superpositioned). In addition, the network highlighted a problem area, which the expert did not mark as a focus of demyelination (it remained brown). In this case, additional validation of the results is required (Fig. 11).

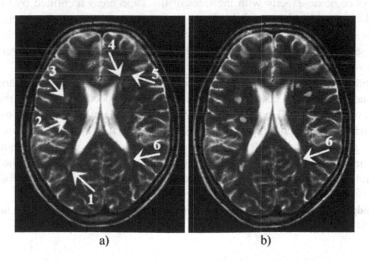

a)   b)

Fig. 11. Myelin sheath lesions: marked on the original T2W image (a); overlay of results of the selection by the expert and the neural network (b). The arrow indicates area 6, identified as an outbreak only by the network

In Fig. 10, the neural network did not identify area 3 as a focus of demyelination, but at the same time found areas 1, 2, 4, which for some reason were not noted by the expert. Additional analysis of the results is required, but neural network extraction looks more promising (Fig. 12).

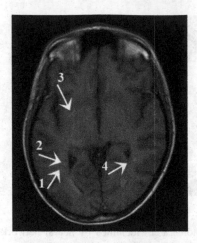

Fig. 12. Myelin sheath lesions: the result of the superposition of the results of the selection of foci by the expert and the neural network. The arrow indicates the areas of non-coincidence

In general, it can be seen that the network successfully detects problem areas on MRI-scans obtained in different modes. The most accurate results are obtained with T2 TSE images. It should be noted that the sizes of the areas selected by the network do not always coincide exactly with the sizes of the same areas identified by the expert. This is due to the ambiguity of the focus boundaries, and the result of network segmentation is not always less accurate, especially when there are many lesions on different sections. Working under severe stress, the expert gets tired and over time his attention weakens.

The proposed solution for the automatic identification of pathological areas using artificial neural networks has significantly increased the speed of analyzing the state of the pathological pattern. Traditional manual isolation of demyelination lesions requires at least 65 min per patient, semi-automatic isolation takes about 23 min, while a automatic segmentation is performed within 1 min. In addition, automatic segmentation using a neural network allows to get hundred-percent repeatability of the analysis results and significantly reduce the workload for neurologists and radiologists.

Acknowledgment. The reported study was funded by RFBR and BRFBR, project number 20-57-00025/BRFFI F20R-134.

References

1. Poser, C.M., Brinar, V.V.: Diagnostic criteria for multiple sclerosis: an historical review. Clin. Neurol. Neurosurg. **106**(3), 147–158 (2004)
2. Filippi, M., Rocca, M.A.: MR imaging of multiple sclerosis. Radiology **259**(3), 659–681 (2011)
3. Shorten, C., Khoshgoftaar, T.M.: A survey on image data augmentation for deep learning. J. Big Data **6** (2019). Article number: 60. https://doi.org/10.1186/s40537-019-0197-0

4. Nalepa, J., Marcinkiewicz, M., Kawulok, M.: Data augmentation for brain-tumor segmentation: a review. Front. Comput. Neurosci. **83**, 1662–5188 (2019)
5. Biswas, A., Bhattacharya, P., Maity, S.P., Banik, R.: Data augmentation for improved brain tumor segmentation. IETE J. Res. (2021). 0377-2063
6. Arslanov, M.Z.: N-bit parity neural networks with minimum number of threshold neurons. Eurasian J. Math. Comput. Appl. **4**(2), 4–13 (2016)
7. Ronneberger, O., Fischer, P., Brox, T.: U-Net: convolutional networks for biomedical image segmentation. In: Navab, N., Hornegger, J., Wells, W.M., Frangi, A.F. (eds.) MICCAI 2015. LNCS, vol. 9351, pp. 234–241. Springer, Cham (2015). https://doi.org/10.1007/978-3-319-24574-4_28
8. Piantadosi, G., Sansone, M., Sansone, C.: Breast segmentation in MRI via U-Net deep convolutional neural networks. In: 24th International Conference on Pattern Recognition (ICPR 2018), pp. 3917–3922 (2018)
9. Tong, Z., Li, Y., Li, Y., Fan, K., Si, Y., He, L.: New network based on Unet++ and Densenet for building extraction from high resolution satellite imagery. In: IGARSS 2020 - 2020 IEEE International Geoscience and Remote Sensing Symposium, pp. 2268–2271 (2020)
10. Huang, G., Liu, Z., Weinberger, K.Q.: Densely connected convolutional networks. In: 2017 IEEE Conference on Computer Vision and Pattern Recognition (CVPR), pp. 2261–2269 (2017)
11. Huang, H., et al.: UNet 3+: a full-scale connected UNet for medical image segmentation. In: ICASSP 2020 - 2020 IEEE International Conference on Acoustics, Speech and Signal Processing (ICASSP), pp. 1055–1059 (2020)
12. Duan, J., Liu, X.: Online monitoring of green pellet size distribution in haze-degraded images based on VGG16-LU-Net and haze judgment. IEEE Trans. Instrum. Measur. **70**, 1–16 (2021)
13. Tran, S.-T., Cheng, C.-H., Liu, D.-G.: A multiple layer U-Net, U^n-Net, for liver and liver tumor segmentation in CT. IEEE Access **9**, 3752–3764 (2021)
14. Rezatofighi, H., Tsoi, N., Gwak, J., Sadeghian, A., Reid, I., Savarese, S.: Generalized intersection over union: a metric and a loss for bounding box regression. arXiv:1902.09630 (2019)

Automatic Tuning of the Motion Control System of a Mobile Robot Along a Trajectory Based on the Reinforcement Learning Method

Kim Tatyana[1,2]([⊠]) [iD] and Ryhor Prakapovich[1] [iD]

[1] Laboratory of robotic systems, United Institute of Informatics Problems
of NAS of Belarus, Minsk, Belarus
tatyna_kim92@mail.ru, rprakapovich@robotics.by
[2] Urgench Branch of Tashkent University of Information Technologies named
after Muhammad al-Khwarizmi, Urgench, Uzbekistan

Abstract. The is a description of the development process of an adaptive motion controller for a two-wheeled mobile robot along a color-contrast line. The learning process of the controller took place on the basis of the digital twin of the indicated robot, with the use of reinforcement learning technology. The digital twin and reinforcement learning implemented in MATLAB/Simulink frameworks, for the latter, the Reinforcement Learning Toolbox library was used. The mobile robot equipped with a differential driver, and the PID-controller adjusted the angular speed of the rotation of both wheels. Therefore, the main purpose of the research work was to determine the coefficients of the PID-controller. The Twin-Delayed Deep Deterministic Policy Gradient Agents was used as a learning algorithm, which used a deterministic actor and a Q-value critic. As a function of reward, the minimization of the distance between the center of the robot and the edge of the nearest section of the color-contrast line was used, as well as the calculation of the angle (γ) between the tangent to the edge of the ellipse curve, where the robot should be located and guided at the current time. The developed environment, which would be influenced by the agent, as well as the policy of the agent, which provides a detailed diagram of the neural network for the actor and the critic. Different methods carried out for the comparison of the results, such as genetic algorithms and reinforcement learning by the TD3 algorithm. The experiments have shown that the founded coefficients of the PID-controller afford control the movement of the robot accurately, even on an unfamiliar track.

Keywords: Reinforcement learning (RL) · MATLAB/Simulink · Twin-Delayed Deep Deterministic Policy Gradient Agents (TD3) · Control system · Digital twin · Neural network

1 Introduction

Reinforcement learning is one of the machine learning methods for revealing control issues in complex technical systems that can be described problematically or have no descriptions in an analytical form.

© Springer Nature Switzerland AG 2022
A. V. Tuzikov et al. (Eds.): PRIP 2021, CCIS 1562, pp. 234–244, 2022.
https://doi.org/10.1007/978-3-030-98883-8_17

The reinforcement learning method is based on the implementation of the process with maximizing a certain rewarding signal (a reward) when enumerating different variants of the behavior of the studied systems - agents. The agent learns to perform the actions that can bring him the greatest reward. The agent's actions can affect not only the local reward received immediately, but also the situation as a whole in the most interesting and important cases [1]. To generate a long-term reward is a rather difficult process, since a correctly formed reward will bring better results and shorten the length of training (the better the learning process is).

At present, in addition to classical robotic manipulators, mobile robots in the form of robotic carts are in high demand in production. The PID regulators tend to be used the most at the lower control level of a mobile robot [2, 3]. The PID regulator allows to adjust the control action of the actuators in such a way as to achieve the required values of the objective function as quickly as possible. Sometimes the selection of coefficients is a rather long process, which does not always lead to success, since there is a chance of overshoot [4, 5]. In a closed-loop control system, the controller uses state observations to improve performance and correct random interferences and errors. There is also a problem related to the fact that each type of the line is required to be found by the corresponding values of the PID coefficients. This problem can be quickly solved by using reinforcement learning.

The object of the research is the RoboCake training mobile robot with a differential drive, which is supposed to be moved along the edge of the flower-trust line. The control system is a classic servo drive, which includes an optical sensor for detecting the edge of the color-contrast line and a PID regulator that monitors the angular speed of rotation of the wheels. Previous experiments were carried out on the automatic tuning of the specified PID regulator using the PID Tuner utility and the application of a genetic algorithm [6]. The aim of this research work is to automatically adjust the motion control system of a mobile robot along a trajectory, based on the training with reinforcement using the Twin-Delayed Deep Deterministic Policy Gradient Agents (TD3) algorithm and compare the obtained implication of the coefficients with the former work [6], where the genetic algorithm was used.

2   Reinforcement Learning Elements

The reinforcement learning elements shown in Fig. 1 are equivalent to a feedback control system. Agent block includes the strategy and the selected algorithm. Agent acts in a certain circumstance, and with the help of sensors it determines the state s in it, and performs some action a, passing into a new state s'. The Agent evaluates how beneficial the action is by using the r-reward. "The reward is scalar utility. Over the time, the agent seeks to maximize (or minimize) the reward, and this reinforces good actions over bad ones, allowing the agent to know the optimal policy" [7].

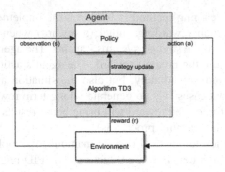

Fig. 1. Expanded reinforcement learning pattern.

2.1   The Description of the Problem

The study of the object of study in reinforcement learning takes place as a result of generation of an artificial neural network, that can simulate the behavior of the desired object. The most important issue in reinforcement learning remains the generation of a training sample for the specified artificial neural network. The experiments were carried out in the MATLAB framework, where it used the "Reinforcement Learning Toolbox" library, with providing a choice of ten Agents (learning algorithms). Actor-critical agents use either a stochastic or a deterministic actor with a significant critic or a Q-significance critic[1].

Following the reinforcement learning methodology to achieve the goal, it is required to describe a software agent that needs to develop a control policy for a supervision object. The term "policy" means a mapping which selects adequate actions of the control object on the corresponding changes in the framework[2].

The Agent uses the following data: 1) the indications of the optical sensor from the edge of the line (consisting of 3 light sensors), 2) the distance from the center of the mobile robot to the edge of the color-contrast line, and 3) the angle between the normal of the nearest section of the line and the direction the movement of the mobile robot itself. The result of observation is the selection of angular speeds of rotation of two wheels of the mobile robot. To form actions correctly, the agent needs to train repeatedly, and to make the training productive for each action, it must be fostered (rewarded) or fined. Cessation criteria is used to reduce the learning time also. Each episode of the learning process could be suspended, if: 1) the simulation exceeds the time allotted for movement along a full ellipse; 2) the robot has exceeded the distance from the edge of the ellipse line. During each episode, the agent chooses an action (forms a policy), after the end, it updates its parameters based on the actions and receives the maximum reward. This process continues until the agent learns to move correctly along the edge of the line with specified conditions[3]. When developing this

---

[1] https://www.mathworks.com/help/reinforcement-learning/ug/create-agents-for-reinforcement-learning.html.

[2] https://www.mathworks.com/help/reinforcement-learning/ug/what-is-reinforcement-learning.html.

[3] https://www.mathworks.com/help/reinforcement-learning/ug/what-is-reinforcement-learning.html.

algorithm, the library "Reinforcement Learning Toolbox" was used, which provides a policy and a reward function using deep neural networks (DNN)[4].

A digital twin [8] of the mobile robot RoboCake, developed in the MATLAB/Simulink packages, is used as the model under study. The specified mobile robot is required to move along the edge of the ellipse curve (color contrast line) at a speed of 1 m/s and with a minimum deviation from the edge of the line.

2.2 Learning Process

Before starting the learning process, it is required to create a virtual environment for the functioning of a mobile robot and an interactive interface with it. Next, it needs to configure the Agent module from the "Reinforcement Learning Toolbox" library. The TD3 algorithm was chosen to implement Agent, which is characterized by the fact that in addition to Agent, offering specific actions of the Actor on certain indications of the sensory system; two new entities are used - two critics, forming a long-term reward and next, Agent is configured and formed. The final stage is training and verification of the results of the trained agent.

After the positive completion of the learning process, using the getLearnableParameters() command, weights are extracted from the trained neural network, which are the desired coefficients of the PID controller.

2.3 Controller Design of the Reinforcement Learning

In Fig. 2 a digital twin reinforcement learning architecture in the MATLAB simulation environment is illustrated. The main block is the RL_agent with response from the environment (RoboCake) directed through the observation vector. The RL_agent block uses the TD3 algorithm, which will be described below.

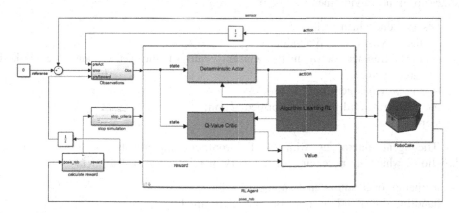

Fig. 2. A digital twin reinforcement learning architecture in the MATLAB simulation environment.

---

[4] Reinforcement Learning Toolbox™ User's Guide 2021a https://www.mathworks.com/help/pdf_doc/reinforcement-learning/rl_ug.pdf.

Implementation of the Environment

The circumstance is a digital twin [8] implemented in the MATLAB application package, which generates the following states for the Agent:

- position of the robot on the line;
- indication from the optical sensor.

Agent Implementation

The agent is based on neural networks that represent the actor and the critic. These networks contain many parameters (Table 1), weights and biases. It is these parameters that determine how neural networks turn off the division into actions or values. They are also updated during training.

There are blocks also: reward, which forms the reward and Stop-simulation, which monitors the end of the episode and reduces the simulation time.

Table 1. Agent hyperparameter settings.

Hyperparamenter	Parameter	Hyperparameter	Parameter
Parameters for actor		Parameters for critic	
Optimizer	Adam	Learn rate	0.0005
Learn rate	0.001	Gradient threshold	1
Gradient threshold	1	UseDevice	gpu
UseDevice	gpu		
L2RegularizationFactor	1e−5		

An agent is a control system that studies a control object and receives the following states from the Environment:

- observation, which includes:
  - the previous formed action;
  - the difference between the current state of the sensor and the desired circumstance;
  - the previous generated award;
- the current reward for the performed action;
- stop criteria.

The agent, interacting with the Environment implements the following basic functions, which are necessary for the work of reinforcement learning:

- formation of action at each moment of time;
- handling status and awards from the environment;
- obtaining the accumulated experience presented in the form of a neural network for the actor and the critic [9].

The list of available actions includes controlling the angular speed of the left and right wheels, where the mobile robot must drive along the curve of the ellipse at a speed of 1 m/s.

The agent receives readings from three sensors such as the encoders of the right and left wheels converted into 1 optical sensor, which determines the speed of the wheels and the location of the robot, as well as the previous action that the agent formed.

The agent receives the current reward when it minimizes the distance (1) between the nearest point on the ellipse and the robot's location, while minimizing the slope between the tangent to the ellipse and the robot's rail (2). The reinforcement learning agent's reward function has been defined as negative when the reinforcement learning agent maximizes this reward, thereby minimizing error.

The conditions are the criteria for cessation, formed in such a way as to shorten the training time. If the robot has exceeded the specified value (20 cm from the line), then the simulation starts over and the learning process continues.

The learning process was built on the basis of TD3. This TD3 algorithm is the next version of the DDPG (Deep Deterministic Policy Gradient) algorithm, which is more reliable, increases the stability [10] of learning and "Eliminates function approximation errors in methods of criticizing actors" [10]. The exceptional nature of this algorithm is that it combines 3 major reinforcement learning algorithms such as Double Deep Q-Learning [11], Policy Gradient [12] and Actor-Critic [13].

This algorithm is based on agent-critic and agent-actor, which uses criticism with Q-value and deterministic actor, respectively.

The advantage of this algorithm is that the TD3 *agent* approximates the long-term *reward*, taking into account the observation (s) and *action* (a), using the 2 presented *critics*. Below is a block diagram of the neural network for the *actor* and the *critic* (Fig. 4). After training, the actor's neural network (Fig. 4, a) forms the values of the coefficients for the PID controller, which are weights for the neural network, then apply to the test model, where the result will be the minimum distance between the robot and the edge of the ellipse and the minimum deviation of the angle (γ).

2.4   Reward Function

The reward process is an important step in RL, as it affects on the performance of the agent in relation to the goal that the mobile robot's control system seeks to achieve. A properly selected reward signal forces the Agent to move in the right direction with minimal deviation from the line and maximize the control system. The total remuneration received by an agent over an extended period of time, stimulating him (Agent) for long-term remuneration. The reward is formed in the form of a scalar signal, which is received by the Agent and generated by the Environment.

As a reward for the performed action, 2 criteria are taken into account. First, the distance (e) from the center of the robot (x_r, y_r) to the nearest unvisited point (x_0, y_0) of the ellipse located on the line is calculated using the formula for calculating the distance between two points (1), a detailed description of this formula and its obtaining is described in the article [6]. The closer the agent is to the edge of the ellipse curve, the greater the reward it will receive. Second, calculate the angle (γ) between the tangent to the ellipse at the point x_0, y_0, where the robot should be, and the robot guide using formula (2). The smaller the angle (γ), the more the agent will receive a reward (Fig. 3).

$$e = \sqrt{(x_c - x_r)^2 + (y_c - y_r)^2} - R \tag{1}$$

$$\gamma = \arctan\left(\left|\frac{-b^2 * \sin(\alpha) * R}{a^2 * \cos(\alpha) * R}\right|\right) \tag{2}$$

where R is the radius of the ellipse, b is the semi-minor axis, a is the semi-major axis, α is the angle between the radius (R) and the semi-major axis (a).

Since our reward signal consists of 2 signals combined into a scalar, we determine that the distance between the line and the robot is of paramount importance, and the resulting angle (φ) we reduce the influence to get the reward by 0.1.

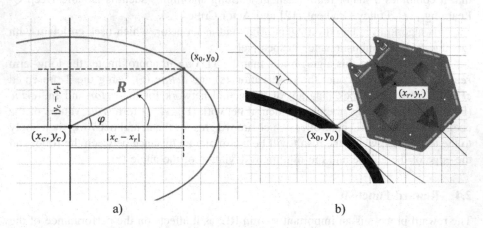

Fig. 3. Graphs demonstrating the formation of the reward function: a) calculating the angle φ of the distance traveled between the abscissa axis and the current position of the robot with coordinates x_r, y_r, R is the radius of the ellipse at the current time; b) determining the minimum distance between the curve of the ellipse and the center of the robot (e) and calculating the angle γ between the tangent of the ellipse and the robot's guide

2.5   Creation of a Neural Network of Actor and Critic

The TD3 actor-critic components have been implemented as shown in Fig. 4. The networks have fully connected layers, they are initialized with random weights of 50 neurons before the start of training.

The output of the actor network is normalized between $[-10, 10]$, using a fullyConnectedLayer, to then extract the coefficients for the PID controller. The first layer consists of 50 neurons, on their basis weights with parameters were formed [50, 3], where the second index 3 denotes the coefficients for the PID regulator.

The output of the network of actors (action A) is normalized between [−5, 5] using a fullyConnectedLayer to give limited impact on the left wheel of the mobile robot.

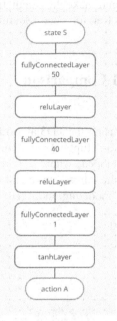

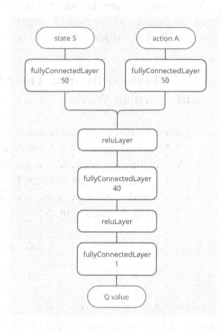

a) Neural network policy for the Actor   b) Neural Network Policy for the Critic

Fig. 4. TD3 network architectures

TD3 Finite Hyperparameters

Table 1 indicates the final set of TD3 hyperparameters. It is worth to pay special attention to the discount factor, which is located on the range [0, 1] and says that if the discount factor is 1, then all remuneration in time is taken with the same weight, the other extreme, when the discount factor is 0, then remuneration is taken into account only at the last steps of training (Table 2).

Table 2. Hyperparameter settings for the TD3 algorithm

Hyperparameter	Parameter	Hyperparameter	Parameter
Parameters for agent		Parameters for train	
Minibatch size	128	Max episodes	500
Experience buffer length	1e3	Max steps per episode	ceil (Tf/Ts), where Ts = 0.1; Tf = 10;
Exploration model	0.01	SampleTime	Ts
Target policy smooth model	0.1	Stop training criteria	Average reward
Discount factor	0	Stop training value	110

At this stage, we have everything ready to train the robot, this is a rather long procedure, and in this case the training process took less than two hours and as a result, everything that had to be done by a specialist in setting up a system.

The control system, in order to set the correct architecture and make the calculation of the parameters of the control system, all this was done by Reinforcement learning using the TD3 algorithm.

3   The Obtained Results, Their Significance and Comparison with Former Work

In the current research work, a software *agent* was developed using the TD3 algorithm for a simulated digital twin of a 2-wheeled robot moving along an elliptical curve in the MATLAB application package. A reward function was developed, where 2 criteria were taken into account: the distance between the robot and the ellipse curve and the angle (γ) of the deviation from the line. The environment for modeling and *agent* for training was implemented (Fig. 5).

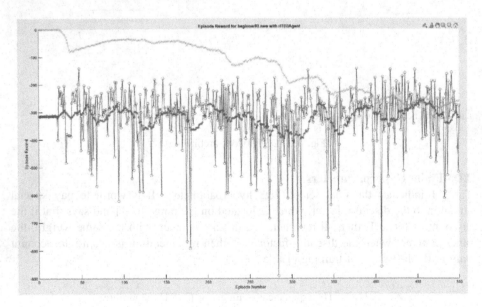

Fig. 5. The result of training a mobile robot after 500 episodes (simulations), Episode Reward - the reward received by the robot for each episode (simulation), Average Reward - the average reward for a window length for Averaging equal to 20, Episode Q0 - a critical assessment of the long-term reward for each episode

Since the trained *Agent* includes criticism, the critic's forecast (Episode Q0) is displayed on the progress graph by default in relation to the value of the reward for each episode. The graph shows that the prediction of the critic approaches the actual reward as the training progresses. This indicates that the critic is learning to accurately assess the value of being in a particular state.

In this graph, it seems that the highest reward is −257.266, the average is −318.154, where the robot can drive the ellipse curve in 41 s, minimizing the distance to the curve.

Due to additional parameter (adding a control angle γ), it is possible to trace the error in the deviation of the robot from the curve in degrees, how much the robot has deviated from the line, that is, its oscillations along the line (Fig. 6).

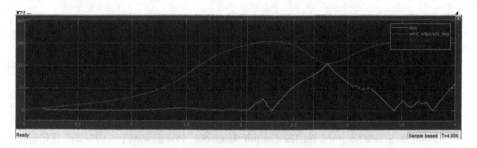

Fig. 6. Robot angle deviation error, where the blue line is the robot's angle deviation after 41 the number of training (in the middle of training), the yellow line is the already trained robot (Color figure online)

Comparing the results obtained earlier by the method of the genetic algorithm [6], with the new results obtained using Reinforcement Learning, we can conclude that the latter method reduces the number of specialties and the mean several times (Table 3).

Table 3. Results of reinforcement learning by TD3 and GA

P	I	D	Learning algorithm	Number of individuals	Elapsed time, ms
1.359	0.406	2.039	TD3	500	41
3.676	−0.159	−4.660		350	48
0.090	0.008	0.769		500	43
0.289	0.022	0.018		110	49
0.667	0.002	0.357		110	45
−4.627	0.150	0.301	GA	1950	61
−1.000	0.000	−0.062		2120	52
−0.416	−0.545	−0.156		1560	54
−3.002	0.156	0.754		1250	52
2.568	0.125	1.265		2100	55

4   Conclusion

In this article, using the reinforcement learning method, such values of the PID controller were selected, which made it possible to accurately control the movement of a 2-wheeled mobile robot along a color-contrast line. For this, an environment was implemented where a mobile robot was functioning, a software agent was configured, a reward function was developed, training was implemented using the TD3 algorithm using a deterministic actor and a Q-value critic. As a result, the tuned PID controller allows the mobile robot to move unmistakably along the edge of the ellipse at a speed of 1 m/s.

References

1. Sutton, R.S., Barto, A.G.: Reinforcement Learning: An Introduction. 2nd edn. The MIT Press, London (2014). https://web.stanford.edu/class/psych209/Readings/SuttonBartoIPRL Book2ndEd.pdf
2. Philippov, A.V., Kosolapov, M.A., Maslov, I.A., Tarasova, G.I.: Автоматизированная настройка ПИД-регулятора для объекта управления следящей системы с использованием программного пакета Matlab Simulink. [Automated tuning of the PID controller for the control object of the tracking system using the MATLAB Simulink software package], Science, Technology and Education 2015, no. 12(18), pp. 53–59 (2015)
3. Levine, W.S.: PID control. In: The Control Handbook, Piscataway, pp. 198–209. IEEE Press (1996)
4. Martins, F.G.: Tuning PID controllers using the ITAE criterion. Int. J. Eng. Educ. **21**(5), 867–873 (2005). 0949-149X/91Printed in Great Britain
5. Ziegler, J.G., Nichols, N.B.: Optimum settings for automatic controllers. Trans. ASME **64**, 759–768 (1942)
6. Kim, T.Yu.,Prakapovich, R.A.: Optimization of the PID coefficients for the line-follower mobile robot con-troller employing genetic algorithms. Informatika [Informatics] **18**(4), 54 −69 (2021). (in Russia). https://doi.org/10.37661/1816-0301-2021-18-4-54-69
7. Siraskar, R.: Reinforcement learning for control of valves. Mach. Learn. Appl. **4**, 100030 (2021). https://doi.org/10.1016/j.mlwa.2021.100030
8. Kim, T.Yu.: Разработка цифрового двойника мобильного робота для исследовательских и учебных целей на базе MATLAB/Simulink. [Development of a digital twin of a mobile robot for research and educational purposes based on MATLAB/Simulink]. In: XVIII International Conference of Young Scientists "Youth in Science - 2021". Belarus, Minsk, pp. 580–584 (2021)
9. Mayorov, M.P.: Reinforcement learning algorithm for solving a robot motion problem. Master's thesis, South Ural State University, National Research University, Chelyabinsk, Russian (2019). (in Russian). https://dspace.susu.ru/xmlui/bitstream/handle/0001.74/29488/ 2019_222_majorovmp.pdf?sequence=1
10. Fujimoto, S., Hoof, H., Meger, D.: Addressing function approximation error in actor–critic methods. Cornell University, October 2018. https://arxiv.org/pdf/1802.09477.pdf
11. Van Hasselt, H., Guez, A., Silver, D.: Deep reinforcement learning with double Q-learning. In: AAAI, pp. 2094–2100 (2016)
12. Silver, D., Lever, G., Heess, N., Degris, T., Wierstra, D., Riedmiller, M.: Deterministic policy gradient algorithms. In: ICML (2014)
13. Sutton, R.S., McAllester, D.A., Singh, S.P., Mansour, Y.: Policy gradient methods for reinforcement learning with function approximation. In: Advances in Neural Information Processing Systems, pp. 1057–1063 (2000)

Author Index

Printed in the United States
by Baker & Taylor Publisher Services

Printed in the United States
by Baker & Taylor Publisher Services